PRAISE FOR *THE RUMI PRESCRIPTION*

"*The Rumi Prescription* is a testament to the healing power
of art and its ability to bring peace to our battered souls.
Sometimes the cure we need is not a pill, but a poem."

—Firoozeh Dumas, *New York Times* bestselling author of *Funny in Farsi*

"As a lover of beautiful sentences and a secret self-help addict, I gobbled
up this groundbreaking book, relishing the language, the wisdom, and the
vivid and moving portrait of a father and daughter. Whether you read it for
its fine translations of Rumi, its engrossing story, or as a practical guide for
self-care, please give yourself the gift of reading *The Rumi Prescription*."

—David Gessner, *New York Times* bestselling author of
All the Wild That Remains and *The Tarball Chronicles*

"Melody Moezzi takes Rumi down from a dusty bookshelf, breathes
life into his ancient wisdom, and makes him our guide through common
contemporary struggles: anger, anxiety, distraction, and more. *The Rumi
Prescription* translates the wisdom of a medieval mystic into the voice of a
wise, honest, irreverent friend who tells us what we most need to hear."

—Krista Bremer, author of *My Accidental Jihad* and *A Tender Struggle*

"A stunning memoir. Melody Moezzi merges medieval poetry with
modern drama, exploring love, politics, and mental health. Original
translations of Rumi's poems are interspersed with ruminations
on fatherhood, feminism, and self-care, offering insights that will
change your life. I wish I could prescribe this memoir."

—Dr. Seema Yasmin, MD, author of *Muslim Women Are Everything:
Stereotype-Shattering Stories of Courage, Inspiration, and Adventure*

T0286565

"This book enlightened, delighted, and actively helped me. It's a love letter sent across centuries, from one artist to another—and decades, from a daughter to her father—and in the here and now, from a writer to her readers. *The Rumi Prescription* is the sweetest medicine I've ever taken."

—Nina de Gramont, author of *The Mystery Writer*

"*The Rumi Prescription* is a joy to read."

—Ellen Forney, *New York Times* bestselling author of *Marbles: Mania, Depression, Michelangelo, and Me*

"[*The Rumi Prescription*] could shatter a variety of prejudices and stereotypes. . . . A heartening narrative of family, transformation, and courage."

—*Kirkus Reviews*

"This is an amazing book, a brilliant read and a pure delight. What I love about *The Rumi Prescription* is how beautifully Melody Moezzi relates it to our everyday lives. If you love Rumi, read it. If you are looking for practical, real, grounded spiritual advice, read it and take it to heart."

—Omid Safi, author of *Radical Love: Teachings from the Islamic Mystical Tradition*

"This is a book that turns the poetic and spiritual quest for love and connection to *the source—Life, God, the Divine*—into something that can ground us in the here and now."

—Persis M. Karim, PhD, Neda Nobari Distinguished Chair, Center for Iranian Diaspora Studies, San Francisco State University

"[Moezzi] makes a case that Rumi has a lot to offer us, in a memoir punctuated with humor, pathos, and often pithy writing."

—Wilmington *Star-News*

"When I picked up Melody Moezzi's latest memoir, I had the distinct feeling this book landed in my hands for a reason. I'd been searching for a work that could nourish my creative soul for some time, a work that could speak to the struggles of our modern life and creating art. *The Rumi Prescription* is the book I've been waiting for."

—Meredith Doench, *Adroit Journal*

"A writer and activist, Iranian-American Melody Moezzi enlisted the aid of her father, who is fluent in the classical Farsi of the mystic poet Rumi, to write her book *The Rumi Prescription: How an Ancient Mystic Poet Changed My Modern Manic Life.* . . . Moezzi shows how [Rumi's] words can help navigate a particular challenge, from anger, to isolation, to depression."

—*Spirituality & Health*

PRAISE FOR *HALDOL AND HYACINTHS*

"Whipsmart but whimsical . . . Moezzi's fierce honesty and comic self-deprecation bind together winningly."

—*The Boston Globe*

"Blistering, brash and irreverent . . . [Moezzi's] courageous postcard from the edge can't come too soon."

—*The Atlanta Journal-Constitution*

"A bold, courageous book by a woman who transforms mental illness into an occasion for activism."

—*Kirkus Reviews*

"Melody Moezzi is an amazing writer, sharp and witty and very funny, describing life as a young Iranian woman raised by her family in the American Midwest, balancing those two sides of her world and cultures in a pre- and post-9/11 world."

—Book Riot

ALSO BY MELODY MOEZZI

Haldol and Hyacinths: A Bipolar Life

War on Error: Real Stories of American Muslims

THE

RUMI

PRESCRIPTION

How an Ancient Mystic Poet
Changed My Modern Manic Life

Melody Moezzi

A TarcherPerigee Book

tarcherperigee

an imprint of Penguin Random House LLC
penguinrandomhouse.com

Brief portions of the writing herein have been adapted from previously published
articles the author has written for different outlets, including *bp Magazine*,
The Christian Science Monitor, *The Guardian*, *HuffPost*, *Ms.*, and NBC News.

The Quranic verse written in Arabic calligraphy
that appears on the facing page is by imransheen.

Most TarcherPerigee books are available at special quantity discounts
for bulk purchase for sales promotions, premiums, fund-raising, and
educational needs. Special books or book excerpts also can be created to fit
specific needs. For details, write: SpecialMarkets@penguinrandomhouse.com.

ISBN (hardcover) 9780525537762
ISBN (ebook) 9780525537779
ISBN (paperback) 9780525537786

Printed in the United States of America

Book design by Ashley Tucker

In the name of God, Most Gracious, Most Merciful

To Baba Ahmad,
for always being my ham-del,
even if we haven't always been ham-zaban

CONTENTS

AUTHOR'S NOTE

Better to be of the same heart than of the same tongue.
—Rumi[1]

My mother named me Melody after a song by Bobby Vinton. It's called "My Melody of Love," and it's bad. Really bad. But my Persian mother was a big fan of "the Polish Prince," and the bilingual pop-meets-polka chorus is so admittedly catchy that unless you're aching for an earworm, I highly advise you not to Google it. Still, in 1979, my mom loved that song just as much as she loved the fact that "Melody" means the same thing in both Persian and English.

My father, on the other hand, wanted to name me Maryam, in honor of the Virgin Mary. But he was still in Tehran, working as an obstetrician delivering *other* people's babies, while my mom had already fled on account of Iran's brewing so-called Islamic Revolution. After her cushy job as a pathologist peering through microscopes in the hospital basement morphed into a decidedly more dangerous one as a makeshift trauma surgeon tending to bullet wounds in the emergency room, my parents got scared. Six months pregnant, my mom swiftly embarked on an American "vacation," so that I could be born here. My father stayed behind to gauge whether we might

---

1   Unless otherwise noted, all of the poems herein are by Rumi, and they are all cited at the back of the book.

still have a future in Iran. I, ever impatient and perhaps taking a cue from my mother, proceeded to flee the womb shortly after we arrived in the States—nearly two months early, fully developed, and sporting a plush Persian head of hair. So it was that halfway across the world, my mother easily won the name debate, and I became Melody, not Maryam.

Ever since, I've been blessed with an intense appreciation for music and cursed with a staggering lack of talent for it. Years of violin and piano lessons proved this definitively. But neither my atrocious sight-reading nor my dreadful recital performances did anything to curtail my love of music—for you need not compose, create, or even read a melody to revel in it. That's the magic of music. It needs no translation. Words, however, do.

While musicians can transcend language, writers are bound by it. Think of all the cheesy lyrics we tolerate and even enjoy in love songs that would induce vomiting if they ever appeared in a book of poetry minus the music. I expect that even the brilliant Beyoncé and Jay-Z know that the real genius behind a song like "Crazy in Love" isn't in the bizarre bridge (*Uh oh, uh oh, uh oh, oh, no, no . . .*) or the captivating chorus (*Got me lookin' so crazy right now . . .*), but in *the notes*.

Eight centuries ago and thousands of miles away, the great Persian mystic poet and Islamic scholar Molana Jalaloddin Muhammad Balkhi Rumi knew this too. For while Rumi's verse is made up entirely of words, it's more than that. In Persian, also known as Farsi, the word for poem—"*shehr*"[2]—means "song" as well. By no coincidence, Rumi's classical Persian verse isn't meant to be read while sitting, but rather sung while spinning. For this is how Rumi composed

---

2 With respect to Persian (and sometimes Arabic) transliterations throughout this book, I use brackets when the meaning of the words is central to the text and footnotes when it's not (or when it's inferable from context). For transliterated words or phrases that appear more than once, I provide translations the first time only—though all of these words are also defined in a glossary at the back of this book for easy reference.

his mystical poetry, whirling and rhyming ecstatically. The miracle here is that this verse isn't just good; it's extraordinary—which is why it has been translated into every major language on earth. It's also why Rumi has become so wildly popular around the world today—especially in America,[3] where he is often identified as the bestselling poet in the country and has arguably earned the highest seal of approval from American pop culture, as Bey and Jay have now named a daughter after him.

There is a reason Rumi's poetry has survived so long and reached so far. His rhymes honor the sublime power of music, begging to be sung, despite and because of the fact that his verse is so exquisite that it stands alone. Even without music and in translation, Rumi's words resonate across time and space, speaking to the unifying force within all of us that transcends language, culture, race, and religion. Herein rests Rumi's notion of "the Beloved," known by countless different names—God, Truth, Light, Nature, Beauty, and the Universe, to name just a few—but sharing a common essence inextricably rooted in love. As such, the Beloved is not a passion we ought to pursue, but a sacred inheritance that lives within each of us, that connects us, and that—*if we let it*—wakes us up.

This book is the story of how—with the help of my father and Rumi—I woke up. Along the way, I faced all of the diagnoses and applied all of the prescriptions that follow, which is why I've organized the chapters largely chronologically and in the order of every diagnosis (Dx) and prescription (Rx) that propelled my journey forward. I still encounter each of these diagnoses daily, for wanting, isolation, haste, depression, distraction, anxiety, anger, fear, disappointment, and pride are all inherent to the human condition. But thanks to Rumi's

---

3   I use the terms "America" and "American" throughout in reference to the United States and its residents, myself included. I do so, however, fully acknowledging the vast and diverse nature of the Americas and the unfortunate limitations of this shorthand.

poetic prescriptions and my father's patience in dispensing them, I finally feel up to the task. In fact, I welcome it. My hope is that this book will help you do the same. Not in the same way or through the same path, but in *your* way and through *your* path.

Whether you are a Rumi expert or never heard of him before picking up this book doesn't matter. The only prerequisite here is love. That said, because Rumi and I are writers, we are both enamored of and limited by words—and therefore subject to all the wonders and dangers of translation. Rumi wrote almost exclusively in Persian, while I write almost exclusively in English. Worse yet, the classical Persian of Rumi's verse is to contemporary Persian roughly what the Elizabethan English of Shakespeare's verse is to contemporary English. In other words, it's *way* different.

And though Farsi was my first language, it's not the one I know best. Growing up in Dayton, Ohio, I spoke predominantly Fanglish at home and English at school. And lest anyone dis Dayton as some backward provincial town, you should know that we had a sizable Iranian-American community, ensuring that I was never the only Iranian kid at school. So please set any "flyover state" stereotypes aside, because the problem with flying over us is that you never get to know us. And for the record, this applies equally to Ohio (go Buckeyes!) as to Iran (go Team Melli![4]).

All this to say, thanks to my parents, Dayton's tight-knit Iranian-American community, weekly Persian lessons, and plenty of summers in Tehran, I speak Farsi—just not nearly as well as I'd like. While I can read and write the language, I do so abysmally and at a glacial pace. And even after five years of intentional study for this book and a lifetime of inadvertent study as the daughter of two proud Persian parents—including a relentless Rumi reciter as a father and a persistent Persian-lesson planner as a mother—my language skills remain deeply lacking.

---

4   Iran's national soccer team.

My father, by contrast, is fluent in both modern Farsi and Ru-mi's medieval variety, which he has been singing to me since I was a kid. Translating whenever necessary, he raised me on a steady diet of Rumi. All the while, I knew these verses were my inheritance. Yet it took me more than thirty years to claim it. Rumi's poetry is epic and untranslatable: full of allegory, commentary, wordplay, and copi-ous literary and Quranic allusions that routinely went over my head growing up and often still do. For most of my life, the idea that some-one like me—with my fourth-grade Farsi reading level—could even begin to translate Rumi seemed laughable, not to mention irrespon-sible. But two visionaries inspired me to approach the task with all the love, courage, humor, and humility it demanded.

First and foremost, there was my father. He believed in me and promised to help, and he did—*a lot.* The short translations sprinkled throughout this book represent a tiny sliver of Rumi's voluminous rhyming couplets, quatrains, and ghazals. Still, translating them was exacting. Some verses took me days, weeks, months, or even years to translate to my relative satisfaction. But I was never alone. Rumi was always there, and more often than not, so was my dad. In fact, all of the translations in this book are by my father, Ahmad Moezzi, and me. He patiently guided me through the Persian of every verse, and I carefully chose which words to use in English. In doing so, I tried to preserve the meaning and musicality of Rumi's poetry. At times, however, I sacrificed some of the former for the latter or vice versa. While I have undoubtedly failed to do Rumi justice here, please know that any such failures are neither Rumi's nor my father's, but mine alone.

The second sage who emboldened me to begin translating this poetry was Coleman Barks. If you've ever encountered Rumi in En-glish before this, then it was likely through Barks' translations. Both my father and I agree that no one has better captured or spread the spirit of Rumi's poetry in English than Coleman Barks. What's more, he doesn't speak Farsi. Barks' more soulful and less literal interpretations of Rumi's verse are based on other translations from the original Persian, most notably R. A. Nicholson's. For years, I didn't realize this, because I have a bad habit of skipping introductions and author's notes. (Yes, I appreciate the irony.) I had always just assumed that translating a work required knowing its original language. Turns out, not necessarily, especially when it comes to Rumi, who adamantly believed that it was *better to be of the same heart than of the same tongue.* And Coleman Barks is undeniably of Rumi's same heart. Indeed, Barks' inspired translations serve as a testament to Rumi's assertion that sometimes language can be a hindrance to love—so much so that the prolific Persian poet noted that *when it comes to love, the pen breaks.*

The combination of my father's faith in my ability and Barks' rightful audacity helped set me free. Because the biggest barrier to writing this book wasn't all the translation, transcription, and transformation that I knew it would require. It was the belief that this poetry, *this language,* was above and beyond me, that despite speaking Farsi and sharing Rumi's ancestry, I was still somehow unworthy of his words. Barks' beautiful translations reminded me that I didn't need to be an expert in classical Persian to claim my own literary inheritance. For if he could claim it without being or knowing Persian, then surely so could I. I could study my father's beloved poetry. I could embrace the name my mother gave me. And I could accept that my humanity makes me worthy.

Nevertheless, as a twenty-first-century Iranian-American who speaks killer Fanglish and decent Farsi, I needed a patient and devoted friend to guide me through Rumi's incomparable lyrical world, full of powerful prescriptions for even the most seemingly modern human dilemmas. Through his life, my father has always been that friend and guide for me, and through this book, I hope to be the same for you.

CHAPTER I

Dx: Wanting
Rx: Go to the Source

Seek the tonic nectar in the bitter sting.
Go to the source of the source of your spring.

I grew up dodging dead Persian poets. Like stubborn evangelists, they knocked on every door and window of my childhood. My father forever let them in, ensuring their safe trespass on nearly every major and minor life event.

Were they alive, he would have cleared each entryway upon their arrival, guiding them inside, treating them like royalty, showering them with effusive Persian idioms, equally bizarre and typical expressions evolved over thousands of years of civilization: asking them to step on his eyes upon their arrival, insisting that he was their servant and the dirt beneath their feet during their visit, and bowing profusely with his hands held to his heart while offering to sacrifice himself for them upon their departure.

Were they solid bones and beating hearts in place of tattered books and ancient rhymes, my father would have happily offered our lyrical ancestors far more than these peculiar perennial pledges of love, esteem, and welcome. Were they still susceptible to hunger, thirst, and fatigue, he would have offered them tea and chickpea cookies; he would have insisted they stay for dinner, and he would have happily prepared the guest room after inviting them to stay for good. If they ever left, he would have held out a Quran for them to kiss and walk beneath and spent hours exchanging well wishes in the foyer, at the doorstep, down the driveway, and at the curb, all before pouring a bowl of water on the ground behind them to ensure safe travels and a speedy return.

Were they still breathing, this is how my father would have honored his beloved Persian poets. Since they aren't, he has taken to breathing for them. He recites their words by heart, tonic ancestral anthems, as though our survival depends on them.

Admittedly, I have not always been so kind to these poets, who— long dead and half a world away—made more appearances in our Ohio home than any living American ever did. But to be fair, my father's love for Sufi poetry is tough to match.[1]

For Ahmad, my father's first name and the only one by which I've ever called him, nothing is more sacred than poetry—specifically, medieval Persian Sufi poetry, and most specifically, Rumi. He recites Rumi's verse with the same fervor and frequency most people reserve for food, water, and oxygen. By all accounts, he is a tried-and-true Rumi addict, and like most children of addicts, I grew up resenting the object of my father's addiction. Rumi was an inescapable presence in our midwestern home: the annoying elder who forever tested the limits of my Persian hospitality, challenging my contemporary kitchen Farsi with his antiquated medieval verse, dismissing my American hunger for brevity with his seemingly endless collections of rhyming couplets and quatrains.

But today, all grown up and painfully clueless about so many

---

1   Sufis are Muslim mystics; Sufism is Islamic mysticism.

things I was sure I'd have figured out by now, I invite Rumi into *my* life, *my* home, *my* heart. Today, I follow my father's lead as I seek remedies for some of the most common human diagnoses around: wanting, isolation, haste, depression, distraction, anxiety, anger, fear, disappointment, pride, and all of the misery they breed. As I finally take the time to explore Rumi's poetry with Ahmad, I see how it applies to these pervasive modern maladies and then some.

I never expected to find twenty-first-century cures in thirteenth-century couplets, but I have. In the process, I have also inherited my father's Rumi addiction, and through this book, I invite you to do the same. For unlike opiates or amphetamines, Rumi's poetic prescriptions defy the rules of dosing and tolerance, as they work better when shared, grow stronger with each successive use, and boast zero harmful side effects. They are meant to be applied repeatedly, in groups and in unison, through song and dance whenever possible, beyond superficial worldly divisions toward eternal sacred connections. It is no coincidence, for instance, that this poetry exists in a language relatively free from gender—with no "she" or "he," no "her" or "him"—for Rumi's rhymes, like the divine, save no room for petty partitions. Instead, they invite us to tear down our barriers and unite through love:

Love's nation of origin is separate from all creeds.
For the lovers, the Beloved comprises all religions and nationalities.

Molana Jalaloddin Muhammad Balkhi Rumi—known simply as Molana (an honorific meaning "our master") to most Persians—was a renowned thirteenth-century Islamic scholar, jurist, theologian, poet, and mystic. He was born in the Central Asian province of Balkh in 1207 CE and grew up in an era of deep political turmoil packed with modern parallels, full of walls and bans and wars.

As a result, Rumi spent much of his life traveling extensively throughout the Middle East before settling in Konya, in present-day Turkey and then central Anatolia, formerly part of the Eastern Roman Empire. This accounts for the moniker Rumi, which simply means "Roman" in Persian and Arabic.

It wasn't until Rumi was thirty-seven, in the winter of 1244, that he finally met the wandering mystic who became his spiritual guide, Shamsoddin Tabrizi, meaning "the Sun of Faith from Tabriz." Commonly known as Shams, he was roughly sixty at the time and acted as a friend, mentor, guide, and mirror for Rumi, reflecting the light of the Beloved within the budding poet so that Rumi too could behold that sacred light within himself, humanity, and the world around him.

In all, Rumi and Shams spent no more than a few years in each other's company, but during that time, the two developed a singular spiritual bond. Shams disappeared from Konya for good in late 1247 or early 1248, when some speculate he was killed by Rumi's own jealous followers. Distraught and devastated, Rumi traveled to Damascus to search for Shams several times. All to no avail. Rumi spent the rest of his life longing for Shams' company, and out of that longing thousands upon thousands of lines of mystical poetry were born. Indeed, so great was the ecstatic love between Rumi and Shams that it sparked Rumi's transformation from a mere religious scholar into one of the greatest mystic poets of all time.

Today, more than seven centuries after Rumi's death, there is no escaping his influence. It is nearly impossible to spend a day walking around any Iranian city, suburb, or village and not hear his echo. Rumi's words live on in everyday parlance: no matter one's station, religion, or occupation, everyone in Iran knows at least a handful of Rumi's poems by heart. They are taught in classrooms as an essential part of the basic curriculum, but more than that, they are learned in homes, cafés, bazaars, parks, and houses of worship.

No current or former Persian territory is exempt from Rumi's influence, which extends deep into the diaspora and far beyond. In addition to all the Iranians I know who will adamantly claim Rumi as their own, I have also spoken with Afghans, Tajiks, Turks, Kurds, Arabs, Armenians, Pakistanis, Indians, and others who lay claim to Rumi as well. For while he composed the overwhelming majority of his poetry in Persian, his influence is far from limited to Persians or the Persian-speaking world. Love was indeed his primary religion and nationality, which is why everyone can lay claim to him. That said, for Persians who speak Persian, like me, this medieval mystic poet is nothing short of a persistent and perpetual presence.

In my case, Rumi followed my family all the way from our Iranian homeland to the American heartland, and within a few short decades, he has become a phenomenon here as well, to the point where this thirteenth-century Persian mystic has now arguably become the bestselling poet in the United States. He has his own misattributed memes and a growing collection of English-language biographies, films, and television specials, not to mention prominent appearances at your cousin's, brother's, best friend's, niece's, and/or sister's weddings. He has even achieved a kind of American celebrity status by association, garnering New Age cred courtesy of Deepak Chopra, pop cred courtesy of Madonna, and hip-hop cred courtesy of Beyoncé and Jay-Z. Still, in my father's eyes, Rumi has yet to gain *remotely* sufficient recognition anywhere. Personally, it has taken decades for me to fully appreciate Rumi's reach, not merely across hundreds of years, thousands of miles, and deep political hostilities, but across my own soul, deftly bypassing my brain and settling in my heart.

Nearly every lesson Ahmad has ever taught me has been accompanied by a poem—recited always with love, regularly from Rumi, and often by heart. It's part habit, part inheritance. Ahmad's father, a devout man whom we all called *Agha joon* ("Dear Sir"), used to pay him and his five siblings to memorize verses—not from the Quran, but from the great Sufi poets. Many an evening was spent gathered around their home's sole heater or under a mimosa tree in the back courtyard, sipping tea through sugar cubes and taking turns reading or reciting from the works of Rumi, Hafez, Saadi, and other mystic lyricists. While Ahmad's upbringing was neither Sufi nor literary in any traditional sense, it was both in a very Persian one.

Though an ocean, a revolution, and a generation away, so was mine. As the daughter of a father who grew up memorizing Sufi love poems for fun and a mother who was so wooed by them as to toss tradition aside and marry for love alone, there was no alternative.

In Dayton, where I grew up and where my parents spent nearly thirty years before moving to the Persian-packed promised land of Southern California, they managed to befriend at least twenty other Iranian families, ensuring my sister, Romana, and me a decidedly Persian upbringing full of adoptive aunties, uncles, and cousins straight out of the Middle East, smack-dab in the American Midwest. Like so many of them, we neither assimilated nor isolated. We improvised.

We were good at making up our own rules, especially when it came to religion. My parents had no problem sending Romana and me to Catholic school, they've always happily added vodka to their pomegranate juice, and for years, they simply refused to believe that pepperoni was a pork product. Though we attended a nearby mosque briefly when I was a kid, we quit going after it was vandalized. Something about the broken windows and swastikas led my parents to conclude that we might not be entirely safe there.

After that, the only events I ever remember my parents attending religiously were Persian parties. Thanks to Dayton's ample Iranian community—mostly doctors who, like my parents, had been recruited to settle and practice in southwest Ohio—there was always a party somewhere, and there were always kids to play with. We may not have had our own mosque or temple, but we had our own tribe and built our own traditions. Our parties were our "services," and there were never any hierarchies of piety. Our primary rituals revolved around music, dancing, food, poetry, tea, and always at least two kisses. Our tribe included Muslims, Jews, Baha'is, Christians, Zoroastrians, agnostics, and atheists. Our chief commandment—the glue that bound us despite passing gossip, quarrels, and rivalries—was simple and consistent: love.

The later into the night our parties ran and the more wine our parents consumed, the more likely they were to share their talents. Seemingly out of nowhere, instruments would appear, ululations would commence, and there would be no turning back. The devotions varied: some sang, some danced, some recited poetry. My father, of course, was forever engaged in the latter.

But it was still Ohio. Sunday morning Farsi classes held in rotating family dining rooms and occasional summer vacations spent in Iran weren't nearly enough to make any of us kids fully fluent. It was too late. English had already become our native tongue. Granted, this is what our parents wanted—for us to adapt to this new land, to escape any discrimination an accent might invite, and above all, to *succeed*.

That's what my steno pad was all about. I couldn't have been more than eight—sitting on our back porch, scrawny legs tucked beneath me, freakishly large eyes devouring *James and the Giant Peach*—when Ahmad handed me my first steno pad. Having recently discovered the magical power of books to transport and transform, I was already hooked, a lifelong addict in the making, and he knew it.

From then on, I was to pay closer attention as I read, not to let a single unfamiliar word escape my grasp. He instructed me to host them all in this strange new narrow notebook bound from above, and I did. Religiously. Words on the left, meanings on the right. Tests on Fridays. I learned countless words this way, and so did Ahmad. Though unspoken, the lesson was clear. For me, in this skin like his, with just enough melanin to arouse suspicion, good English wouldn't suffice. It had to be pristine. It wasn't enough to read, write, and speak as well as my non-hyphenated American classmates. I had to do better.

So Persian took a backseat while I dutifully documented every new English term that entered my life as though it were a prophet seeking revelational refuge in my steno pad. Every week, my father tested me on the ever-expanding scripture, all in English; every week, I failed to appreciate just how much of it was new to him, and every week, Persian lost priority. Until now. Although admittedly, the catalyst for hearing and heeding the call of my Persian roots couldn't have seemed any less likely.

It happened on a Monday. After six back-to-back radio interviews to promote the paperback release of my latest book, a memoir about living with bipolar disorder, something cracked. This was no minor hairline fracture of the tibia or fibula. It was a complex compound fracture of the human soul.

All had gone well on air: I kept things conversational, I remembered each host's name, I dropped the book's title whenever appropriate, and I got all my relevant facts and stats straight. But by the end of the last interview, I felt utterly drained. And not just physically and emotionally, but *spiritually*. I had no idea what was happening. All I knew was that I felt empty and stuck.

An off-air aside from a producer right before one of my segments—

perhaps the world's worst attempt at a pep talk to date—kept playing inside of my head like a broken record: "Remember, you're a brand, and you're selling a product."

I wanted to say, "Remember, you're a fool, and you're selling a farce." I wanted to say, "I'm not just some brand, and my books aren't just some *products*." I wanted to say, "I'm an artist, and my books are my *children*." But I didn't. Instead, I unwittingly allowed his insidious words to infect my soul through the phone line. I know better than to believe that this sole producer was responsible, but it seems easier to blame him than myself for what ensued.

Within days, I was struck with the most ruthless case of writer's block I'd ever experienced. And it just got worse from there: migraines, backaches, a random case of tendinitis, and some weird foot injury. Still, none of it troubled me nearly as much as the writer's block, for writing has always been my sanctuary: the place where I find meaning and purpose, the place where my prayers are formed and heard, the place where I connect with myself, the universe, and everything in between. But something had invaded my sanctuary and shattered my creative morale, and I couldn't figure out what it was.

After that wretched midsummer Monday afternoon, I spent months trying to string words together, constantly battling the urge to delete every single one. It was as though some invisible demon had taken up residence on my shoulder, ceaselessly whispering into my ear every time I pressed the space bar: *Not good enough! Garbage! Delete!*

The rest of that year was excruciating, and I say this as someone who is intimately acquainted with a wide variety of pain—so much so that for years, I never believed I'd see thirty. Between a wounded gut and a wayward brain, I knew the odds were against me. I was eighteen the first time I nearly died, and I spent the next dozen years cheating death over and over again. As a young adult, I survived a rare pancreatic tumor, myriad medical hospitalizations, chronic pain, major surgery, and a wicked case of undiagnosed and untreated manic depression that led to a suicide attempt, an acute manic episode, a psychotic break, and three inpatient psychiatric hospitalizations. My early adulthood wasn't about risk-taking or self-discovery. It was about survival and legacy. The goal was simple: keep my lungs breathing and my heart beating, keep my hands paddling and my legs kicking, keep my head above water just long enough to *do* something with my life, to *make* something of myself, to *count*.

So I hurtled through my twenties determined to make the most of what little time I had left, desperate to matter, collecting degrees and accolades, writing, praying, publishing, protesting, falling in love, getting married—all the while, expecting death to soon come knocking. But it didn't. It hasn't.

By some miracle, I'm still here, and no one expects me to check out any time soon, not even me. Having made it all the way to thirty-five, I'm stunned. For the first time in my adult life, I can quit hurrying and take a moment to look around and process the world and my place in it. The view is both terrifying and exhilarating.

After learning that my medical conditions can be managed and treated, I feel hopeful but adrift. I've been coping well with my psychiatric illness. Properly medicated and in weekly therapy, I've even become an outspoken mental health advocate committed to combating the stigma and discrimination surrounding psychiatric disabilities. But never had my soul felt more restless, nor my creative spark more extinguished. And I'm slowly beginning to understand why.

Unable to write after that unfortunate radio interview, I shifted my focus almost entirely from writing to publicity. In effect, I did what so many of us do when faced with the rigors of our twenty-first-century market economy: I treated myself as though I were indeed just a brand selling just a product. I soon realized, however, that in the land of brands and products—where numbers talk and words fail—*nothing is ever enough.*

My reviews were excellent, speaking invitations poured in, plenty of media appearances ensued, and where I feared people might see me as weak on account of my psychiatric condition, they saw me as strong on account of my candor; strangers sent heartfelt messages insisting the book had saved their lives. I should have felt grateful and gratified. Instead, craving ever more acclaim and affirmation, I felt perpetually slighted and unsatisfied. Careening along this twisted ego trip, I felt at once full of myself and empty inside. The more I got, the more I wanted, and the more I wanted, the worse I felt.

I had fallen victim to the most common modern mental ailment in the so-called developed world, an illness so conventional the *DSM*[2] makes no mention of it and so widespread it's considered normal: wanting. And not just wanting, but wanting *more.* Voracious for validation—more likes, more followers, more readers, more comments, more fans, more sales, more *more*—I tried to keep my ego well-fed. But the effort only deepened my insecurities, starving my soul and corroding my heart, proving that insanity is *not* exclusive to the insane.

Sure, there is the rare clinical variety, rooted in chemistry and electricity, prompting hallucinations and delusions. But there is also the routine societal variety: rooted in ego and ambition, prompting fear and insecurity. I know both firsthand. The former led me to a series of locked psychiatric units and a world of isolation, while the latter led me to a successful literary career and a world of aspiration. Though distinct, both worlds have proven equally disorienting.

2 The *Diagnostic and Statistical Manual of Mental Disorders* is the so-called bible of psychiatry. Compiled by the American Psychiatric Association, it is now in its fifth edition, and it lists detailed diagnostic criteria for currently recognized psychiatric disorders.

But having already survived the more scarce and stigmatized clinical species of lunacy, I failed to spot the more standard and celebrated societal one at first. Consumed by an insatiable longing for more and bigger and better successes down the line, I lost track of the present and grew so addicted to affirmation that I had no energy left for creation.

What little I could write, I quickly deleted, certain it wasn't good enough, certain *I* wasn't good enough. A noxious cloud of self-doubt spread within me like a swarm of insufferable fruit flies, expanding exponentially with every fresh accolade. Each new glowing review or speaking invitation or media request or sales bump, or like or mention or follow or share, simply further eroded my sense of self-assurance. Unbeknownst to me, this ruthless swamp of self-doubt was the direct result of ego: a beast born of neither courage nor confidence, but of dread and dubiety.

By the time I finally recognized the insanity in my own debilitating ego and ambition, however, I was already surrounded. My once-shimmering creative well had morphed into a fetid Superfund site, and I was stranded, smack-dab in the middle of this sickening morass of my own making, swatting at a heavy haze of ravenous red-eyed vermin, sinking into toxic sludge, desperate for a way out. I was stuck, and my own relentless wanting was to blame.

To make matters worse, I was also haunted by the terrifying realization that, with my medical conditions in check, I would now likely outlive my parents, doomed to suffer what seemed an unbearable loss. Recognizing that no parent should ever have to bury a child, however, I then quickly grew consumed with guilt for being so petrified at the prospect of an average life expectancy. Caught in a cycle of insecurity, creative inertia, terror, and shame, I broke.

For nearly a year, I grappled with depression, trying and failing to jump-start my creativity: to get on with my next project, to quit deleting thousands of sentences that deserved a chance, to adhere to my calling, to embrace my new lease on life. I even ran off to a remote cabin in the woods, hoping to revive my creative spirit by emulating one of my American literary heroes. But once there, it was clear that I was no Henry David Thoreau. Where he found a way "to live deliberately" in the woods, I found a way to get my Corolla stuck in a frozen creek. Where he found a way "to front only the essential facts of life," I found a way to front only new and greater self-loathing. Where he found a way to learn what the woods could teach, I found an intense new longing for the beach. As much as I adored Thoreau, he was not the source of my lyrical lineage, and my disaster in the woods merely confirmed it. Where writing was once my refuge, it had become my torment. The woods held no cure for me. For that, I would have to head to the sea.

When you're dealing with a madness so painfully prevalent that most people would rather revere than renounce it, effective prescriptions can be hard to come by. You may need to travel through time and space. You may need to rewind seven centuries and cross a continent. You may need to exchange a language where you've learned to shine for another where you're sure to stumble. You may need to track down the wisest guide you know, and you may need to do it *now*, while you're both still here.

Just to be safe, I resolved to do all of the above, traveling westward to find my way eastward, reaching outward to find my way inward, and going backward to find my way forward. Creatively and spiritually spent, feeling more rootless than ever, I heard a faint call from within my heart—a gentle plea from the stubborn Sufi poets turned perpetual houseguests of my childhood—and I followed it. I turned to my source, starting literally, with my parents, the bearers of my distinctly Persian past and its majestic mystic poets.

Don't retreat, come near.
Don't lose faith, adhere.
Seek the tonic nectar in the bitter sting.
Go to the source of the source of your spring.

So I plotted a pilgrimage. Not around the Kaaba,[3] but alongside the Pacific. Not in Arabic, but in Persian. Not to study Quranic verses, but mystical ones. In search of a cure for searching—to want, take, and consume less; to appreciate, give, and create more—I decided to immerse myself in the ancient poetry I grew up taking for granted, to learn it by heart and by history and under the expert tutelage of my father, a physician by trade and a connoisseur of Sufi poetry by tradition.

Still, I never chose Persian poetry; it chose me. Personally, I'm partial to prose and my English is worlds better than my Farsi. But this poetry had sought me out before, saving me from myself when nothing else could. Perhaps, I thought, it could do it again.

Six years prior to plotting this pilgrimage, at twenty-nine and in the midst of what I would later learn was an acute manic episode, I became illiterate. Shortly after finishing a seemingly endless formal education, my mind quit. No two weeks' notice. No resignation letter. No retirement party. Just here one day, gone the next. It wasn't that I had forgotten how to read. It was that no text could sit still long enough for me to interpret it. Cracking open a book was like blowing

---

3   Often referred to as the most sacred site in Islam, the Kaaba is the cube at the center of Masjid al-Haram (AKA the Sacred Mosque or the Great Mosque) in Mecca. Described in the Quran as the first house of worship, it is central to the performance of pilgrimage (*Hajj*) and establishes the direction (*qiblah* or *ghebleh*) for daily prayers.

up a can of alphabet soup on the moon. For each word or letter that mercifully stayed put, dozens of others refused. Every page of every text—however sacred or profane, brilliant or mundane—took on the same incoherent windswept shape, like a word search in microgravity.

Nearly overnight, I had transformed from a hyperliterate author and attorney into an illiterate ecstatic. Provoked by a spiritual experience I had neither pursued nor prepared for, my metamorphosis was simultaneously manic and mystical, scary and sublime. Unlike my first and only other mystical experience to date, this one was messy.

The first had occurred years earlier, absent any adverse side effects. As I stood, deep in prayer, atop a mountain in the Canadian Rockies, the Beloved whispered sweetly to me. Not in words, but through a beam of sunlight that penetrated my soul, reminding me where I'd come from, what I was made of, and where I was bound to return. The exhilarating encounter lasted a few minutes at most, but having lit me up inside, fleetingly filling me with more love and wonder than I ever imagined possible, it stuck with me.

So when, nearly a decade later, on the twentieth-floor balcony of my home in Atlanta, I encountered that same piercing light, I recognized it at once. But this time, the light lingered, so long that it burned me. The Beloved was no longer whispering, but clamoring. Transfixed, I couldn't pull myself together long enough to do the sensible thing and look away. I stared into the sun as it rose over Stone Mountain, feeling its rays permeate every cell in my body, and fell into a trance.

I hadn't slept for days, and my sanity was slipping. Within hours, I was struck illiterate and incoherent. Certain I could fly, off that balcony or anywhere else, I became my own worst enemy. To prevent my delusions from killing me, my husband called 911, and soon, it was official: I was crazy. Then restraints, then isolation, then medication, then psychiatric hospitalization.

There is perhaps no greater blow to the ego than losing one's mind, and having lost mine so completely, I no longer had any sense of a distinct self, separate from Creator or creation. However clumsily or unwittingly, I had stumbled into the land of mystics.

At the time, I didn't know this land had a name, let alone that it was the subject of so many of the poems my father had recited to me since I was a child—poems by Rumi, Hafez, and other Sufi lyricists; poems that always revolved around love. The word Ahmad's cherished Persian poets reserved for this borderless territory, the word I wouldn't learn until years after first experiencing it, was simple and profound: *fana*. It denotes a unique kind of "passing away" or "ceasing to exist," a sublime state of self-annihilation: the death of the ego, or *nafs*, before the Beloved. That day, I was briefly privy to it. A place where there was no "I" or "me," no "her" or "him," no "they" or "them," no "you" even; a place where there was only the transcendent We and Us, united and inseparable from the Beloved.

For maybe an hour before descending into madness, I stood on that small balcony, my soul soaking in the sun's rays like some irresponsible teenager on spring break—too drunk to apply sunblock, too young to consider the future, too mad to be reasonable. An intense calm washed over me, a sense that everything was and would be as it should be. More than ever before—more than even on that stunning sun-drenched afternoon in the splendor of the Canadian Rockies—I felt a deep connection to every atom back to Adam and before, to the divine spirit within each one of those atoms, composed entirely of love and dancing inside of me like a holy kaleidoscope of butterflies.

But I had entered this land unprepared, with neither a map nor a guide, and this, it turns out, can be fatal. Sufis prepare for *fana*—through prayer, meditation, charity, fasting, and pilgrimage—and they do not approach it alone. They bring a guide, a sheikh, a guru, a *friend*. This way, they can take in the light of transcendence without being burned by it.

I, however, had arrived alone and unready, so despite catching a glimpse of that glorious glow on my way down, I was scorched by it and quickly descended into clinical insanity, ultimately landing inside the locked psychiatric unit of the same hospital where my father— an obstetrician/gynecologist—had conducted thousands of surgeries and delivered hundreds of babies. It would take years to even admit, let alone appreciate, but what my doctors eventually identified as acute mania and psychosis brought on by bipolar disorder, I first experienced as acute love and union brought on by an expired ego.

In the hospital, my father continued—as he has done throughout my life, particularly in times of great joy or crisis—to offer me poems. But this time, they weren't just poems; they were sustenance. Stripped of my sanity, pride, and liberty, I gained a new appreciation for Ahmad's random poetic recitations. Suddenly, they weren't so random. Suddenly, they made sense. Suddenly, they *spoke* to me.

My father's cherished poets had once again come knocking, but now, for the first time, *I* was the one to let them in. *I* was the one to clear the entryways. *I* was the one to beg them to stay. All their endless talk of love and lovers and the Beloved, everything at the heart of their ecstatic poetry: it finally clicked. What modern medicine lacked by way of explanation, these ancient Sufi poets provided. My break from the rest of the world's notion of reality was clinical, painful, and terrifying. But it was also mystical, soulful, and electrifying. At long last, I was beginning to understand this poetry that has so spoken to my father since he was a child in Shiraz—not because I was reading or studying it, but because, having lost the ability to read and study, I had *felt* it.

> *In love with insanity,*
> *I'm fed up with wisdom and rationality.*

Such are the words of a man who spent much of his life fleeing war and invasion, perpetually displaced, yet never lost; a man who, in a different time or place, could just as easily have found *himself* locked inside a psychiatric facility. Prone to spinning and spontaneous singing, Rumi—the first of the whirling dervishes—would have fit in quite well on that ward. And in a way, he did. Thanks to my father's frequent lyrical offerings, Rumi's rhyming couplets soon became my constant companions on the unit.

While this transcendental calm in the eye of my mind's manic storm did nothing to erase the damage left behind or avert the horrors still ahead, it scattered flickers of peace and clarity like merciful moonbeams across the tempest of my psychosis. Inside those ephemeral rays of reflected light, I felt my *self*—my ego, my separateness—disintegrate. In its place emerged the Beloved. Not up on some cloud or out in some mosque, but under my skin, traversing my veins, hugging my heart, and filling my lungs. Such is the terrain of mystics, and for some, the upside of madness. But in a territory as fleeting as it is unpredictable, amnesia abounds. And so our souls must constantly seek reminders, for it is far too easy to forget the holiness within our hearts.

This is why I now pursue pilgrimage. Sane but stuck, I'm after a reminder. Like a virologist deriving a vaccine from a virus, I seek to derive mysticism from madness, transcendence from trauma. Now I pursue the Beloved with *intent*. I don't yet know that it will be years before I begin to understand the full scope and purpose of my pilgrimage. But I do know that I will need a guide to travel safely, and without hesitation I choose my father.

Though the conscious mind may be able to forget being torn from its roots, the soul cannot. Trying to heal a broken brain while dismissing a fractured soul is like trying to build a house while dismissing a shoddy foundation. Build your home on quicksand, and it will sink no matter how sturdy or stunning the roof.

Rumi dealt with this same dilemma centuries before I crashed headlong into it on a locked psychiatric ward. He begins his six-volume masterpiece of some twenty-five thousand rhyming couplets, the *Masnavi*,[4] with the legendary cry of a reed flute torn from its reed bed. Ahmad says I could spend my entire life exploring just these opening lines, and in a way, I feel as though I've been doing exactly that, over and over again, largely without realizing it. The poem starts with a simple command to *listen*, then it continues:

> *Lamenting a separation gone on too long,*
> *The reed flute sings its tender song:*
> *"Ever since I was torn from the reed bed,*
> *My cry has multiplied and spread . . .*
> *All those severed from their source*
> *Yearn to return as a matter of course . . ."*
> *But the message of this melody stands classified,*
> *Reserved only for those who in madness reside.*

Today, years since residing in that delicate, dangerous, and delusional space, I return to my roots to learn this poetry that played such a vital role in my recovery and inspired countless ancestors before me. Now in my mid-thirties—nearly the same age as Rumi when he met his beloved friend, guide, and teacher, Shams—I sing the song of the reed flute as I cross a continent, from my home in North Carolina to my parents' in Southern California, in the hopes of a safe reunion. This time, with less mania and more intention. This time, free from re-

---

4   The *Masnavi*, or *Masnavi-e Manavi*, translates as "Rhyming Couplets of Deep Spiritual Meaning" or "The Spiritual Couplets."

straints and isolation. This time, with my father to guide me and a new steno pad in hand, one of my own choosing. This time, no red lines printed down the middle. This time, I draw my own borders, wildly off-center. This time, words on the right, meanings on the left, as I seek to narrow the chasm between past and present, Source and soul.

Having now made a career out of playing with words from left to right, my Farsi still leaves much to be desired. Given a Persian translation or equivalent rendering of *James and the Giant Peach*—say, *Jamshid and the Modest Pomegranate*—it could easily take me a year to read. In short, I'm slow in Farsi. *Really* slow.

But Ahmad thinks I'm smart. He always has. Growing up, I never played team sports, but straight A's were always my thing. Whenever my report cards arrived, Ahmad would proudly post them on the refrigerator and cheer as though I'd just scored a winning goal at some sport I couldn't play to save my life. His choice praise: "You are number vohn!"[5]

Still, all of my A's were in classes taught in either English or Spanish, both languages that use almost entirely the same letters and move in the same direction. By contrast, Farsi has none of the same letters, moves in the opposite direction, and is entirely absent from the Ohio public school curriculum. All this to say, I excelled at slacking off in Farsi class. I never did my homework and dreaded reading aloud. The moment my parents let me stop going, I did. So, when I first mentioned wanting to study classical Persian poetry with Ahmad, *in*

---

5   Ahmad's English, like my Persian, is accented and laced with grammatical errors. While I make no effort to "fix" such errors here, I've taken liberties in choosing when to reproduce accents. For the most part, I don't, so for reference, some of the most common features of the Persian-American dialect include: dropping or adding articles unnecessarily, confusing gender (because again, there is none in Farsi), mixing up singular and plural, occasionally replacing the sounds of *w*'s with *v*'s ("vohn" here, for example, is "one") and the sounds of *th*'s with *t*'s or *d*'s, and often adding an "eh" before certain words beginning with *s*, as in "eh-svimming pool."

Persian, he should have laughed. Anyone even remotely familiar with the complexities of medieval Persian verse or the inadequacies of my Persian language skills should have laughed. He didn't, likely because his belief in me has always bordered on delusional.

"You really think I can do it?" I asked. "I just feel so far behind, like a *lifetime* behind."

"Of course you can do it! Are you kidding? You are number vohn! You just come to San Diego, and I teach you. You will see."

I pray he is right, that there's still time, that I'm not irreparably stunted, that it's not too late to learn this poetry that continues to play such a routine and indispensable role in my father's everyday life. Whether he is reciting it aloud or under his breath, alone or in company, by heart or from books, Ahmad is forever consumed by this extraordinary addiction, and Rumi has always been his primary drug of choice. It's equally enlightening and endearing for those who bother to truly listen. But for most of my life, I refused, so I just found it irritating. Growing up, my response to Ahmad's poetic recitations was often swift and obnoxious. Eyes rolling, having possibly heard the same poem before, I would say so: "Ahmad, I *know,* I *know.* I've heard this one twenty times."

And perhaps I had. But amid all the "I know"s and eye-rolls, I had also missed nearly everything. Caught up in ego and a false sense of knowing born uniquely of familiarity, I spent decades foolishly dismissing these poems, like some ever-growing unclaimed inheritance that could always be retrieved at a later date. But such inheritances are bound. They cannot be distributed after death. They must be transmitted in life.

Now, as a grown-up finally taking the time to reclaim this literary legacy, I'm drawn back to my childhood. For only by looking back can I begin to grasp the powerful role my father's treasured poems have always played in my life. Even before I came to recognize them as anything more than charming trivialities at best, they have always served as sacred remedies, reminders of my roots, connections to my Source.

Take the time I was ten, playing at a construction site behind our home in Dayton. I stepped on a nail that pierced through my flip-flop, deep into the sole of my foot. As Ahmad tended to my wound in the kitchen, I begged him to take me to a hospital like "normal people."

"Who is *normal* people?" Ahmad asked as he sat at the breakfast table, calmly pulling a nail out of my foot, unfazed by the blood pouring onto our white marble floor.

"*Not us,*" I yelped.

As he tried to apply a butterfly closure to the bottom of my foot, carefully pulling the flesh from either side of the wound together, I writhed in pain. Instead of lidocaine, my father—a skilled surgeon who always beat me at Operation, even left-handed—chose to apply poetry. In the original Persian first as always, translating specific words into either contemporary Persian or English at my request, he offered me these words from Rumi:

> If a thorn gets stuck under a donkey's tail,
> The ass knows only how to neigh and flail.
> But this drives the spike deeper still, the flesh further torn.
> It takes a sage to dislodge that pesky thorn.

Given this poem makes me out to be the ass and my father the sage—a fact proven throughout my life more times than I care to recount, but one that nonetheless took me years to accept—you may understand my early aversion to verse, and why it took the temporary annihilation of my ego via insanity and illiteracy for me to begin to appreciate this ancient ecstatic poetry that so permeated my childhood.

All the same, having stood squarely at the intersection of madness and mysticism, I can neither ignore nor romanticize their connection. I don't recommend insanity any more than I do illiteracy. At the depths of depression, I slit my wrist, and at the heights of mania, I nearly jumped off a high-rise. I thank God and every scientist responsible for the invention of antipsychotics. I believe in the power of modern medicine and always have. Still, I can't forget the intensely spiritual nature of my earliest manic experiences. They allowed me to bypass my brain, sidestep my ego, and open a door to my heart, straight to the Beloved. They nearly killed me, but they also showed me salvation, briefly freeing me from the tyranny of my own ego and filling me with more love than I knew possible.

For all the pain my mind has caused me, for all its ordinary and extraordinary fissures, I cannot dismiss the fact that it has also summoned a light, transforming my wounds, guiding my steps, imparting a distinct spiritual hunger, if not aptitude—a compassion, a creativity, a connectedness. This propensity, along with my history, is at the heart of who I am and why I now seek pilgrimage.

I arrive in San Diego on Halloween, my favorite American holiday by far: the one day of the year when being a freak is not only socially acceptable, but encouraged—a holy evening reserved for honoring the dead. On the five-minute drive from the airport to my parents' home, we pass a pirate, two witches, a band of Teenage Mutant Ninja Turtles, Alice in Wonderland, the Mad Hatter, Dorothy, Toto, SpongeBob, and a handful of zombies. As we drive by the latter, I ask Ahmad, "Are you excited about our pilgrimage?"

"Of course," he replies. "Just ask Jazbi."

"You have no idea, Melody *jan!*[6] I never see him this excited, except maybe when we got visa to come to United States. You make him so happy," my mom answers before I even have a chance to ask.

"But you know what Molana says when he sees a group going for *Hajj,*"[7] Ahmad continues, taking full advantage of the unrestricted poetic license the word "pilgrimage" has afforded him. "He calls them to come back. He says to them that the Beloved is your next-door neighbor." In other words, which we had yet to translate:

> *Why seek pilgrimage at some distant shore,*
> *When the Beloved is right next door?*

"So why the hell did I cross two time zones to get here?" I ask, only half kidding.

"Ahh, because," Ahmad replies, laughing but not kidding, "one day I will be dead."

Thus begins the first lesson of my trip. The Prophet Muhammad advised and Rumi took heed and repeated,

> *Die before you die.*

For Rumi, a devout Muslim and an Islamic scholar, this vital teaching isn't just about remembering death in order to appreciate life. It's about shedding your respectable worldly attire and discarding your ego before the divine presence. In that holy space—where

---

6   *Jan* (sometimes *joon*) is a term of endearment and reverence, often added after someone's name. It literally means "soul" and serves as the rough equivalent of "dear" in everyday conversation. In effect, instead of calling someone "my dear," we call them "my soul."

7   Pilgrimage to Mecca. Muslims who are capable (physically, emotionally, and financially) are expected to perform *Hajj* at least once in their lives. Along with faith, charity, prayer, and fasting, *Hajj* is one of the five pillars of Islam.

there is no room for two egos, as only the One will fit—reason and respectability become a hindrance. Indeed, it's no accident that my pilgrimage begins on Halloween.

By the time we arrive at my parents' harborside condo, it's late. But the table is set, and Rumi once again awaits. On my plate sits a prescription slip and a fork turned makeshift paperweight. The prescription is in Persian, but my name, suggested intake ("Twice a day"), and address ("Universe, Milky Way, solar system, Earth, USA") are all in English. The prescription, roughly translated, reads:

> *Your wounds may summon the light hereto,*
> *But this sacred light does not come from you.*

For as long as I can remember, my father has been scribbling poems on his old prescription pads, signing them as though they were for any ordinary pharmaceutical. My entire life, he has been writing me these prescriptions, leaving them like pearls at my feet. And my entire life, I have failed to fill them, too distracted and distraught by the thorns piercing my soles and the wounds left behind to notice the treasures lighting my path.

Like the verses on my countless unfilled prescription slips, many of my wounds have been inherited, some for generations. But every puncture, sprain, and laceration has led me here, on a pilgrimage of my own making, after a bandage that lets through the Light.

Dx: Wanting ♣ Rx: Go to the Source

Love's nation of origin is separate from all creeds.
For the lovers, the Beloved comprises all religions and nationalities.

—

Don't retreat, come near.
Don't lose faith, adhere.
Seek the tonic nectar in the bitter sting.
Go to the source of the source of your spring.

—

In love with insanity,
I'm fed up with wisdom and rationality.

—

All those severed from their source
Yearn to return as a matter of course.

—

If a thorn gets stuck under a donkey's tail,
The ass knows only how to neigh and flail.
But this drives the spike deeper still, the flesh further torn.
It takes a sage to dislodge that pesky thorn.

—

Why seek pilgrimage at some distant shore,
When the Beloved is right next door?

—

Die before you die.

—

Your wounds may summon the light hereto,
But this sacred light does not come from you.

CHAPTER 2

Dx: Isolation
Rx: Invent, Don't Imitate

Become the sky and the clouds that create the rain,
Not the gutter that carries it to the drain.

The next morning, thanks to the wonder of jet lag and the terror of a nightmare revisited, I'm up before the sun. I reach for my husband, Matthew, but my hand lands on an empty pillow. The orange quilt and floor-to-ceiling windows overlooking the San Diego bay quickly remind me that I'm in my parents' house.

It's the first time I've had this nightmare in months. For nearly a year after my last psychiatric hospitalization, the misery replayed weekly, if not more: I'm locked in solitary confinement with no windows, no clock, no books, no music, no rationality, no hope, no company. What makes this so disturbing is that it's not as much a nightmare as a flashback. In fact, nothing about this dream is fictitious. It happened to me, in a hospital isolation cell in Atlanta, where I was held for nearly twenty-four hours. If that doesn't seem long to you, then you've never been locked in seclusion while acutely manic and psychotic. It was not only long enough to scare the hell out of me, but it was also long enough to prompt a year of steady nightmares and a lifetime's worth of sporadic ones. This morning's is especially unnerving, because it's the first time I've awoken from this recurring horror show without Matthew here to hold and comfort me in its wake.

My parents are fast asleep down the hall, and it's too early to call Matthew or anyone else in the Americas for that matter. So I try my closest friends overseas: Sanam in Lausanne, Shireen in Milan, and Roja in Dublin. I even try some cousins in Iran and Australia. Anyone to make me feel less alone. But no one picks up.

So I turn to the first thing I always turn to when I'm feeling alone and human contact is unavailable, an art form for which I hold zero talent and endless affection, my name's blatant inspiration, and a powerful balm forbidden in isolation: music. OMD keeps me company through my headphones as I unpack, the sky silently staging its diurnal coup, ousting onyx for sapphire. I'm too busy singing "Walking on the Milky Way" to perceive its pageantry unfold before my eyes.

Feeling better, I freely extend my occupation of my parents' twenty-seventh-floor condo, moving on to what will serve as my "office" for the next month: the dining room. My mom has graciously agreed to temporarily abdicate her reign over this sacred space, home to panoramic views of the harbor and a round glass table that routinely seats eight to twelve guests several times a week. For Jazbi, a passionate perennial party host, this represents an extraordinary sacrifice—one for which I feel grateful as I turn on her latest shining addition to this place, a contemporary crystal chandelier straight out of *Architectural Digest*.

After rolling in my suitcase full of books and rolling out my yoga mat beside the table, I remove my headphones and with them the psychic remnants of that isolation cell in Atlanta. I set foot on the squishy cerulean rubber, face the ocean, and do my dawn prayers *on time* for the first time in years.

As usual, I pray in what many orthodox Muslims would consider the "wrong" direction, but given the world is round—and more important, that God is everywhere—I refuse to believe that there is any "right" or "wrong" direction for prayer. Wherever I am, I simply pray toward whatever I'm most drawn to within that space. Here, it's the ocean, so naturally, I face west.

I fully understand that the sight of an unveiled woman in Hello Kitty pajamas bowing westward on a yoga mat could easily cause some orthodox Muslims to lose their damn minds, but thanks to a steady dose of Sufi poets growing up, I couldn't care less. Plenty of people dissed Rumi's ecstatic chanting and whirling as wildly heretical, and he too couldn't have cared less. So the way I see it, I'm in good company.

Upon completing my prayers, I hear my father's voice and Rumi's verse wafting in from the kitchen.

Your homeland flows in every direction.
Why pray facing one minuscule section?

"The *universe* is your homeland!" Ahmad says after repeating this verse in Persian several times, an enduring echo from my childhood. "Your *ghebleh*[1] is everywhere. *Afareen* [well done]*!*"

Yes, my dad just praised me for praying in the "wrong" direction. Yes, he's actually proud of me for it. Yes, I know this is a ridiculous privilege few can claim—and I'm determined to quit taking it for granted. I've never envied my friends who grew up in strict religious households, forced to pray or dress a certain way, dragged to church when they'd rather stay out and play, driven to fear fun as though it were a sign of going astray. I always felt bad for those kids, and while

---

1   The direction Muslims face during daily prayers, toward the Kaaba in Mecca.

in Dayton most of them were Christian, this kind of inanity infiltrates all religions. Still, I never fully appreciated my good fortune in growing up in a home where God was never associated with fear or shame, nor reduced to religion, but always expressed and elevated as Love.

That said, I understand the temptation to get caught up in minutiae: focusing on the precise angle at which we pray or the houses of worship we frequent or the attire we don is way easier than focusing on *what* we worship and *why*. It takes so much less work to focus on the physical than on the spiritual—on our surface than on our souls, on our clothes and orientations than on our hearts and foundations.

Fixating on façades, moreover, is a recipe for emotional isolation, for where our souls connect us, our egos divide us. Comparisons born of ego foster separation, imitation, and jealousy, while connections born of love foster communication, invention, and community. Union with the divine—whether through prayer or nature or human interaction—demands that we look beyond the superficial in favor of the spiritual, that we use intuition to unite us instead of religion to divide us, and that we actively employ an increasingly scarce resource: focus.

"I can't believe you're *awake*," I say to Ahmad as I sit down at the dining room table. I can tell he's about to dive into another poem, so I open my laptop for documentation. He immediately shuts it as he sits down next to me.

"What are you doing? I wanted to take notes," I say.

"Why?"

"For the book."

"*Mageh kholeey?* [What are you, a fool?] This is not for a book. This is for your *life*. You cannot record everything. You do not even know what I am going to say. Anyway, sometimes you have to remember. And if you care and focus, then you will remember."

I'm not so sure, but recognizing how distracted I can get in front of a screen and how unlikely it is that Ahmad will budge on this, I leave my laptop shut.

"Molana says . . . ," Ahmad goes on, and I proceed to zone out, thinking, *I knew it*—too busy congratulating myself in my mind for predicting that another poem was pending to actually pay attention to said poem. Lucky for me, my father is both prone and amenable to repetition.

"Tell me again," I say, picking up a pen and opening my notebook. For the record, I've heard this particular poem dozens, if not hundreds, of times before. I've just never paid it my full attention. Ahmad grabs my pen and notebook.

"We have *time*, Melody *jan. Hala* [now], just *listen!* Before you leave, you will know this poem by heart. You will not need any pen or recording. I promise."

"Fine," I say, irritated, as I place my hands in my lap and stare at him, widening my already oversized eyes. "Can you just recite it again then, so I can *listen?*" I ask, oozing fifteen-year-old brat from every pore in my thirty-five-year-old body.

And of course, he does. Again, and again, and again—over the next month and the years to come. And yes, he is right; soon enough, I *will* have it memorized. I will also eventually learn that this couplet, though prevalent in the Persian oral tradition, cannot be found in most authoritative versions of the *Masnavi*, as many scholars deem it apocryphal. When I point this out to Ahmad, he immediately sides with the oral tradition over the scholarly interpretation, insisting that this must be Rumi. Personally, I don't care much where the verse originated—only that it survived long enough in Farsi to make its way to my father and me:

We have taken the fruit of the Quran, the marrow of its verses.
We have left the rinds and the bones, the waste for the asses.

Many choose to define Sufis simply as the mystics of Islam, and while this is true, it is also reductionist and incomplete. This brief couplet provides a better description. The "we" here refers to the Sufis, the mystics, the lovers. Like American transcendentalists, Sufis concern themselves only with the heart of all matters; they don't bother with refuse. They prefer the fruit to the rind, the marrow to the bone. They believe that union with the divine isn't exclusive to some afterlife, but that it can be achieved here and now, through abandoning one's ego and surrendering to the Beloved within each of us. For Sufis, everything boils down to love. While others peddle in worldly trifles, trading and arguing over rotting rinds, Sufis enjoy the fruit of devotion, savoring its sweetness.

To so-called Islamic fundamentalists trying to pervert and politicize Islam to spread violence, oppression, and hatred, this Sufi mentality represents a vast and undeniable threat from within. To the rest of us, it represents hope. Whether it's ISIS in the Middle East or the KKK in the American South, the aims and tactics of religious fundamentalists of all stripes remain indistinguishable: to divide humanity by using religion for personal and political gain. Sufis, like mystics across so many religious traditions, seek the exact opposite: *to unite us through love.*

"Well, you'll have to recite it again later," I tell Ahmad as the sun rises behind us, reflecting off the waves before us, "because I know I'll forget it."

"Of course! Why do you think I always repeat these poems? If I do not repeat them, *I* forget them too. Human being is like this: we forget the *maghz* ['marrow,' 'center,' or 'brain'] and remember only the *poost* ['skin,' 'peel,' or 'rind']. Really, we are such dummies," Ahmad says as he stands up and pops a dried fig into his mouth.

"Great. I'll try to keep that in mind," I reply, rolling my eyes as I open my laptop again in an attempt to jot down what I'm convinced I'll forget if I don't.

"*Boro baba!*[2] I try to help you, and you only want to write everything down. I tell you, this is not for a class or a book. *This is for your life.*"

"Yeah, I get it. And for some reason this great new life has no pens or notebooks or computers in it. No big deal. It's not like I'm a *writer* or anything."

"Rumi was a writer too, and you know what he says?"

"Seriously, this is like the third poem in less than ten minutes, and you won't let me write anything down?"

"Okay, this one you can write. Get ready," he says, cracking open a pistachio and laughing as he proceeds to recite this couplet in Persian:

> *The pen writes and writes in frantic haste,*
> *But when it comes to love, the pen breaks.*

"Sure," I reply, "from a man who wrote a gazillion lines of poetry *entirely* about love. Just perfect."

Now we're both laughing.

"Seriously though, why are you even *up* so early?" I ask again. "And where's Mom?"

Before Ahmad (a classic snoozer) can answer, my mom (a classic lark) walks into the room carrying a giant poster board with my face and the cover of my latest book plastered across it. It's so big, and she's so short, that it actually looks like the poster itself is walking. Ahmad and I laugh harder.

"What? You don't like it?" she asks.

---

2 Literally "Go Dad," but the connotation of *boro baba* is roughly equivalent to a playful "Get outta here!"

"No, Mom. I *love* it. Thank you!" I say, hugging her and kissing her cheeks.

Apparently, Matthew took it upon himself to create and email her a template for a poster, which she then had printed to surprise me.

My sole bit of business here in California is an appearance on the "Breaking Taboos" panel at the 2014 Iranian American Women Foundation conference tomorrow in LA, and this poster is meant to sit in front of the table where I'll be signing books after my panel— presumably so people can tell me apart from other Iranian-American overachievers who will no doubt be peddling their wares as well.

Honestly, I'd rather stay in my pajamas and let the poster rest in its secure future home under the bed in the guest room, but I can't. My parents are too excited for the conference; a bunch of their friends will be there, and I don't want to make them look bad—or worse yet, to fulfill any stereotypes by being the flighty bipolar girl who bails at the last minute. No, I am reliable, and so is my family.

For an incalculable cost, they have all set me up to succeed in a world that was designed to watch me fail. My parents left their homes and families in Iran so that Romana and I could have every free- dom and opportunity afforded to anyone of equal intelligence with a Y chromosome. They paid for every cent of our college, my law school, my master's, and her medical school. They left us debt-free in a land defined by debt. And they did it after relocating with next to nothing to the same country that effectively ruined theirs, the same country that staged a coup that led to the so-called Islamic Revolution and the shitstorm that followed, and the same country that would wait nearly sixty years before admitting to it.

Ironically enough, my parents chose America because there were more freedoms for us here, in the land that sold out Iran and Irani- ans for cheaper gas prices. They swallowed their pride when people berated them for their backgrounds, insisting that their education would save them, that their degrees would eventually lead Americans to consider them equal. Two MDs from the best medical school in Iran, however, have proven insufficient. My mom is still a woman, my dad is still brown, they both still have accents, and they both still come from extended Muslim families that will be banned from visiting us in the US by the time I finish writing this book.

Nonetheless, I am lucky, and I know it. No matter how many strangers consider me "less than" on account of my gender, ethnicity, religion, disability, and/or skin color, I remain far more privileged than oppressed, more blessed than cursed, more loved than loathed. Of the dozens of hospital beds I've occupied, I never sat in a single one uninsured or alone if my family and friends could help it. My parents and my sister showed up at hospitals in Ohio, Illinois, and Indiana; Matthew showed up at hospitals in Connecticut, New York, and Georgia. And when they needed a break, my friends and extended chosen family were always there to relieve them.

Because of this extraordinary and diverse community of friends and family, I was never alone. Because of them, even as I sat in that isolation cell in Atlanta—manic, psychotic, and terrified—some part of me *knew* that I would eventually be healthy and free, that I had advocates who were fighting for me. Because of them, I have not only survived America, but I have thrived in it. In other words, because I was loved, I am alive.

So yeah, I'm getting out of my pajamas and going to this conference. Too many people have invested too much for me to bail. I mean, there's a fucking *poster board* for God's sake!

We arrive at the Beverly Hilton that afternoon following a five-hour drive that should've taken less than half that. Thanks to traffic and an epic Wholesome Choice grocery stop in Irvine that included more eggplants than your average white American family eats in a year, we get to the hotel well past Ahmad's nap time. For reference, my father naps longer and more consistently than any human I have ever known. With the exception of koalas, cats, and coma patients, I can think of no one more deeply devoted to dormancy.

Every afternoon, he sleeps for one to three hours—and just to be clear, this is *on top of* averaging a good eight to ten hours at night. Even during med school and residency, even while running the largest ob-gyn practice in Dayton, even as a rambunctious kid and an active bike-riding, Starbucks-frequenting senior citizen—my dad has always taken his naps *very* seriously. I used to think this had to do with the thirty years he spent as a practicing obstetrician, when we often received middle-of-the-night phone calls, because Ahmad, in a pre-cell-phone era, insisted on sharing our home number with patients. But my mom—a pathologist who had the privilege of pretty much zero patient contact, unless you count cadavers—insists that Ahmad's legendary naps long predated his obstetrics practice, and my father readily admits as much.

The moment the concierge hands us our keys, he grabs a copy and makes a beeline for the elevator. Within less than five minutes, Ahmad is already passed out on one of the two queen beds. My mom and I hang up our outfits for tomorrow to minimize wrinkling, re-apply our lipstick (L'Oreal Persistent Plum for me and MAC Russian Red for Jazbi), and head out to tour the hotel. It's no surprise that a group of Iranian-American women would choose such a posh venue for their conference, just as it's no surprise that Gucci is sponsoring it.

As a diaspora, we're suckers for brand names and elaborate parties. When you've lived through war, revolution, and exile, knowing how to dress up and celebrate becomes all the more important. And when you're subject to misrepresentation, vilification, and discrimination, you seek security wherever you can find it. For plenty of Persian women, this means wearing the "right" clothes or having the "right" nose. So much so that not only is Tehran considered the nose job capital of the world, but Los Angeles, arguably the most image-conscious city on the planet, is also called Tehrangeles on account of being home to more Iranians than any other city outside of Iran.

While I prefer to focus on our saffron, pistachios, and poetry, I can't deny that Persians are also known for some considerably less delicious and high-minded proclivities defined more by excess than by taste. Indeed, there is a subset of Iranian-Americans that has actively sought equality not merely through education, but through affluence and all the obnoxious status symbols that come with it. To learn more about this contingent, you need only turn on your TV and tune in to Bravo's nightmare known as *Shahs of Sunset*—though I beg of you, please don't. The fact that this mortifying reality television show is a step up with respect to popular depictions of Iranians is due entirely to a media landscape where the only available roles tend to be "Terrorist #1," "Terrorist #2," and "Terrorist #3."

The gaudy *Shahs of Sunset* stereotypes are few and far between here, but touring the Beverly Hilton with my original nose and consignment clothes, I still feel acutely out of place among these women who are supposedly just like me.

"We should go soon," my mom says, as if reading my mind.

"Yes. Let's go *now*," I reply.

Thankfully, my cousin Nousha has invited us all to dinner at her home in Pacific Palisades, so I'm able to spend the rest of the evening catching up with her instead of dreading tomorrow.

My "Breaking Taboos" panel doesn't begin until 2:30, so I have plenty of time to register, set up my booth, and attend other sessions in the morning. It's my first formal encounter with this particular pride of *sheerzan*s, or lionesses, as they call themselves, and I have to admit, they're impressive: hypereducated, hypersuccessful, hyperpolished. I genuinely feel honored to be here, but I also feel intensely isolated— partly because being invited to represent a cultural taboo doesn't exactly foster a strong sense of belonging, and partly because the LA Iranian scene has just never been my thing. It's *so* not Ahmad's thing either, but he somehow manages to fit right in. In fact, he seems downright ebullient, proudly joining my mother and me as one of only a handful of men in attendance, despite lacking a ticket, as they'd already sold out by the time he tried to buy one.

"It's okay," Ahmad insists, "they will not even notice me. Anyway, I can help with your books." And he does. He rolls around my suitcase full of hardcovers and paperbacks and follows me to my booth, neatly setting out every last book on the table provided. I teach him how to use Square, so he can accept credit cards while I'm signing books, and miraculously, he picks it up right away.

By two o'clock, Ahmad has already sold nearly a dozen books before I've even spoken, merely by bragging about "the author" to strangers while my mom and I attended conference sessions.

"Are you ready for my panel?" I ask Ahmad as I squeeze behind the poster of myself so I can sit down next to him.

"Are *you* ready?"

"I think I'll manage," I say as we soak in the scene before us. "I've never seen this many *irooni* women in the same place before—I mean outside of Iran or a wedding or something. Definitely not for an organized conference without an open bar. It's weird."

"I think it is great to see all of these women who are so smart, talented, and *irooni*. Just like you."

"Really? *Just like me?*" I ask, nodding toward a woman who looks more feline than hominid thanks to excessive elective surgery.

"How much money you think she pays to look that bad?" Ahmad whispers in English, because this is one of the few places in America where you can't use Farsi as code to dish about strangers "behind their backs" in front of their faces.

"We're horrible," I reply, and we both agree.

"You know, Rumi says—" Ahmad starts.

"That you shouldn't talk shit about people?" I interrupt.

"You two always are laughing," my mom says as she walks toward us. "Are you ready? It's time for your talk, Melody *jan.*"

"It's just a panel, Mom. But yes, I'm ready."

The conference room is packed, standing room only. Oddly enough, taboo breakers draw a good crowd. I can't help but think that just by being here I'm inviting all of these strangers to start talking shit about me to my face.

"I have to pee," I say a little too loudly to no one in particular the second we walk in.

"You have time," my mom whispers. "We find a seat and hold your bag. You go."

I book it to the bathroom, only to find a massive line snaking outside the women's restroom, well into the hallway. Then I do what I often do when confronted with lines like these: I use the men's room. Immediately the only man in this giant restroom begins freaking out: "This is the *men's* room!"

"Then be a gentleman, avert your eyes, and quit yelling at me," I say, holding up my hands like blinders on either side of my face as I gallop to one of the many empty stalls.

"This is the *men's* room!" he repeats. "For *men!* You understand?

Men!" Hell-bent on throwing a hissy fit over a girl who won't stay in her place, he refuses to shut up. But as a woman who writes and speaks her mind for a living—as well as a person who simply gets an inordinate kick out of crossing all sorts of socially constructed boundaries—I am well versed in the art of ignoring hysterical men. I ignored the pale, pimply Ohio schoolboys who told me to go back to I-rack when I beat them on the basketball court. I ignored the alleged men of God who tried (and failed) to kick me out of the "men's section" of a West Virginia mosque. And I ignored and continue to ignore pretty much anyone who wants to school me on where I do and do not belong.

Thus, undeterred, I proceed to take a long and satisfying piss despite this man's ardent and redundant protest. When I walk out of the stall, he is still there, and I interpret the look of disgust frozen on his face as an invitation to tear into him.

"Sir," I say as I wash my hands, being sure to speak slowly and enunciate, "you are at a *women's* conference. There are maybe ten men here *total*. You will have to share the restroom. It will be okay. We are not violent."

The man storms out, and I feel oddly serene, taking my sweet time checking my eyeliner and reapplying my Persistent Plum before I walk out of the bathroom and inform all the women in line that the men's restroom is now officially unisex. The women take me at my word, and the line is no longer.

As I walk back to the conference room and take a seat onstage with my fellow panelists, I feel a fleeting sense of solidarity with these *sheerzan*s, and for the first time, I'm excited to be here.

It helps that I'm sharing the stage with two extraordinary Iranian-American women: the honorable Shahla S. Sabet, a brilliant jurist and the first Iranian-American judge to be appointed to the superior court of the state of California, and Dr. Foojan Zeine, a fierce and gifted psychotherapist, author, and television host. But my sense of excitement and solidarity soon fades, as I remember that none of us is here to speak about her talents or accomplishments. Instead, we are here to share our traumas. Whatever brilliant legal, psychotherapeutic, or literary insights the three of us may have to impart, they're not on the menu. Though we're all successful women who've managed to thrive amid highly hostile environments, we're not here to talk about that. Rather, we're here to talk about how society interprets our traumas as taboos.

So I speak about living with bipolar disorder, Shahla speaks about living as an out lesbian, and Foojan speaks about living as a survivor of childhood sexual abuse—all within an Iranian-American community that is far from eager to discuss mental illness, homosexuality, or rape. By the end of the session, I feel weary and depleted, certain the last hour was more about voyeurism than veracity. Maybe it was the misdirected focus on taboos. Maybe it was the inept moderator, perpetually interrupting panelists at the most inopportune moments to insert the most irrelevant commentary. Maybe it was Tehrangeles. Maybe it was me. I have no idea. But whatever the cause, at the conclusion of our panel, I feel more like a traumatized misfit than a burgeoning mystic, and I want out of here. Before I can reflect further on my exit strategy, I see Ahmad heading toward me.

"That was great, Melody *jan!*" he says, holding out his hand to help me step down from the stage. He clutches it tightly and leads me through the crowd in what I swear feels like a skip.

On the way out, several audience members inquire about whether I'm selling books, and Ahmad answers for me: "Yes! Follow us. She signs them too!"

I nod and smile at the strangers who keep complimenting me for being "brave." I get this a lot, and I find it equally flattering and insulting, a reminder that what I do is risky—that more rational people would veer away from revealing a highly stigmatized mental health condition to the world. It's much like being complimented on a "brave" outfit—as if to say, "*I* would never wear that, but good for *you!*" Whether it's revealing a serious mental illness or sporting a fuchsia spandex bodysuit, there are certain actions and apparel that people claim to appreciate in "brave" strangers but would never adopt for themselves. As such, these compliments have always struck me as unsettling. And after receiving roughly a dozen of them back-to-back during our skip to my booth, I feel thoroughly nauseated the minute we sit down. Still, I manage to sign about thirty books while Ahmad gleefully swipes credit cards and Jazbi chats up the women in line, keeping them sufficiently entertained to withstand the wait. Though my self-elected chiefs of financial affairs and public relations couldn't seem happier, I can't wait to get the hell out of this place.

The last book I sign is for a woman who keeps asking, "How do you *do* it?" as if I'm scaling Everest or curing cancer. Before she leaves, she leans down and whispers, "I would be *so embarrassed.*" Then, without so much as a transition, she turns to Ahmad and adds, "You must be so proud."

"So proud," he confirms, beaming sincerely.

"Yes," I chime in, "he is very proud of his embarrassment."

"Oh no," she says, laughing nervously as she literally clutches her pearls. "I just meant that *I* would be embarrassed. *You* shouldn't be at all."

"Of course," Ahmad replies, shooting me a raised eyebrow, "she was just kidding."

"Yeah, totally kidding," I lie.

"Look," Ahmad says as the pearls walk away, pointing to my empty suitcase, "we sold out!"

"You're telling me," I mutter under my breath.

Heading back to San Diego, Ahmad drives, I sit shotgun, and my mom sleeps in the backseat. Even as a kid, I nearly always got to sit in the front—partly because I was spoiled, but mostly because I was chronically carsick.

The last time I remember sitting in the back as a child, my mom was driving and my dad was in the passenger seat. Thanks to me, my parents always kept plastic bags in the car, but on this unfortunate occasion, there was either no bag to be found or even less warning than usual. Whatever the case, my father's immediate instinct was to cup his hands under my mouth, and mine was to promptly puke straight into them. I know of no more simultaneously revolting and heartwarming expression of unconditional love. Ever since, the same cupped, outstretched hands that signify the standard Muslim prayer pose have doubled as Ahmad's own custom sign language for me. Translation: "I love you so much that I'll catch your vomit."

"Are you okay?" Ahmad asks, extending a cupped hand to my chin.

"I'm fine," I lie, but as usual, my face betrays me. It's one of those highly expressive faces that can't control itself to save its owner's life. In fifth grade, before I knew what it meant to roll your eyes but long after I'd perfected the maneuver, I earned more than a week's worth of detention because I kept rolling my eyes in class, even after Mrs. Geyer told me to stop. Instead of telling her I didn't know what the phrase meant, I just kept saying "fine" while simultaneously rolling my eyes. She wrote my name on the board and put what seemed like a million check marks next to it: a check for every inadvertent eye-roll. After class, a friend explained what "rolling your eyes" means, and I realized that you could be an expert at something without even knowing it had a name.

"You are not fine. What is wrong? Is it that woman? Forget about her. She was a dummy."

"It's not just her. It's that I don't feel like I fit in with so many of those women."

"Why you want to fit in? Fit in for *what*? You know what Rumi says?"

My pilgrimage seems to have given Ahmad greater license to be fully himself. This translates not only into crashing women's conferences, but also into a deluge of poetic recitations, far more than usual. Since he's always been so quick to recite a relevant poem in any given scenario, I never considered the possibility that Ahmad might actually be *holding back*. But now, after a weekend of a seemingly endless torrent of couplets, quatrains, and ghazals, I realize that he has spent much of his life exercising extreme poetic restraint. This isn't as much a new Ahmad as a *liberated* one, and I envy him for it. I couldn't have felt more confined, surrounded by women who, despite being so much like me, felt nothing like me. But as out of place as I felt at that conference, Ahmad couldn't have seemed more at home—not because he felt like he fit in, but because he was happy to stand out.

"You hear me? You know what Molana says?"

"No, tell me," I reply, and he does.

> *Though the song of the nightingale you may learn to compose,*
> *You still can't know what it sings to the rose.*

"You see," Ahmad says, "always it is better to sing your own song than to copy someone else. Invent, don't imitate, Melody *jan*."

This is one of those verses I've heard at least a hundred times, a lesson I've learned repeatedly from personal experience, but one that I am still struggling to fully internalize. By creating my own pilgrimage here in California instead of going for *Hajj* in Saudi Arabia, I've begun to apply this lesson.

But Ahmad is an expert, and as such, he can feel at home anywhere, even as a super-minority, while I still feel at home nowhere, not even among my own. Like Ahmad, I'm an original, but unlike him, I can be self-conscious about it.

It's easier to imitate than to create, but imitation builds cults, not communities. True community demands originality, for invention is the most powerful antidote to isolation. Any sort of new creation—be it a book, a painting, a hairdo, a chocolate mousse, or a human life—connects us to one another, and in doing so, to our Creator, which is ultimately the goal of any mystic.

Rumi advises,

> *Become the sky and the clouds that create the rain,*
> *Not the gutter that carries it to the drain.*

Becoming the sky and the clouds, however, requires a certain perspective—one we're born with, but one that often gets lost in the ridiculous rush to become an adult. In my case, to follow Rumi's advice and my own creative spirit, I will have to quit seeing my writing as a means of achieving sustenance and status, and I will have to start seeing it the way I *first* did: as a way to connect—with myself, with others, and with the Beloved.

I wrote my first book while I was in law school. No one assigned it; no one was paying me for it, and no one expected it, least of all me. But I started writing, and I couldn't stop. It wasn't about seeking wealth or approval. It was about having something to say and saying it. Eventually, I realized that writing was my way of making sense of the world and doing my part to change it. I never expected money or accolades to follow, but they did—and with them, a sense of self-importance that soon enough became self-defeating. For ego has a way of crushing creativity—stopping us before we even start.

Contrary to popular myth, humans cannot be divided into "creatives" and "non-creatives," for to be human is to be creative by nature. Even if all you're creating is compost, you're still *creating*. Even in death, left to decompose, we feed the plants and animals that once fed us. In effect, we're genetically programmed to be creative, and we'd be dead wrong to think otherwise. At the very least, every one of us is perfectly capable of becoming fertilizer. Whether we recognize it or not, creativity is in our DNA—and it extends far beyond our capacity to nourish the soil.

Within each of us lies the potential to create something unique and valuable, and by doing so, we not only produce novel contributions to the world, but we also foster meaningful community. Being human, however, we often waste time trying to make the *same* thing, act the *same* way, or sing the *same* song as someone else—all in an effort to be accepted, to fit in, to find love. But any semblance of community that arises from these efforts is a sham. It may seem counterintuitive, but real community demands originality, not conformity.

I know this firsthand, because every time I write something new it helps me feel less alone. For one, no matter how odd and lonely I may feel in any given time or place, my readers form a kind of community for me, but even before my words make it onto anyone's nightstand, the act of writing them down, of creating something from nothing, connects me with all that has been written before and all that will be written after.

"If you do not sing your own song," Ahmad will say to me on a crisp September morning four years later as I read portions of this chapter to him over FaceTime, "you do not understand it and nobody else will understand it. You hear the sound, but you do not know what does it mean. Only the *bolbol* knows what it says to the *gol.*"

I know what Ahmad means. Not because I know that a *bolbol* is a nightingale and a *gol* is a flower, but because he has always sung his own song and encouraged me to sing mine.

Within days of returning to San Diego, I will find myself writing— *and enjoying writing*—again. It won't be a lot and it won't be my best work, but it will be more and better than anything I've written all year. Inspired by the subtlest change in perspective, I'll stop writing for everyone else and start writing for myself: to create something new and different, to cultivate community, to find my way home.

Such is the power of perspective to inspire, and it's far from exclusive to the arts. No matter your vocation or situation, there is room to be creative and find community by nurturing invention and connection in our everyday lives. When we choose to create instead of imitate—to focus on fostering more homemade relationships and experiences instead of accumulating more mass-produced stuff, on collecting more adventures than artifacts, and on amassing more friends than followers—we find true connection and community with ourselves, the world around us, and the Beloved. And not so coincidentally, if you trust the scientists who study this, we also find joy[3]—along with a priceless insight for any creative (AKA human): *we need not be miserable in order to be creative.*

We are constantly presented with opportunities, big and small, to act in ways that cultivate both joy and innovation, ways that recognize that building meaningful connection isn't the consequence of blandly blending in, but rather of boldly standing out. Like all of the

---

3   A. Kumar, M. A. Killingsworth, and T. Gilovich, "Waiting for Merlot: Anticipatory Consumption of Experiential and Material Purchases," *Psychological Science* 25, no. 10 (October 2014): 1924–31; G. E. Vaillant, *Aging Well: Surprising Guideposts to a Happier Life from the Landmark Study of Adult Development* (New York: Little, Brown, 2008).

lessons herein, it's one that I'm still learning—and in fact, one that I'm learning *with you* as I write this.

Were I *not* still learning and somehow convinced that I had it all figured out, then I would hope that you'd quit reading now, because while I neither have nor believe in having all the right answers, I do know this: to live well, we can never stop learning. The moment we quit and insist we know it all, we're screwed. After all, that's the recipe for fundamentalism: mix a ton of pride, a gallon of ignorance, and a bucket of insecurity with a cup of a simple answer you've convinced yourself is right for everything and everyone, then add hefty fistfuls of fear until . . . *voilà!* Instant fundamentalist.

Where fundamentalism perpetuates crass imitation, mysticism invites creative invention. Where fundamentalists seek to shrink their God through hostility and conformity, mystics seek to expand theirs through love and ingenuity. As a mystic who fostered his own form of worship that revolved more around whirling and singing than kneeling and whispering, Rumi understood the power of mysticism and originality to combat fundamentalism. And while he inspired an entire Sufi order that modeled its rituals after his whirling and chanting, Rumi never set out to start a religious order, for to follow Rumi's teachings isn't to follow at all. It is to investigate, to create, and always, in the process, to love.

> *Since hearing my first love story,*
> *I pursued the Beloved with every part of me.*
> *But could lover and Beloved ever be separate, subject to division?*
> *No, they are one and the same. I just had double vision.*

A consummate Sufi, Rumi forever finds the Beloved within, and in doing so, he boldly declines to distinguish between lover and Beloved, humanity and divinity, as he finds each within the other. Rumi's God isn't up in the clouds looking down on us; Rumi's God is inside each of us. Rumi's God isn't He or She; Rumi's God is We. Rumi's God isn't declaring judgments; Rumi's God is declaring love. And Rumi's God *isn't merely God*; Rumi's God is *the Beloved*. Now, *that's* a deity I can get with. And it's the One I meet again and again in Rumi's poetry.

Because any hindrance to love isolates us from the Beloved and all creation, Rumi provides a clear prescription for the petty pride and propriety that prevent us from fully expressing the divine gifts we hold within, hindering our hearts from accepting and offering all the love we can:

Toss timidity aside and leave your reputation behind.

To reconnect with the indivisible and irresistible Beloved within, we need only stop pretending to be someone else and start rejoicing in being the wildly unique and deeply connected creatures we always were and always will be. It sounds easy enough, but humans are a chronically forgetful bunch, easily seduced by the comforts of con- vention, myself included.

"*Reseedeem* [have we arrived]?" my mom asks, sitting up as we pull into the garage.

"Yes, Jazbi *jan*," Ahmad responds into the rearview mirror. "We are home, Your Majesty."

"*Boro baba!* One nap and suddenly I'm 'Your Majesty'? You nap every day! What does that make you?"

"A hypocrite," I tease as we get out of the car.

"I am not a hypocrite. I am a *Shirazi*," Ahmad says proudly, hold- ing his right index finger up to my face as a means of driving his point home.

"Way to fulfill the stereotype then," I joke, grabbing his finger and waving it in his own face. Among Iranians, Shirazis have a reputation for indolence, and Ahmad's notorious napping does nothing to defy the popular dis, not that he's trying to.

"Why always you are on your mom's side?"

"What do you expect? Paradise lies at the feet of the mothers, *not the fathers*. I didn't make the rules," I say, citing the Prophet Muhammad as we board the elevator.

"Let's go shopping," my mom says, tired of both of us.

"*You* go shopping," Ahmad replies. "I go sleeping."

"You thought you were invited?" my mom counters. "Neiman Marcus has a sale, Melody *jan*. We have some lunch and then we go, okay?"

"Sounds perfect," I reply as we step off the elevator, and I mean it.

Like my mother, I adore fashion, and while on my own I tend to buy my designer apparel secondhand, I always look forward to hitting Neiman's with my mom. It's basically her mosque, and honestly, when we're together, it's mine too. I'm not proud of it, but I've spent my fair share of time worshipping at the altar of consumerism and engaging in retail therapy—at least long enough to know that neither offers any long-lasting results. Still, ever a sucker for instant gratification, I partake. But I recognize today's shopping excursion as more: an opportunity to connect with my mother on her terms and territory, in a place where we both find beauty.

"So 'paradise' *yani*[4] Neiman Marcus?" Ahmad asks, chuckling.

"*Eh, velam kon,*"[5] I protest as he unlocks the door. "I'm a work in progress."

---

4   "Means" or "meaning" or "as in."

5   "Leave me alone." "*Eh*" is more of an exclamation with a meaning akin to "oh" than a word unto itself.

Dx: Isolation ❧ Rx: Invent, Don't Imitate

Your homeland flows in every direction.
Why pray facing one minuscule section?

—

We have taken the fruit of the Quran, the marrow of its verses.
We have left the rinds and the bones, the waste for the asses.

—

The pen writes and writes in frantic haste,
But when it comes to love, the pen breaks.

—

Though the song of the nightingale you may learn to compose,
You still can't know what it sings to the rose.

—

Become the sky and the clouds that create the rain,
Not the gutter that carries it to the drain.

—

Since hearing my first love story,
I pursued the Beloved with every part of me.
But could lover and Beloved ever be separate, subject to division?
No, they are one and the same. I just had double vision.

—

Toss timidity aside and leave your reputation behind.

CHAPTER 3

Dx: Haste
Rx: Quit Keeping Score

Quit keeping score if you want to be free.
Love has ejected the referee.

Born in Shiraz—a city famous for its gardens, mystics, poets, philosophers, and of course, naps—Ahmad developed an intense appreciation for all of the above at an early age. Nonetheless, he was an unruly child. A jokester and a slow reader who earned poor grades in everything save literature up until high school, Ahmad preferred soccer fields to classrooms and often got into fights.

"I think if I was in *this* society," he says now, nearly seventy, finally submitting to my digital voice recorder the day after we return from LA, "they would have labeled me, I have no question, as probably somewhere between dyslexic and retarded . . . and they would put me on some kind of medication."

As a properly labeled and medicated product of said twenty-first-century American society, one who winces at words like "retarded" and welcomes words like "neurodiversity," I can't entirely disagree. My best guess as to Ahmad's likely diagnosis, with all of my zero medical training, would include a couple conditions in or around the dyslexia and ADHD departments, but given the growing buffet of labels and subjective diagnostic criteria recognized by modern medicine, there's really no telling. Depending on the day and the psychiatrist, psychologist, learning specialist, or social worker involved, he might have been diagnosed with any number of disorders within or across the attention, learning, mood, and/or conduct spectra. Growing up in Iran in the 1950s and '60s, however, Ahmad easily avoided any such labels, while eventually managing to stop fighting and start studying.

For this, he credits three friends, adding, "After I met them and start studying with them, I become one of the best students in the class. I started really working hard, and all of the sudden, I notice I am not retarded."

"Ahmad, you can't say that word! It's *really offensive*. It's like someone calling me psycho or calling you a terrorist or something like that."

"Okay. I did not know. I never say it again. Thank you for telling me."

I still can't get used to Ahmad thanking me for correcting his English. Had I done this as a kid, I'm sure he would've called me a *pedar sag* (a choice curse among many Iranian dads despite the fact that it literally means "Your dad is a dog"). More recently, however, after I asked Ahmad to start correcting my Farsi, he not only agreed, but he told me to do the same for his English.

Even after explicitly asking him to correct my mistakes though, I still tend to get annoyed when he actually does it. By contrast, Ahmad is genuinely grateful when I correct him. "Thank you for telling me" is now one of his signature taglines—right alongside "I know you love your mom more than me," "Tanks God," "This is a fact," and, naturally, "*Pedar sag.*"

"Sorry for interrupting you. Go on," I say.

"No, it's good you interrupt me. Thank you for telling me. Please always keep telling me. What I was saying was that I really always thought that I have a"—he pauses—"mental disability. And my father always was telling me, 'No, you are smart,' da da da [Ahmad's version of 'et cetera'], all those things. I studied so hard for the entrance exam to Tehran University. At the time, I think there were close to forty or fifty thousand people applying; they accepted only the top two hundred fifty people to study medicine. I was one hundred eighty-five or so. That was a huge success, *huge* success."

Though Ahmad is prone to hyperbole, this is not that. His score was indeed a huge success: a ticket to the country's most prestigious university to study its most prestigious profession. While there, he met my mom, also a medical student. When I ask him about it now, sitting at the kitchen table as my mother expertly peels a tangerine, preserving the rind for jam, Ahmad smiles at her and adds, "But my biggest success, *of course*, was to marry Jazbi."

"*Boro baba!*" she says, raising her head and handing me a slice. Ahmad takes this and the red light on my voice recorder as an invitation to continue.

"You know she score higher on *Konkour* [Iran's notoriously grueling university entrance exam] than almost everyone, and way higher than me."

I do know. My mom never brings this up, but my dad loves to—and he will, to anyone who'll listen. More than any man I've ever known, he can't stand when people underestimate women. Unlike me, my mom, and my sister, Ahmad doesn't believe that men and women are equal. He believes women are superior. And he can go on for days about it if you let him.

A tiny snippet of his extensive reasoning: "Because when you go and see the accomplishment of women and their ability, you see nature gave them more. Their connection between the right brain and the left brain—it is proven, you can Google it—is far more than man, so woman can do many more things at the same time. This is a fact. Man sees only what is in front of him. But woman sees everything. In nature, men do not do as much. Woman has to be ultra-conscious of everything, to protect herself and her babies. Otherwise, predator eats them up. If the male sheep tries to take care of the babies, then all the babies would be dead. The brain of the woman is better. This is a fact. I have no doubt."

Despite actually Googling his facts and finding evidence to back them up, I still don't buy Ahmad's conclusion or find it nearly as straightforward or unproblematic as he seems to. I do, however, appreciate having been raised by a father who is so deeply convinced that women's brains are superior to men's, as it has helped me better navigate a world where so many seem so deeply convinced of the exact opposite: a world where reviewers routinely refer to women's books as "sassy," "fierce," and "feisty," while reserving words like "genius," "definitive," and "groundbreaking" for our male counterparts. This is a fact. Google it.

"We meet in pharmacology class," Ahmad continues. "I keep asking to walk her home and she keep saying no, but one day she say yes, and for one year, we walk together like that. Then, it was the first of Farvardeen [March 21], so the school was closed for two weeks for Nowruz [the Persian New Year]. Since I did not have any excuse to see her, I called her for the first time. I say to her: 'Do you want to go to mini-golf?'"

"Are you kidding? Mini-golf?!"

"So what? It was fun for us. At that time I really knew I wanted to marry her. After one year walking back and forth together and having maybe ten or fifteen dinner together, always at the same place by her house, getting one order of chicken for both of us because I did not have money, that day she said okay and we did some pitt-putt golfing—"

"It's putt-putt, Ahmad."

"Oh, thank you for telling me. So we did some putt-putt golfing, and then we went to a very good restaurant for that time, and we ordered pizza. I told her, 'I want to live the rest of my life with you.' Then she said, almost right away, 'It's okay, but I have to ask my mom and brother.' I told her, 'Let's go ask.' And we did. Same night. We were twenty-two years old."

After some persuading, both elders approved, and my parents were married less than a year after pizza and putt-putt. Not exactly your standard Iranian courtship—no parental prescreening, no chaperoned meetings, no dowries, none of that—but it worked. Nearly fifty years, four countries, thousands of miles, and two grown children later, they remain happily married. Shining examples of Iran's post-revolution brain drain, they are now both naturalized American citizens who've spent more than half their lives in the US. But only since moving to California have they come to feel truly at home in this country.

In Ohio, they were Iranians who lived in America. In California, they *are* America. Here—with their own restaurants, grocery stores, bookshops, radio stations, hair salons, magazines, plays, concerts, and streaming television shows—they don't have to choose between being Iranian or American. Here, they can be Iranian-Americans.

One of the greatest joys of spending this time with them in San Diego has been the opportunity to witness my parents' finally feeling genuinely welcome in America. I never expected I'd live to see this day, so I am grateful for it.

Every morning, Ahmad and I sit at the round glass dining table and spend hours poring over poetry in between sips of tea and bites of fruit and *noon-o-paneer*.[1] We've been doing it for weeks now, and despite the fact that we can spend four hours straight discussing verse after verse in the mornings, most of Ahmad's poetry lessons remain as they always have: impromptu. Couplets, quatrains, and ghazals join us on our frequent evening walks along the harbor, or as we run random errands throughout the day, or over dinner at one of the dozen-plus Persian parties my mom insists we attend while I'm here.

We are both enjoying our formal and informal poetry lessons more than I ever imagined, but the month races by, and before I know it, it's nearly Thanksgiving.

My parents leave for Denver to visit my sister, brother-in-law, niece and nephews for the holiday, and despite everyone's persistent pleas for me to join them, I stick to my guns and stay in San Diego alone, just as I had planned when I first booked this trip. My admittedly flawed reasoning: the solitude will inspire me to write. Before my parents leave, they beseech me one last time to join them, insisting they'll buy me a ticket at the airport. I again resist.

"Then at least let's do some *bayt*s [couplets] before we leave," Ahmad insists, picking up one of his many "notebooks," AKA spiral-bound index cards where he copies down his favorite poems in painfully illegible script when he isn't scribbling them on random Post-its or prescription pads.

"But you only have a few hours. We'll do this when you get back."

"She is right, Ahmad *jan*. Do it when we get back," my mom says.

"No," he insists. "I have some *bayt*s I want to tell her before we go. There is time." Every day now Ahmad reminds me that we will be continuing our lessons over video chat when I return home to

1   Bread and cheese, standard Persian breakfast fare.

Raleigh. Today is no different. "We do this *at least* once a week, but probably two or three times is better. And not just on the phone, but on the Skype or the FaceTime, so we can *see* each other."

Ahmad is clearly going to miss our face-to-face lessons, and he's not alone. As frustrating as I find this archaic language at times, I have treasured the opportunity to ponder this poetry together—and not because I've learned a lot about classical Persian verse, as I still have tons left to learn, but because I've learned a lot about Ahmad.

"Of course we will," I assure him, "and we still have almost an entire week after you get back from Denver. Once I've written some more of the book over Thanksgiving, we can get a lot more done."

"But there is no rush, Melody *jan*. You can come with us to Denver. You can write *there*. You don't need to do everything so fast. That is why I say we keep doing our lessons after you go back to North Carolina. We have *time*. When you try to go so fast, to do so much, you slow yourself down. Really, it is crazy for you to stay alone for Thanksgiving."

"I'll be fine," I say, and like a fool, I even believe it.

Right before heading to the airport, Ahmad leaves me with another reminder to slow down and look around:

> *I have spoken the language of madness,*
> *full of whys and hows and wherefores.*
> *Obsessed with reasons, I spent a lifetime knocking at this door.*
> *When at last it opened, my soul replied.*
> *All along, I had been knocking from the inside.*

Know it or not, knocking or still, we are—all of us—already home, already loved, already whole. The trick is to notice, even if it means surrendering some sanity—or more precisely, some of the madness that the world deems sane. Our obsessions with reason and status keep us separated—not only from each other, but also from the Beloved. And this separation—this failure to recognize how deeply connected we are to every living organism—is a sign of an acute societal madness born of ego and ambition run amok. It's the same madness that first led me on this pilgrimage, and it's a madness for which the only viable prescription is love.

But still being a novice on this journey, I fail to appreciate the love in front of me, so I stay alone in San Diego and embark on the least productive writing retreat in all of human history. The moment my parents leave, a pathological procrastination takes hold of me. It begins with a seemingly innocuous walk to the newly built San Diego library, where, instead of writing, I take a two-hour self-guided tour of every floor, read *Darkness Visible* for a second time, and check email.

Since planning my pilgrimage, I have fantasized about best-case scenarios that might result from this near-week of solitude. The dominant dream/delusion ends with my having written most, if not all, of this book. The reality, however, is that I write none of it.

Instead, after my tour of the library, I spend an entire day nursing a migraine from hell, and several more reading *Women on War* when I'm not streaming sappy Christmas movies (a long-standing autumnal guilty pleasure; don't judge), Skyping with Matthew, or crashing the American Academy of Religion conference down the street courtesy of my friend Levi, a professor of Japanese religions who happens to be in legitimate attendance.

It isn't until Thanksgiving morning that I realize I have never actually *spent* a Thanksgiving alone, and I don't want to start now. Knowing that I'm on my own, allegedly writing, my friend Lilly, a San Diego native whose parents are tight with mine, graciously invites me to join her and her family at a friend's home in Elfin Forest. After learning that this is a real place and not a Disney set (and thoroughly mocking it accordingly), I spend the holiday there with Lilly and several other Iranian families, most of whom know my parents but are relative strangers to me. None of them understands why I'm not in Denver, and at this point, neither do I.

There is indeed something worse than the prospect of enduring the inescapable excess of human depravity born of celebrating genocide via Thanksgiving and bracing yourself for its demon spawn (Black Friday, Small Business Saturday, Sofa Sunday, Cyber Monday, Giving Tuesday, and Weeping Wednesday): the reality of enduring it *alone.*

But my parents return tomorrow, and for now—however hard it is to swallow my wasted week of self-imposed solitude combined with all this turkey, rice, *khoresht,*[2] and kabob—I am grateful to Lilly for letting me tag along.

"What is your *heart* feeling?"

I'm barely awake, but I know it's Ahmad. I can hear him through the wall. My parents just got back from Denver, and he's already on the phone, talking to a contractor, asking questions about expanding an entryway. I laugh, knowing he means *gut* feeling and hoping the contractor doesn't take it the wrong way. The word *"del"* in Persian means both "heart" and "gut"—hence the mix-up.

Personally, I don't trust my *del,* no matter how you translate it. My gut has nearly killed me, and my heart beats way too fast, guiding my blood through an obstacle course of excess cholesterol. But bound by a condition lacking either a clear cause or cure, my brain wins the prize for least trustworthy organ by far. No contest. Nevertheless, I

---

2   *Khoresht* is Persian stew; it comes in many varieties and is traditionally served over rice.

remain in the habit of almost always trusting my mind over my heart, gut, and most everything else.

This is apparent as Ahmad and I begin the day's poetry lesson. Within the first hour, we come across a dozen Persian words that are entirely new to me, and I grow frustrated. For the millionth time Ahmad tells me not to get caught up in words, that *meaning* is what matters most. But as I think about all that has been lost in translation between us over the years, all the words we don't share in common, a tear wells up in my eye and plops onto my steno pad. The letters of the word "*johaar*"—meaning "essence" or "heart" in a literary context and "ink" in an everyday one—surrender to the saline, bleeding into one another on the page.

"There are just so many words I don't know. It's too much," I say, feeling overwhelmed and defeated.

"Remember," Ahmad says, citing Rumi, "*ham-deli az ham-zabani behtar ast.*"

Better to be of the same heart than of the same tongue.

Shortly before leaving California, I inscribe this in a bilingual copy of Rumi's *Divan-eh Shams* for Ahmad, adding: "Thanks for always being my *ham-del* [of the same heart], even if we haven't always been *ham-zaban* [of the same tongue]."

I began this journey full of ridiculous expectations: wanting to squish a pilgrimage that was inherently lifelong into a single month, and in that time, wanting to perfect my Farsi, crush my writer's block, bang out this entire book, and learn as many couplets and quatrains as humanly possible by heart.

But before I can as much as blink, it's December, and I haven't learned nearly as much as I had hoped. Ahmad keeps telling me to slow down, to aim toward less measurable and more meaningful goals: to forget about learning these poems by heart and focus on getting more heart out of every poem—which of course sounds lovely, but to be honest, I don't actually know what the hell that means in practical terms. And practically speaking, I need to make a living. Having chosen to pursue one of the least lucrative and most unreliable professions on earth means that I am forever on a deadline. If I want to keep up this insane dream of paying my rent as a writer, then I have to keep writing books, and while I've begun writing this one here in California, I still have far more left to write.

After spending nearly a month in San Diego, I'm beginning to remember what I so detested about poetry before losing my mind. Growing up, I hated how so much of the stuff made so little sense to me, all those obnoxious adjectives and adverbs squeezing out perfectly good nouns and verbs, words that might have imparted real meaning had they just been given the chance. Most of all, I hated the way that poets—with their seemingly special license to be vague, redundant, and contradictory in some purported pursuit of profoundly profound profundity (presumably above and beyond the modest powers of prose)—often sounded like world-class bullshitters to me.

Such was my perspective on poetry before losing my mind six years ago and finding myself on a locked psychiatric unit, spontaneously illiterate and bearing a brand-new bipolar diagnosis. Abandoned by reason and intellect, all I had left was my heart, but I needed nothing else for Rumi to win me over. And he did. Though I can't pinpoint the exact moment it happened, a single encounter stands out.

One afternoon, my father visited me on the locked unit, and we sat together next to a wall that should've been a window, talking and eating homemade sugar cookies—a gift from one of his patients who had just given birth. They were delicious, but the idea that a woman could somehow find time to bake and drop off cookies at her obstetrician's office just days after tearing her body apart to bring a new human into this world made me feel that much more pathetic. For I had done nothing even remotely challenging or notable, and here I was, insane, illiterate, and immured. I bit the head off a blue butter-cream giraffe and asked Ahmad if he thought I was crazy. True to form, he replied by dispensing a dose of Rumi:

> *On the road to enlightenment, wise and mad are one.*
> *In the way of Love, self and other are one.*
> *For those who drink of the wine that connects souls,*
> *In their religion, the Kaaba and the house of idols are one.*

Miraculously, I needed no translation, as I had drunk of the wine that connects souls just days prior. After sipping from the well of the Beloved, I had undeniably lost touch with a whole host of worldly truths, but I had also stumbled upon a deeper and equally valid one: we're all connected. From labor to delivery, from infirmity to recovery, from expiration to immortality. We are inextricably linked to and through a sacred spark within each of us, delivered from stardust, tending toward hope, and lit by love.

This poem that made such immediate sense to me in the hospital is also the last one that Ahmad and I try to translate together before I leave California. As always, I want to be precise with my translation. And as always, Ahmad is more concerned with meaning than precision. So much so that he insists that I translate "Kaaba" in the last verse as "church," so that the majority of my presumably Christian and English-speaking readers will more readily relate to these verses.

"But that's wrong—and offensive," I respond, appalled. "Islam is the second-largest religion in the world: everyone should know what the Kaaba is. And regardless, it's just *not* 'church.' That's not what the poem *says*."

"Forget what it says, Melody *jan*. Think what it *means*."

"So you just want me to dumb everything down and whitewash it? People should know that Rumi was Muslim, that he was an Islamic scholar, that his poetry was inspired by the Quran. It will show them how Islam is really about love. And if they don't know what the Kaaba is, then they can learn. What's wrong with that?"

"Only the heart do they need to learn, Melody *jan*. Everything you say, maybe it's right, but it's only ego and politic and religion. I promise, you just focus on love and the rest will work out. Don't let religion confuse you. Of course, Rumi was Muslim. But he was a *true* Muslim. This is why he says that he is not a Christian or a Jew, not a Zoroastrian or a Muslim, not of East or West, not of land or sea. This is why he says, 'I belong to the soul of the Beloved.' Does the Beloved have a *religion*?"[3]

"Of course not, I get it. But people need to see this poetry as serious *Islamic* philosophy, as something that reflects the *real* Islam. If only to counter all the ISIS garbage in the news every day. They have to learn. It's how they'll stop hating us."

"Stop being so serious and stop thinking of hate. So what if they hate us? Let them hate us. We just keep speaking of love. Only love. And soon, they see it too: they are one of us, and we are one of them. You just keep speaking of love, Melody *jan*. Rumi understood this. *You* need to understand this."

But now that I am free, sane, literate, and medicated, I *don't* understand this. At least, not fully. Not yet. As I return to this simple quatrain in the midst of my pilgrimage, it's hard to be patient. These verses don't seem so simple anymore. And they unnerve me

---

3   Some scholars suggest the verses my father references here are apocryphal. Nevertheless, they appear often in the Persian oral tradition, and my father refuses to accept that they are not by Rumi, as they reflect a unifying sentiment prevalent in his poetry.

for reasons having little to do with the Kaaba or the translation or even love.

It's that first line—"On the road to enlightenment, wise and mad are one"—that most intrigues and terrifies me. Ahmad has no trouble with it, as unlike me, he has never been struck mad or illiterate, nor has he ever had a mystical experience. So now, looking back at how I arrived here, I can't help but wonder if I'm way off track.

Perhaps the fact that it took acute mania and psychosis for me to begin to appreciate this poetry should *tell* me something. Perhaps I was misguided in even pursuing this pilgrimage in the first place. Perhaps I've lost my mind again, and my renewed affinity for Rumi is the result. Perhaps this time I've finally lost it *for good.*

As all these possibilities flash across my brain like an obnoxious chyron caught in the same interminable loop, it's clear that my pilgrimage isn't turning out the way I expected. I came here determined to learn so much. But now, after a month of intense daily poetry lessons, I still feel a lifetime behind and, bonus, at least twice as ignorant as I did when I arrived. Ahmad insists this is a good sign, but I'm not so sure.

"Isn't that just a cop-out?" I ask him.

"Cop-out?"

"An excuse, a, a—" I can't remember how to say "excuse" in Farsi. Then it comes to me: "*Bahaneh!* A *bahaneh* for not learning enough to get rid of this language barrier between us. Have you ever thought about how we're both communicating with each other in languages we don't fully understand? Don't you ever wonder how much we lose in translation?"

"Lose? Are you kidding? Don't you ever wonder how much we *win* in translation?"

"No," I reply, having genuinely never considered winning as an option. "What could we possibly *win*?"

"*Everything!* Just you imagine we are like those in Ohio who speak only English and that's it. You think it's easier for them? It's not. It is harder. Each language is like a new universe. Even if it's not perfect, who cares? It's an extra *universe* you win!"

"But doesn't that just leave us in two separate *universes* then? There will always be a barrier. Don't you get it?"

"*Boro baba!* Stop exaggerating. I don't know this barrier. And even if it exists, you build it yourself. You really think you can cross something like that with *words*? This is what I keep telling you, Melody *jan.* Words only get in your way."

"But, Ahmad, I'm a writer. Words are all I *have!*"

"*Eh, pedar sag, cheshmet ra baaz kon* [open your eyes]*!* You have your *heart.*"

It will take far more than a month of poetry lessons to trust my "heart feeling," but years later, when I finally start, I realize that all of my best decisions have been the result of trusting my *del.* It was my heart, not my head, that led me to marry Matthew at twenty-three, to retire from legal practice less than a year after passing the bar, to adopt a series of increasingly ungrateful cats and love them anyway, to pursue a full-time writing career despite a considerable pay cut, and to fly out to San Diego to study Rumi with my father years before this ever became a book.

Even from a purely rational perspective, it's clear in retrospect that my heart has provided a surprisingly steady return on investment. Though this calculation allows me to begin to trust it more, I'm still *calculating,* still *analyzing,* still relying more on intellect than intuition. To begin to lead with my heart, I will have to slow down and reconnect with my ancestry.

For while the notion of intergenerational trauma that's so fashionable among socially conscious academic circles is admittedly real, so too is the notion of intergenerational resilience, which we are far less likely to label, study, and appreciate. By surviving colonialism, revolution, war, migration, and discrimination, my parents made *my* survival possible. Sure, there are wounds associated with descending from that kind of trauma, but then again, plenty of wounded souls descend from persistent privilege. And whatever the case, as Rumi reminds us, it is our *wounds* that summon the Beloved's light, and in doing so, our most sacred source of resilience. Modern psychology has only recently begun to recognize this ancient bit of wisdom. For years, scientists have focused on studying post-traumatic stress, while all but ignoring its natural alternative or corollary: post-traumatic growth.

But growth—whether post-traumatic or post-ecstatic—requires time. And as my stay in Southern California comes to a close, I begin to realize just how naïve and delusional I was to think I could fulfill this pilgrimage in a mere month.

I still speak kitchen Farsi, I still require tons of help with classical Persian, and I still need a guide. So as I pack my bags to return to Raleigh, I'm still disappointed at my lack of progress. But if this balmy November has taught me anything, it's that the Beloved has no respect for earthly timelines.

> *Be it an hour or a hundred thousand years,*
> *They are one and the same, however the math appears.*

Any spiritual journey worth taking is inherently never-ending, for the soul resides outside of time and space. Still bound to my physical body, however, I rely on that anchor, because I am not prepared for oblivion. Recognizing this shortly before my departure, I grow even more determined to learn as much as I can from Ahmad in whatever time we have left on this planet together, and not knowing how much that will be, I once again find myself rushing.

On my last day in California, fearful I've failed at this pilgrimage and still in a useless rush to succeed in every arena, including the spiritual one—where, of course, concepts like "success" and "failure" don't even apply—I find myself feeling far more stressed out than blissed out. So I go for a walk across the street, along the harbor at Seaport Village. It's a walk Ahmad and I have taken together nearly every day that I've been here, but in an effort to clear my head and to avoid waking him up from his nap, I go alone. On my way home, I notice a "pop-up" yoga studio in the middle of the Headquarters.

It's a small freshly built square of shops and restaurants that earned its name on account of being the site of San Diego's old police headquarters. The city even restored several jail cells, filled them with allegedly historic memorabilia, and left them open for tourists to take creepy selfies. The Headquarters' website instructs visitors, "Don't forget to snap a photo at our lineup wall," and if that's not sufficiently nauseating for your tastes, no worries, there's a Cheesecake Factory right next door.

The pop-up yoga class is right behind the Cheesecake Factory, which ought to serve as an unequivocal warning sign, but I nonetheless manage to miss it. While I am considerably less spiritually and creatively blocked than I was at the start of my trip here, I am still light-years from enlightened. There have been no grand mystical epiphanies or creative breakthroughs, and being in such a perpetual rush to get things done as fast as humanly possible, this seriously bugs me. So at a loss, I somehow forget how much I hate sweating with strangers, succumb to Southern California's relentless knack for misappropriation, and give yoga a go.

Halfway through the class, I am even more deeply confused than I was at the start: despite being surrounded by white people, I detect a distinct *eau de* stinky foreigner. Since I arrived, my mother has been spoiling me with my favorite foods, including *ghormeh sabzi*: a dish full of every green imaginable that takes forever to make and even longer to exit your system. Aside from the near-daily doses I've consumed since stepping off the plane on Halloween, I also downed several extra helpings at Thanksgiving.

Still, it doesn't occur to me that *I* might be the stinky foreigner until I turn my head on a downward dog and am assaulted by my own brutal *ghormeh-sabz*-stench. Amid this sea of white people draped in freshly laundered Lululemon, there is no doubt: *I am the stinky foreigner.* A bomb of herbs and spices just waiting to explode right in the middle of this unsuspecting provisional yoga studio. The fenugreek alone ought to be enough to demolish the entire class and give new meaning to the final savasana, AKA corpse pose. But somehow, by the end, everyone is still breathing, myself included.

As I roll up my yoga mat, the instructor, all blue eyes and blond dreadlocks, approaches me: "Are you from India? I just got back from Goa," she says. All I want to do is shower. I tell her I'm from Ohio, which yields a look of confusion while affording me a quick exit. As I walk outside, I overhear two women discussing "competitive yoga." I laugh at the contradiction, certain it's a joke, but I am quickly set straight. Turns out, it's a *thing*.

After a welcome shower, I Google it, and within a few clicks, I'm on the United States Yoga Federation's website, where I find sixteen single-spaced pages of rules and regulations for their annual championship competition. I'm surfing the site in disbelief when Ahmad wakes up from his nap and suggests heading to the driving range, his favorite pastime since knee-replacement surgery.

Despite detesting golf, I agree. Unhampered by the burdens of form, aim, and interest as we tee off, I am now free to focus on *my* favorite pastime since preschool oral arguments (see *Chocolate v. Vanilla*, 1 Ohio 1, Discovery School, 1983): words.

After swinging and missing the ball twice in a row, I ask, "What's the word for this?"

"Uncoordinated," Ahmad says, laughing.

"Seriously, there must be a *real* word for it," I insist, hitting and missing again. "What is it?"

"Whiff," Ahmad replies, "or air shot."

"Whiff? Really? What, because it stinks?"

"I don't know. They just call it that," he says as he swaps spots with me to sincerely attempt to practice his swing.

"So you won't believe what happened at yoga today," I say, and proceed to tell him, skipping the *ghormeh-sabz*-sweat and focusing on the competitive yoga, because it's still bugging me. "Can you believe that there even *is* such a thing? I mean, it's like competitive *namaz* [prayer]!"

"Ameri-can," Ahmad replies, driving a ball straight into the netting. "Everything for them is a competition."

"And you're any different? Making fun of my whiffs and showing off with your . . . What's the opposite of a whiff?"

"*Man cheh meedonam.*[4] I play for fun. Never I play to win. Molana says to compete is like to live in a jail. Next time you go sit inside the Headquarters, you think about *that*."

> *Quit keeping score if you want to be free.*
> *Love has ejected the referee.*

For Rumi, competition is a trap, bloating the ego and obscuring the Beloved. Love is our only ticket out. But you won't find it on Ticketmaster, and it's sure to decline any Visa, Mastercard, or American Express. Here, the only acceptable currency is devotion, and it deftly defies basic economic theory.

---

4   "What do I know?" or "How should I know?"

The only way to keep this ticket is to give it away, and the only way to lose it is to save it. But far too often, we unwittingly deprive ourselves of love in our mad rush to seek it, forgetting our sweeping stockpiles within. This frantic search for what we already own—a vast resource that defies cost-benefit analysis, growing only by being given away—reflects a collective madness and the polar opposite of mysticism, as it makes all kinds of conflict and separation possible, a catalyst for extremism, war, and environmental devastation. Personally, it has led to a whole host of self-made hurdles for me—chief among them, an intense fear of imminent death that left me rushing through much of my life.

But unlike so many clinical psychiatric conditions, this maddening tendency toward haste has a clear—albeit hard-won—cure: quit competing, so we can slow down and look around long enough to remember where we're from and what we're made of, our ultimate indivisible source and structure, the Beloved.

Naturally, as with all of Rumi's prescriptions, this isn't one I can fill once and be cured. I need regular refills, because I'm human, and as a species, forgetfulness is by far our most stubborn heritable habit.

"Aren't you excited to see Matthew?" my mom asks, presumably discerning my disappointment at the end of my trip as she hands me a saffron-rosewater ice-cream sandwich.

"Of course I am," I tell her, and I mean it. Matthew and I have spoken every day since I got here, and every day I miss him more. "I'm just disappointed I didn't learn or write as much as I had hoped."

"You expect too much too fast, Melody *jan*," Ahmad says before reciting this couplet in Persian:

Patience, not haste, gets you where you belong.
Slow down and heed the Beloved's song.

"He is right. *Slow down,*" my mom adds. "Always you were like this: you were born two months early and the delivery was less than one hour. From the beginning, you were in a rush."

"And? Wasn't that a good thing? Less pregnancy, less pain?" I reply, ignoring her point entirely.

"Of course. But you do not need to always be in such a hurry," she says, picking up my empty plate and offering me another ice-cream sandwich from the freezer.

"No thanks. I'm good," I reply.

"That's what I keep telling you, Melody *jan!* You *are* good," Ahmad says, and recites Rumi to me again: "*Zar talab gashti. Khod aval zar bodi.*" In other words:

You went out in search of gold far and wide,
But all along you were gold on the inside.

"Remember," he continues, "love is not about competition; love is about *connection.* And if you want to connect, then you have to *slow down.*"

"You're right. I'll try. Thank you for telling me," I reply, reciting Ahmad to Ahmad.

Though my father's literary lessons have always revolved around Rumi and poetry, I realize upon leaving California that they have never in fact been *about* either. Rather, they are and always have been about prayer. Not the kind that requires a temple or a church or a mosque, but the kind that requires a soul and nothing more, a devotion that supersedes religion while sustaining faith, singing of love through countless incomparable melodies.

It underlies the Christian teaching that the kingdom of God is within you, the Zoroastrian teaching that the divine can be found inside your own heart, the Sikh teaching that the Lord lies within you like the fragrance in a flower or the reflection in a mirror, the Buddhist teaching that enlightenment relies upon awakening to a condition that already awaits within, the Baha'i teaching that you can find God standing within you by turning your sights inward, the Hindu teaching that curbing your mind can reveal the Almighty within your heart, the Jewish teaching that the Lord's candle shines inside your soul, and the Islamic teaching that the Beloved is nearer to you than your jugular vein.

While it is the latter Quranic teaching with which Rumi, my father, and I are most familiar as Muslims, every one of these parallel revelations resonates in the same ecstatic key, all part of a single sacred symphony. *This* is the language of mystics—the vernacular of those who slow down to speed up, who bow down to rise up, whose only rush is in seeking the Beloved within—and it is everyone's native tongue.

Dx: Haste ♣ Rx: Quit Keeping Score

I have spoken the language of madness,
full of whys and hows and wherefores.
Obsessed with reasons, I spent a lifetime knocking at this door.
When at last it opened, my soul replied.
All along, I had been knocking from the inside.

—

Better to be of the same heart than of the same tongue.

—

On the road to enlightenment, wise and mad are one.
In the way of Love, self and other are one.
For those who drink of the wine that connects souls,
In their religion, the Kaaba and the house of idols are one.

—

Be it an hour or a hundred thousand years,
They are one and the same, however the math appears.

—

Quit keeping score if you want to be free.
Love has ejected the referee.

—

Patience, not haste, gets you where you belong.
Slow down and heed the Beloved's song.

—

You went out in search of gold far and wide,
But all along you were gold on the inside.

CHAPTER 4

Dx: Depression
Rx: Welcome Every Guest

Welcome every guest,
No matter how grotesque.
Be as hospitable to calamity as to ecstasy,
To anxiety as to tranquility.
Today's misery sweeps your home clean,
Making way for tomorrow's felicity.

Matthew meets me inside the Raleigh-Durham airport, which is weird. We're both more the curbside, airport-police-taunting, drive-in-circles-texting-'til-you-get-there, kiss-and-fly type. For us, greeting each other in airports is for soldiers, migrants, and saps, and given we are none of the above, it seems like a waste of time.

Nonetheless, here stands Matthew. Waiting. Flanked by eager military families, church groups, and delusional romantic comedy addicts, he actually *hops* when he spots me and my leopard-print carry-on. We rush to hug one another before I realize we look exactly like those delusional rom-com addicts I just made fun of a sentence ago. Apparently, the only thing that separates us from every other sad sap is a month apart—a fact that becomes all the more evident when we get home.

"You did *not!*" I say as I walk through our front door.

"Oh, I *did,*" Matthew beams.

The living room is immaculate and despite the fact that it's barely December, the Christmas tree is already up—fully decorated, fully lit. For background—and even more evidence that I'm not the sensible cynic I apparently imagine myself to be—I *love* Christmas. Yes, I'm Muslim. Yes, Muslims don't do Christmas. And yes, I don't care.

By contrast, Matthew's Christmas spirit vacillates between indifferent and insurgent. He was raised categorically Catholic, with trees, presents, lights, Midnight Mass—the whole Yuletide package. I was raised vaguely Muslim, with none of it. Christmas at our house was about celebrating my mom, because it happens to be her birthday, and pillaging the pantry, because there's apparently a law in Dayton that requires you to send a box of Esther Price chocolates to the doctor who delivered your babies every year at Christmas for the rest of your life. So while my sister and I were singing happy birthday and bingeing on Buckeyes as we tossed aside photos of all the kids my dad had delivered since what felt like the beginning of time, Matthew and his brother were singing carols and opening gifts they had actually requested.

Astoundingly, despite all the Christmas cheer at his childhood home in the Catskills, Matthew was decidedly agnostic by the time I met him at Wesleyan. I was a freshman studying philosophy and Latin American literature. He was a sophomore studying economics and Russian. I'd never noticed him before he chased me out of Olin Library to ask me out, and only a few months into my college career, I had no interest in dating anyone. Still, his nerve and humor impressed me, so we became friends, and three years later, we fell in love.

I'd like to say that it was my example that inspired Matthew's conversion to Islam, but it wasn't. He converted because he read the Quran, and it spoke to him. We were nearly engaged by then, but apart from suggesting decent translations, I had nothing to do with Matthew's conversion. Even still, Ahmad was livid and blamed me when he found out. First, he insisted that I should've forbidden Matthew from converting, as though that were something I was capable of doing. Then he urged Matthew to respect and embrace the faith into which he had been born, insisting that there was no meaningful difference between Christianity and Islam. But Matthew never identified as Christian as an adult, and he had been studying the Quran for years by that point, so his mind was made up.

Personally, I was happy he had found a faith that resonated with him and that we happened to share it, but his conversion neither made nor broke the deal for me. For one, both of us were adamant about never wanting kids and didn't anticipate getting into any religious debates over how to raise our cats. And more important, I was already so in love with Matthew by then that he could've worshipped dandelions, and I still would've married him. Aside from my father's vocal protests, which subsided with time, the rest of my family cared even less than I did about Matthew's religion. My sister had already married a white Southern Baptist from South Carolina, so my marrying a white Muslim convert from upstate New York was far from radical.

All this to say, with no intended disrespect for Matthew's convictions, I highly suspect that one of the greatest perks of converting to Islam for him has been the ability to more fully dismiss the Christmas holiday. He can go on for days about why Christmas sucks: the commercialism, the eggnog, the murdering of trees, the sweaters, the massive historical inaccuracies, the crowds, the exclusion of religious minorities, the creepy Santas, the lies we tell children, and the fruitcake.

While I dispute none of these horrors, I'm still a sucker for Christmas: the lights, the evergreens, the sugar cookies, the glitter-dusted pine cones, the snow, the holly, the carols, the steaming hot chocolate, the gingerbread houses, the crackling fireplaces, and of course, the endless filmography. Much to Matthew's dismay, I start watching Christmas movies right around Halloween, and I don't stop until weeks after New Year's.

"I can't believe you put up the *tree!*" I say. In a dozen years of marriage, not once has Matthew put up a Christmas tree on his own. I'm always the one dragging it out a couple weeks before Thanksgiving, and he's always the one begging me to wait.

"I know it's not my thing, but I thought you'd like it."

"I *love* it," I say, wrapping my arms around his neck and planting a scatterplot of kisses across his face as I notice a shiny snowman floating in the middle of my office.

"You got me a *balloon?* What am I, ten?"

"Yes. *Duh,*" Matthew replies, and he's right. At thirty-five, I still purchase an embarrassingly large portion of my clothes from the children's department, and I retain a strong affinity for bright colors and anything Hello Kitty. "*And* I packed the fridge with Kit Kats and pomegranates," he adds, puffing out his chest for emphasis.

"Way to pull out all the stops! Let's start with the Kit Kats," I proclaim, plopping down on the couch between our corpulent cats, Keshmesh and Nazanin. Matthew hands me an opened Kit Kat bar.

"It must be defective. It only has three sticks," he says, visibly chewing on the allegedly absent one as he picks up Keshmesh and sits down next to me. He cradles her in his arms like a newborn, a move most cats would violently resist, but one she seems to relish. Presumably feeling neglected, Naz proceeds to take up residence on my chest, forcefully nudging and licking my face.

"Look," I announce between licks. "We're all here. We can take off!"

"Where do you want to go?"

"Nowhere," I reply, nuzzling my head against Matthew's shoulder. "I'm happy at home."

But happy never lasts. Not for me, and not for anyone who lives long enough to notice. Mine ends in January. I'd give up Christmas trees, balloons, Kit Kats, and pomegranates forever for it to have ended differently, but I can't. Death doesn't make deals. No trades, no tallies, no take-backs. Dead is dead. You can't fix it.

Mary's obituary says she "passed away . . . after a twenty-year battle with bipolar disorder." But Mary was my friend, so I know better. She didn't "pass away." She died in pain, alone, by a bullet. And her life wasn't a "battle with bipolar disorder." It was a triumph, a testament to the fact that people with mental health conditions can live flourishing and fulfilling lives.

When I met Mary, she was working as the director of recovery initiatives at a Greensboro mental health organization, where she invited me to teach a writing workshop after reading my last book. The clients adored her, and I did too.

Aside from being a smart, funny, and inspirational mental health advocate, Mary was also a licensed counselor, a mother, a writer, and a genius at handling broken pieces: forever rescuing and resuscitating them, creating a perfect whole from imperfect parts. Indeed, her brilliant mosaic artwork was as much a metaphor for her recovery as it was a means of creative expression.

From the moment I met Mary, I recognized her as a friend and a force of nature. She did more than "cope" or "struggle" with bipolar disorder. She thrived with it, determined to use her experience to help others to do the same. In short, Mary was a mentor and a role model for countless people living with mental health conditions, myself included. But sometimes when you're so busy looking up to someone, you forget to look out for them. You assume they have it covered. And maybe they do. Until they don't.

It's tough enough to seek help when you need it, but when people consider you an exemplar of wellness and recovery, the fear of letting them down can make it damn near impossible. If that's what happened to Mary, then I absolutely get it.

Ever since I began writing and speaking publicly about having a psychiatric condition, I've been routinely identified as someone who has "overcome" bipolar disorder—despite the fact that it's a chronic condition and I've never claimed any such thing. Sure, like Mary, I learned to manage and even thrive with this illness, but like Mary, I was also never foolish enough to think that this meant I had *overcome* it. Bipolar disorder isn't something you just "get over" like a cold or a flu. It's something that requires regular and responsible psychiatric treatment, and it's something you manage every single day, some days better than others.

Like me, Mary realized all of this and more. She knew that seeking help was a sign of strength and intelligence. She knew that treatment was available. She knew that recovery was possible. But somehow, for a split second, under the influence of acute clinical depression, this fierce artist and activist I had so grown to love and admire *simply forgot.*

The last time I saw Mary was in September, when we rode trails together. True to form, she insisted I ride her horse, Mystic, while she rode another less tame and less beautiful one. A majestic gray gelding, Mystic was a dream to ride, but he hadn't always been. When Mary first began working with him, he had already been banished to pasture twice on account of being deemed unsafe and unmanageable. But Mary loved lost causes, so despite having only recently returned to riding herself, she soon adopted the rescue saddlebred. With her gentle and patient encouragement, Mystic became not only safe to ride but friendly.

That sun-drenched early autumn afternoon was my first time back in the saddle in more than a decade. We rode and talked for hours, and miraculously, Mary's company and Mystic's confidence kept me upright and stable the entire time. It was a perfect day, and before leaving the stables that evening, I told Mary as much. I thanked her and gave her a big hug, entirely unaware that it would be our last. As I drove away, I watched her in my rearview mirror, waving and smiling in the shadow of a golden Carolina sunset. We planned another ride soon, but soon never came.

The last I heard from Mary was in an email she sent a few weeks before she died. In it, she asked me to share a list of writing prompts for a class she was teaching that afternoon. She also mentioned that she'd had a "steep descent since we last saw each other," which led to a "nosedive into a deep, dark, suicidal depression." But she closed her message with hope and reassurance, adding, "I like to think I'm on the upswing. A visit to Mystic this weekend will surely help."

I replied that same morning, attaching the prompts Mary requested and telling her not to hesitate to call if she ever needed to talk. I closed my message with love and gratitude, along with a reminder for Mary: "You inspire more people every day than you recognize, including me. Please don't forget that—and thank you for it."

That was our final point of contact. I tried calling once, but she didn't pick up. I figured I would call her back later, or that she would call me. I trusted that if she was well enough to volunteer to help other people manage *their* mental health conditions, then she must've been managing *hers*. I never thought for a second that she would buy a godforsaken gun a month later and shoot herself with it. But she did.

And now I'm left with all these questions: *How did she get a gun? What fool sold her a gun? Why is it so fucking easy to get a gun? Why didn't I keep calling? Why didn't I drive to Greensboro the minute I read her email? Why did an hour-and-a-half drive seem like too much time out of my precious day? What on earth was I doing that seemed so much more important? What will happen to Mystic? How did I let "I like to think I'm*

on the upswing" outweigh "deep, dark, suicidal depression"? How was I
clueless enough to miss so much?

Lacking any satisfying answers, I spiral into a depression of my
own. Ahmad and I have stuck to our pact since I got home, meet-
ing for weekly poetry lessons over Skype. But when I find out about
Mary, I call to cancel our lesson.

"I can't today," I tell him, my voice quivering.

"What's wrong?"

"A friend died."

"Who?"

"Mary. She's the one who invited me to speak in Greensboro last
year, the one who got me back on a horse. She had bipolar too." I start
sobbing.

"I'm so sorry, Melody *jan*. What happened? Was she old?"

"No. She was fifty-six. It was suicide."

Silence.

"Are you okay?"

"I'll be fine. I'm just sad that *she* won't be," I say, already hating
myself for getting into this. I don't want to worry Ahmad, and I know
that hearing about someone with my diagnosis who died by suicide
will send his mind to ugly places. I just wanted to call and cancel
our lesson and hang up. But over the past few months something
has shifted in our relationship. Where before we both always tried to
shield each other from bad news, we now actually talk about what's
going on in our lives, good *and* bad. In short, we're friends now. So I
can't *not* tell him what's happening with me.

Of course, he is still my father, and I still want to protect him.
I can hear the concern in his voice now, and I so want to put his
mind at ease—to promise that I'll never do what Mary did—but I
know it won't do any good. I've attempted suicide once before, so my
credibility is shot. Understandably, I can't be trusted with promises
like that.

Sure, I have no plans to kill myself *today*, but then again, seven years ago, when I *did* try to kill myself, I was out of my damn mind. Though I had a meticulous plan in place, I followed none of it. In fact, my suicide attempt was spontaneous, and to this day, I remember it as an out-of-body experience. Floating above my curiously crouched frame in the corner of a busy waiting room, I watched my right hand slit my left wrist with a pocketknife, and I felt utterly powerless to stop it. By all reliable accounts, I was still very much inside of my body. It just didn't feel that way.

"She used a gun," I tell Ahmad, knowing it's far too late to protect him. "A *gun*! Mary wasn't a gun *person*. She went to *Smith*! How the hell did she get a *gun*?"

I can't stop asking this question, and I can't stop coming up with ridiculous rationalizations for why it would be impossible for Mary to shoot herself. Like the Smith thing. For some reason, I keep latching on to that, imagining that somehow a top-notch liberal arts education and suicide by gun must be mutually exclusive. I know this is absurd, but I can't help it. I know that suicide strikes all sorts of demographics, I know that more than half of all suicides are gun related, and I know that nearly two-thirds of all gun fatalities are suicides. I know this, because these are stats I've cited in nearly every mental health workshop and keynote I've ever delivered. Nonetheless, standing face-to-face with the reality of what these numbers actually *mean*, I am gobsmacked.

"Did you call Dr. Spiro?" Ahmad asks, referring to my psychiatrist.

"No. You know I meet with him every week. I'm seeing him again Tuesday."

"But maybe you can see him sooner. This is a lot. You should call him."

"Why? What can he say to fix it? What can anyone say? What would Rumi say?" I ask, almost as a taunt.

"Rumi says to listen to your father and call your psychiatrist," Ahmad replies, entirely as a taunt.

"I didn't care before, but now I'm curious. Seriously, what *would* Rumi say?"

"You *know* what he would say. I taught you this."

"What do you mean?"

"You ask me why bad thing happens. I taught you twenty poems for this. Already you know. *You tell me.*"

"I told you, I'm not up for this. We're not doing a lesson today. Just tell me," I say, annoyed.

"Melody *jan*, I promise you know this. Just think." This command only further irritates me. Ahmad knows I don't want to think, but as I'm thinking about how aggravating he is for telling me to think, it hits me.

"You mean *ganjeh bee-maar o goleh bee-khaar?*"[1] I ask.

"*Afareen!* That is one," he replies, vindicated.

Where there is treasure, snakes come round.
Where there are roses, thorns abound.
In the grand bazaar of life, joy without sorrow cannot be found.

"But how does that *help*? Sure, you can't have good without bad, but so what? How does that *fix* anything?"

"It does not fix anything—only it helps you understand. Nothing can fix this, Melody *jan*. Already you know that. But your friend is not lost. You see her again. Now you have to take care of yourself. Listen to Molana," he says, reciting Rumi as he once again ignores the fact that I'm trying to *cancel* our lesson and not expedite it:

---

1   My shorthand for the poem that follows: "Treasure without snakes and flowers without thorns."

For a viable cure, pain is the key.
Your injury invites the remedy.

"In medicine, a cure does not come from nowhere," Ahmad continues. "The disease teaches you the cure. Think of the polio vaccine. It comes from the *polio virus*—and so many vaccines they work this way. Think of Ebola or smallpox. They can kill *all of us*. Human being thinks they are *sooo* big, *sooo* important. But really, you ask any physician and they tell you we are *nothing* compared to one tiny virus. If you want to stop a virus you must appreciate its genius. Only then can you learn from it."

"What, so I should look for a weakened strain of grief and inject myself with it?" I ask, missing the point entirely.

"*Pedar sag!* No. You have to *respect* grief, because it teaches you. Pain is *important*. You must listen to it. That is what Rumi is saying, and that is my professional opinion as a physician. You can learn from pain, but first you have to respect it. Like the virus. You see?"

"I get it, but I don't *want* this pain. I just want Mary to be alive again. I should've called. I should've gone to Greensboro to see her. I should've helped her. She said she was depressed, but I just didn't think it was that bad. If I'd just gone to see her, maybe I would've noticed and could've actually *done* something." Tears pool in my eyes. Several drop onto the couch, and I watch them expand on the gray microsuede.

"Don't do this to yourself. This is why I say you should call Dr. Spiro. Maybe he can't remove the pain, but he can help you learn from it."

"I know. You're right. I'll call him," I tell Ahmad, and in the moment, I mean it.

But after hanging up the phone, I'm tired. My limbs feel like lead, and I don't want to learn anything. I just want to stop feeling this

way. So I turn to my drug of choice whenever I want to go numb:
television.

Instead of calling Dr. Spiro, I spend days glued to the couch, pet-
ting cats, sleeping, and streaming episodes of *Dexter* like an alcoholic
downing vodka by the bottle.

*I'll call Spiro when I finish season 6. But if I make a basket in the trash
with this ball of Ferrero Rocher wrappers I can wait until I finish the first
episode of season 7. And if Nazanin curls up behind my knees and Kesh-
mesh plops down in the space between my stomach and the edge of the
couch, I'll watch some more episodes just to let them stay until they want to
leave. I wouldn't want to disturb the cats.*

By the time I actually get up the energy to call Dr. Spiro, it's only
a couple days until my next appointment anyway, so I hold off and
once again melt into the microsuede. Despite being exceptionally flat,
my ass has spent so many hours sinking into the left side of the couch
this week that the cushions are now wearing unevenly. A deep hole
is forming in my preferred corner, which ought to be a warning sign,
but all it has done is motivate me to switch sides periodically.

"Should I be worried?" Matthew asks the morning of my ap-
pointment, after I go straight to the couch from the bed, not even
showering or brushing my teeth first.

"Nah, I'm fine," I lie.

"Nah, you're not," he replies. "Even Dexter can see that, and he's
a sociopath."

"He's *not* a sociopath! He's a complex character with hopes and
dreams just like the rest of us."

"Do you hear yourself?"

"Yes. I know. I should be writing my own complex characters."

"That's not what I'm saying. Do what you need to do. Take all the
time you need to take, but just promise me you'll go to your appoint-
ment today, that you won't cancel. I'll even drive you if you don't feel
like it."

"I can *drive*. I'm not an infant. I'll go," I assure him, and I do. I don't shower or even brush my teeth, but I do manage to turn off the TV long enough to throw on some pants and drive the thirty minutes to Chapel Hill to see Dr. Spiro.

I tell him about Mary and how sad I've been this week, and he assures me that this is normal. I tell him I'm scared of what sharing a diagnosis with her could mean for me—of what I might do when *I'm* fifty-six, of how many more depressive episodes *my* mind and body can handle—and he assures me that this is normal too. Last, I tell him that I'm afraid of slipping into clinical depression—and while he confirms that this too is normal, he also asks if I'm experiencing any symptoms. I'm suddenly intensely aware of the fact that I haven't brushed my teeth in at least twenty-four hours, and I wonder if he can smell my breath from his desk.

"You know, the usual," I tell him, trying not to exhale too heavily. "I've been sleeping a lot more, watching a lot more television, eating a lot more garbage. I'm not writing or exercising or socializing. I'm avoiding phone calls. My inbox is out of control. Basically, I just don't want to do anything ever again. So yeah, the usual," I repeat, laughing nervously. "But it's just been a week, so I don't think it's a big deal."

I add this last tidbit as a direct nod to the *DSM*'s diagnostic criteria for clinical depression, which require that symptoms be present for at least two weeks to rise to the level of pathology. Of course, this is a somewhat arbitrary delineation. Nevertheless, it makes me feel better to know I haven't hit it yet.

Dr. Spiro catches the reference immediately, but he has been down this road with me before, so he suggests that I consider starting back on an antidepressant that has helped me in the past. I suggest waiting, and in response, he writes me a prescription to fill "just in case" I want to start taking it before our next appointment. I thank him, hoping I won't need it but knowing I might.

I'm barely out of the parking lot when Ahmad calls and puts me on speakerphone.

"Did you see your psychiatrist? How did it go?" he asks.

"Tell us. What did he say?" my mom chimes in.

Perhaps you're reading this and thinking, *Boundaries, people. Boundaries!* And sure, there's a part of me that agrees with you. But my parents don't do "boundaries"—and just to be clear, neither does any other set of immigrant parents I've ever met. They've given up their families and their homelands to give us kids a shot at this elusive, fantastical American dream, and they're not about to let us go and screw it up.

Once, when I was in high school, after my parents refused to let me go to a concert, I made the asinine move of advising my dad to "let me make my own mistakes." He lost it. That single sentence earned me an hour-long lecture about how smart people learn from other people's mistakes while stupid people make their own. He topped it off with one of his signature monologues about how America works, concluding: "This country was not made for us. We cannot make as many mistakes as them."

Because this land was, indeed, *not* made for us, my parents have spent their entire adult lives working to ensure that we all survive it. This meant urging Romana and me to speak better, act better, dress better, learn better, and score higher than all of our non-hyphenated counterparts at school. Our parents weren't being mean or harsh. They were being practical. Surviving America is punishing, all-consuming labor. It leaves no room for self-imposed restraints on how much or how often to interfere in your children's lives. In other words, my parents will never understand the concept of "boundaries." Just throw it in the box with prom, potlucks, and peanut butter as yet another curious American phenomenon that makes zero sense to them.

"The appointment was fine. I got a prescription so I can start the Wellbutrin again if things get worse."

"Fill it *now*," Ahmad says. "Even if you don't need it. It does not hurt to have it."

"He is right, Melody *jan*. Better to have it just in case."

My parents' acute interest in my mental health is no doubt the result of years of experience surviving America. But it's also the result of my suicide attempt nearly a decade ago and my manic episode a few years later, both of which led to hospitalizations, so *I get it*. That said, both also occurred when I was misdiagnosed with unipolar depression and, at times, on medication known to *exacerbate* bipolar disorder. Today, I have an accurate diagnosis; I know what's wrong; I know how to treat it, and I have access to quality mental health care. As I write this though, I am keenly aware of the fact that Mary had and knew all of this too. So again, *I get it*. Still, Ahmad and Jazbi's prying annoys me.

"I'll fill it. I was going to fill it anyway. You don't need to worry about me," I say, trying to stay calm.

"*Pedar sag!* 'You don't need to worry about me,'" Ahmad says, mocking me. "Don't you know *my life* is to worry about you? That is all I do: worry about you and Romana."

"Leave her alone," my mom says, and for the first time possibly ever, I'm grateful to be on speakerphone. "I am so sorry about your friend, Melody *jan*."

"Thanks, Mom. But I'm at the pharmacy now. I have to go."

"Good. Go get your medication," Ahmad says, and I do. But I don't take it. Instead, I try my best to shake this on my own, but it's too late. My will is no match for my double helix. Although this started out as perfectly normal grief and guilt over Mary's suicide, it has since morphed into something else. Three weeks in, it's clear that my mood has evolved from situational to clinical.

I'm still watching too much television and wearing out the couch unevenly. I'm still oversleeping and overeating. And I'm still not writing. Maintaining even the most basic standards of daily hygiene feels like an epic chore, testament to my slide from subtle melancholy into full-blown disability.

So I finally agree to start the Wellbutrin again as part of a large-scale effort to stage a respectable resistance. Ahmad and I are doing our poetry lessons nearly every day now over video chat. Matthew keeps calling it "research" to make me feel better about all the un-written words piling up, and I'm trying to share his perspective and reserve a bit more patience and mercy for myself. To that end, I commit to becoming more consistent in my daily prayers and getting out-side more often.

Competitive yoga with strangers clearly not being my thing, I've taken up leisurely walks with friends. Sometimes those friends are people, and other times they're just the local fauna and flora. Oaks, squirrels, cardinals, and bluebirds routinely meet me on my daily walks, and connecting with them has become just as much a part of my regular spiritual practice as my daily prayers. It's a simple act that takes less than an hour a day, but slowing down to convene with nature connects me with the Beloved next door, within every living organism I encounter, myself included. While the walks don't cure my depression, they combine with the meds, prayers, and poetry les-sons to make it more bearable and less suffocating.

After a stroll around Lake Johnson today, I come home to find a Pri-ority Mail box on our doorstep. It's from my mom. She has stuffed it to the hilt with four gallon-size freezer bags of meat and potato cutlets, six pairs of chenille socks, a box of cardamom tea, a pair of fleece penguin pajama pants, a tin of hot chocolate, two toy mice for Keshmesh and Nazanin, and a giant bag of *zereshk*. The latter are tiny dried, superbly sour berries. They're called barberries in English, though I've never met an English-speaker who knows what they are. Sane Iranians cook them in sugar and mix them with rice, but ever since I was a kid, I have eaten them alone, raw and in fistfuls. This thoroughly disgusts everyone who knows about it, but my mom indulges me.

The package also includes one of Ahmad's old blue prescription slips. On it are some couplets from the *Masnavi* that we studied together when I was in San Diego. Ahmad's handwriting is equally atrocious in every language, but miraculously, I make out *"mehmankhaneh"* (guesthouse) in his Farsi chicken scratch, and immediately, I know the poem. In it, Rumi compares the human form to a guesthouse, and he advises,

> *Welcome every guest,*
> *No matter how grotesque.*
> *Be as hospitable to calamity as to ecstasy,*
> *To anxiety as to tranquility.*
> *Today's misery sweeps your home clean,*
> *Making way for tomorrow's felicity.*

I loved this poem when we studied it on a mild Southern California November afternoon, but revisiting it now, on a freezing central North Carolina February morning, it's hard to entertain the idea of treating depression as a welcome guest. After all, some of my previous "guests" have so shamelessly overstayed their welcomes that they nearly killed me—and Mary's "guest" actually *did* kill her. How could that kind of lethal misery warrant a *welcome*?

I ask Ahmad as much that night during our Skype lesson.

"When you see depression as the enemy, then it *becomes* the enemy. When you see it as the friend, then it *becomes* the friend," he explains.

"This is why people hate poetry," I reply, frustrated. "Sure, it sounds nice, but it doesn't actually make sense. I mean, if I could meet Mary's depression, I would kick its ass. *It killed her.* I wouldn't welcome it anywhere. I would kill it back."

"Of course you would, but you can't. Don't you think this is what your friend was trying to do? She did not want to kill *herself*. She wanted to kill *her illness*. But there is no way to kill this kind of illness without killing yourself. It is part of your life and your gene. That is why you welcome it, so you can survive it, so that it does not kill you."

"But how do I get rid of it if I'm inviting it for dinner and tea?"

"Melody *jan*, the only way to kill depression is to live through it, to respect the illness. Just like a scientist respects a virus. Remember? That way you can learn from it and build your immunity. That way you can find a vaccine."

"So how do you respect depression? By crying all the time?"

"Yes, if that's how you feel. Crying is *good* for you: the best natural tranquilizer on earth. Ten times better than Valium or Ativan. Never be afraid to cry. You cannot pretend you do not feel sad and expect the sadness to go away. You have to feel it. Remember Molana," he says, reciting this couplet in Farsi:

> *Wherever streams go, life grows.*
> *Wherever tears go, mercy flows.*

"So you're telling me to cry?"

"No. I am telling you to *feel*. If that makes you cry, then cry. If that makes you laugh, then laugh. Welcoming the guest does not mean you love depression. It means that you *feel it*, so you can let it teach you something. Just you try it."

"Okay, I'll try," I promise, and despite intense skepticism, I do.

. . .

To date, I've experienced over a dozen depressive episodes, and they've all deeply sucked. I haven't learned much from any of them—apart from the fact that, if you wait long enough, they end. As a result, my instinct has always been to fight these episodes, to make them end as soon as humanly possible—certainly not to study, let alone learn from, them.

But now, I begin to genuinely consider this radical alternative, and it leads me to a weekly Rumi seminar at Duke. The class is taught by my friend Omid Safi, an Islamic scholar and professor of Asian and Middle Eastern studies, as well as a fellow Iranian-American and a bona fide Rumi expert. The fact that Omid happens to be teaching this seminar now and that he has welcomed me to attend strikes me as nothing short of kismet.

Early on, he instructs us to pair up with another student and look into one another's eyes. Then he tells us to let him know when we get it. Before anyone can ask, "Get what?" Omid says, "Go." Soon enough, despite not knowing what we're looking for, we *do* get it. When you're close enough to stare into someone else's eyes and when you pay attention, you can see yourself inside their pupils—a reminder that we are all potential mirrors for one another, learning through the reflections we see and cast.

Thanks to Rumi, Ahmad, and Omid, I'm able to become a student again. In doing so, I entertain the possibility that my depression could mean something, that poetry could serve as a potent antidepressant, and that tears could be as sacred as Rumi describes them, as reflective as Omid exemplifies them, and as medicinal as Ahmad identifies them.

Perhaps in the past, had I not been so quick to judge the loyal and hideous guest I call depression—had I not immediately labeled it an invader, detestable and meaningless; had I been even *remotely* welcoming; had I attempted to discern its message; and had I wept with abandon for as long as I felt like it—then maybe things would have been different. Maybe, in return, my depression would have treated *me* with more respect. Maybe it would have quit chronically overstaying *its* welcome. And maybe it would have left me stronger and less terrified of its inevitable return.

Now, as I commit to becoming a dedicated student of my own depression—allowing myself to fully examine, feel, and even welcome it—I soon find all these "maybes" becoming realities. It's not easy, but for the first time, I manage to neither fight nor flee from depression. I sit with it instead of rushing to banish it—for once, treating it as a guest, not a trespasser. I listen and learn what it wants. To my surprise, it seeks neither suffering nor submission, but transformation. Relieved, I allow this depression more patience, reverence, and tears than any before it, and by spring, it's gone. In its wake, I uncover a novel parting gift: a subtle, yet seismic, spiritual shift.

Without fail, every one of my prior depressive episodes has always left a mess behind. But this one is different. It actually *cleans up after itself*. What's more, it sparks precious renovations, allowing me to replace judgment and self-doubt with curiosity and self-love. By recognizing that every emotional guest carries a message rooted in love and purpose, I've become a more gracious and grateful host, as I've found mercy in even the most seemingly merciless emotions.

Indeed, the Beloved's affection knows no bounds, but as humans, we are intensely forgetful. Despite the fact that every one of my prayers begins with a reminder of the Beloved's supreme and all-encompassing grace and mercy, despite the fact that all but one of the 114 suras of the Quran begin with this exact same reminder, and despite the fact that providence has permeated my every human experience, I'm painfully prone to forgetting all of the above from one minute to the next. And it's not because I'm irredeemably slow, selfish, or sadistic. It's because I'm human. As a species, our capacity for spiritual amnesia is staggering. Fortunately, so is the Beloved's patience.

Rumi reminds us:

> *Every storm the Beloved unfurls*
> *Permits the sea to scatter pearls.*

By respecting the physical, psychological, and spiritual nature of my latest personal storm—absorbing medication, therapy, prayers, love, nature, and poetry to weather it—I've stumbled upon a bevy of pearls. Among them: accepting that none of these remedies need be mutually exclusive, learning that no emotion or mood is meaningless (even, and perhaps especially, those that turn clinical), and finding comfort in unexpected places—in tears, in virology, and in lyrical snakes, thorns, and storms.

But respecting and recovering from this latest depression requires more than welcoming it as a guest. It also requires going to my source, favoring invention over imitation, and slowing down. In short, respecting this depression—and thereby learning how to better read and receive the next—requires all of the lessons I've learned on my extended pilgrimage thus far. Applying these lessons not only leads me through—and, ultimately, out of—my depression, but it also leads me back to another storm, one I never thought I'd willingly revisit.

With Ahmad's encouragement, I agree to teach a weekly writing workshop inside a locked psychiatric unit in Raleigh. Though it takes some convincing, as part of me can't help but feel like a patient every time I approach the ward. The first few times I try, in fact, I can't even walk in, because I'm too terrified they might not let me out. I know it's irrational—as I've been invited here to teach—but reason is no match for memory. For weeks, I simply can't get my legs to carry me through those double doors.

"I keep freezing," I explain to Ahmad after my third failed attempt. "This isn't a good idea. I should just tell the hospital I can't do it."

"Are you kidding? Of course you can do it—and you *should*."

"I know. That's why I said yes in the first place, but I just have so many bad memories of places like this. They're *horrible*. There are never any windows, and there's always someone screaming. I get close to those doors, and I remember what it was like to be locked in a place like that, hopeless and humiliated. I remember the restraints and the seclusion and the strip searches. I remember feeling like I wanted to die. I remember being a hundred percent sure that I'd never do anything useful with my life again. With memories like that, why should I go back there? Why should I *voluntarily* subject myself to that?"

"Because, Melody *jan*, you can make it *less* hopeless and humiliating for patients who are there *now*. Just that they see your example—that you can have something like bipolar and still have a job and a family, that you can be a lawyer and a writer—it means so much. They see that, and they think they can do whatever they want too. They see they are *somebody*. And they see that someone cares about them and believes in them. They relate. This is the best prayer you can do: to help people like you."

"I get it, and you're right. But somehow I need to make myself walk through those doors first, and that's just so much harder than I expected."

"You can do it. You just keep trying. Even if it takes ten tries. You keep trying. It will help them so much to have you there—and it will help you too. I promise. And if you cannot do it today, then that is okay. You just try again tomorrow."

. . .

So I try again—and again, and again, and again. Then, just when the whole thing begins to feel like a fool's errand, Mary comes to my rescue, appearing to me in a dream for the first and only time since her death. She is standing in front of the double doors I have yet to walk through, and she looks so beautiful, smiling and serene in a flowing cerulean gown. Mary takes my hand and whispers in my ear: "Go on. It's safe. I'm with you."

I jolt awake and for a split second, I can still feel her hand in mine, her voice echoing in my ear. That same afternoon, I drive to the hospital, and before I know it, I'm breezing through those double doors. From the moment I enter the unit, I know two things for sure: I am not alone, and I am exactly where I need to be.

I teach this workshop every week for nearly two years, and by the second year, I begin to see some of the same faces return. Among them is Elena, a young transgender woman whom I've since befriended. Like me, Elena has bipolar disorder. Unlike me, she grew up in foster care, battered and berated by people who had promised to protect her. I first met Elena when she was manic and then a year later, when she was depressed. She has endured more trauma in her twenty-odd years on this planet than most of us will in a lifetime. But despite all of the abuse, ignorance, and discrimination she has suffered, Elena still shines brighter than most anyone I know.

The first time she was locked inside the drab, windowless ward, she made her own windows, filling the bland white walls of the unit with colorful drawings of clouds, hearts, and butterflies. But there were no windows when she was admitted again the next year for suicidal ideation, and I feared that she may have lost her light. Upon

Elena's release, I took her out to dinner to celebrate. My plan was to remind her of that light within. Instead, she reminded me.

"How does it feel to be free?" I asked her as we shared a vegetarian pizza.

"Honey, you can't confine me," she replied, pulling at a long string of cheese as she lifted another slice of pizza onto her plate. "I'm *always* free."

And there it was, that light again, as bright as ever, ready to turn every wall into a window. Basking in Elena's glow and that of so many patients I've met on the ward has allowed me to shine brighter simply by reflecting their radiance back at them. Bound together by our common wounds summoning the same sacred light, the patients and I see ourselves in one another—not through our eyes, but through our hearts. Where reason has failed us, we find love. And where we find love, we find hope.

> *With Love, bitter turns sweet and copper turns gold.*
> *With Love, pain becomes healing manifold.*

Having survived suicidal depression and manic psychosis, I constantly tell my students that recovery is possible, that medication works, that faith works, that love works, and that having an atypical brain can be as much an asset as a liability. Because I've been there, they believe me. Because they're where I used to be, and could just as easily be again, I can't help but believe in them.

Surrounded by brave and kindred spirits who understand what it's like to lose your mind and find your soul, I've discovered purpose and community. If that makes me crazy, then it's fine by me. For even on a locked ward, I can now feel free.

Dx: Depression ♣ Rx: Welcome Every Guest

Where there is treasure, snakes come round.
Where there are roses, thorns abound.
In the grand bazaar of life, joy without sorrow cannot be found.

—

For a viable cure, pain is the key.
Your injury invites the remedy.

—

Welcome every guest,
No matter how grotesque.
Be as hospitable to calamity as to ecstasy,
To anxiety as to tranquility.
Today's misery sweeps your home clean,
Making way for tomorrow's felicity.

—

Wherever streams go, life grows.
Wherever tears go, mercy flows.

—

Every storm the Beloved unfurls
Permits the sea to scatter pearls.

—

With Love, bitter turns sweet and copper turns gold.
With Love, pain becomes healing manifold.

CHAPTER 5

Dx: Distraction
Rx: Go Beyond the Five and Six

Love has no business with the five and six.
Only upon the Beloved are the true lover's eyes fixed.

Distractions abound on this curious pilgrimage I now recognize as my life. But I didn't actually notice them *as distractions* until I first followed Rumi's advice to go to my source and found myself perpetually sidetracked in Southern California, struggling to focus on this peculiar Persian poetry I'd spent my entire life taking for granted.

By the time I got to San Diego, after months of preparation, I was brimming with hubris and ambition. I genuinely believed that this book could have been researched in a month and written in less than a year. In other words, I was in a rush without realizing how futile and counterproductive it is to be in a rush. As it turns out, Rumi's prescription for haste applies just as readily to distraction, so it bears repeating:

> *You went out in search of gold far and wide,*
> *But all along you were gold on the inside.*

Indeed, I began this journey by rushing out into the world, seeking answers that I had yet to realize were already in my heart. That ridiculous rush, combined with my attraction to distraction, made it seem like the entire world was conspiring to divert my attention away from Rumi—and ultimately, away from every ember of divinity within me. No, I'm not trying to be melodramatic. I'm just trying to say that the things we choose to pay attention to affect our bodies, minds, and souls.

From the start, this whole venture has been riddled with distractions seemingly intent on sabotaging my journey. Of course, like any other sucker with an internet connection, I am constantly battling the draw of every cat, dog, sloth, penguin, hedgehog, koala, pygmy goat, sea otter, platypus, turtle, panda, kangaroo, and dancing lemur on YouTube. Then, even if I *do* miraculously manage not to become one of the millions of innocent victims who've lost up to twenty minutes and twenty-seven seconds of their lives to "Animals Being Jerks," there's always more and worse to reckon with.

In San Diego—which I now refer to as the city that always beeps, because every semitruck in the world seems drawn there for the express purpose of backing up as loudly and frequently as possible— further distractions included: an overflowing inbox and interminable texts, because I'm addicted to getting the last word; unrelenting NPR, BBC, *New York Times*, and AP news alerts; enough outstanding orders and returns to convince the people at Amazon and Etsy that I'm effectively a recluse; my mom's blaring hair dryer from the bedroom; my dad's blaring cable news from the living room; the steady hum of jet planes from above; and the tireless ringing of trolley bells from below.

Recognizing the spiritual danger in such petty preoccupations, Rumi created his own shorthand for all the worldly distractions alienating us from the Beloved. He called them "the five and six," referring to the five bodily senses and the six worldly directions (cardinal, plus up and down).

Love has no business with the five and six.
Only upon the Beloved are the true lover's eyes fixed.

But averting your eyes from the five and six isn't easy, because they're *everywhere*. A more accurate and less poetic description wouldn't be "the five and six," but "the infinite and infinite," because that's how many distractions our senses and the world around us can create. Not long after I first arrived in San Diego to study Rumi with Ahmad, my phone rang at 6:30 in the morning as yet another reminder of this.

Upon hearing the peppy Persian pop song that has been my ringtone for years ("Melody" by Arash, for obvious reasons), I rolled over in bed, reached for my phone, and hit "accept" almost as a reflex. By the time I noticed the number had no name attached, it was too late. I was already being assaulted by a Pakistani scammer posing as an American IRS agent who was now warning of my imminent arrest. I knew it was a scam, but I was up and irritated by that point, so I kept him on the phone as long as possible to conduct a full investigation for which I have never been trained—and of course, to mess with him.

"So, *what's* your name again?" I asked, grabbing a pen to take thorough notes for what I expected would be a lengthy and detailed FTC complaint.

"Maxwell Smith," said a man who sounded way more Mahmoud than Maxwell. At that point, I'd already Googled the phone number and discovered that this was a scam originating in Pakistan. "Maxwell" proceeded to recite my old Atlanta address (and he was right, which I found deeply creepy and mildly impressive). Then he insisted that the IRS had sent multiple notices to me at this prior address and that because of my failure to respond to said nonexistent notices, the police were now "on their way" to arrest me.

"On their way *where*?" I asked, laughing and putting the phone on speaker as I walked into the kitchen. My parents looked up from their *noon-o-paneer* as I pointed to the phone and said, "*Ein kolah bardarhayeh pedar sookhteh daran telephone meekonan.*" Literally: "The people who take off hats and have burnt fathers are calling." Meaning: it's a lowlife scammer. For the record, I have no idea what hats have to do with fraud or what burnt fathers have to do with being a lowlife. Just add these to the hefty pile of Persian idioms that defy direct translation.

As the exasperated con artist halfway across the world tried to explain how the police knew my whereabouts (despite the fact that *he* clearly didn't), my parents and I had an entire conversation cursing and mocking him in Farsi. Ahmad called him *lamazhab* (one lacking religion), I called him *beeshoour* (one lacking sense), my mom called him *beetarbiyat* (one lacking upbringing), and we all meant exactly the same thing: "Maxwell" is a prick.

Still unsatisfied, however, my mom leaned into the phone and just before tapping the red icon at the bottom of the screen, she proclaimed, "The FBI will be at your home in an hour to *behead* you!"

IRS imposters aside, the world is brimming with an endless supply of distractions from every direction vying for every ounce of our attention. And we can't just get the FBI to behead them all. Resisting the pull of the five and six requires a scarce and sacred act: introspection. We must dismiss as many petty distractions as we can through our own *personal* bureau of investigation, one that isn't afraid to favor heart over head, love over logic, intuition over intellect. After all, how can we ever learn that we're gold inside if we refuse to *look there*?

Never in history has it been so easy to seek answers from outside of ourselves: just ask Google or Siri or Alexa. But so too, never in history has it been so easy to forget the questions we were asking in the first place, plummeting into an endless abyss of links to links to links. Don't get me wrong. I'm not just a *member* of the twenty-first century; I'm a *fan*. But connecting with the world online doesn't diminish our need to connect with the divine inside, however we understand or define it. As humans, we are natural seekers, and our instinct is to seek *outside* of ourselves, imagining that the farther we travel, the greater the reward. But Rumi's rhymes—meant to be sung while spinning, not spoken while sprinting—are precious reminders that the greatest reward, the seat of the divine spark within each of us, cannot be outsourced. In other words, your Fitbit may tell you how many steps your feet have taken today, but it will never tell you how far your soul has traveled.

> *The Beloved has expanded your heart with divine light,*
> *Yet you still seek answers from outside to feel right.*
> *You are a fathomless lake, yet you complain of drought incessantly.*
> *Why settle for a puddle when you have a channel to the sea?*

Rumi urges us to turn inward, toward the sublime sustenance the Beloved has planted within all of us, our greatest source of spiritual nourishment, but one that we chronically overlook thanks to the countless distractions heaped upon us courtesy of the five and six. Remember Rumi's call to pilgrims bound for *Hajj*. He does not bless them and wish them well, as others might. Rather, he pleads with them to stay, to return to their homes, asking:

> *Why seek pilgrimage at some distant shore,*
> *When the Beloved is right next door?*

In an era when it's so much easier to turn outward, Rumi guides us inward, toward our inner sage's gold over some scammer's fool's gold, toward our Source over some source code, toward our transcendent treasures within over some worldly riches without. Such is Rumi's antidote to the modern manic distractions that abound in our increasingly digitally connected and spiritually disconnected world.

But more than merely looking inward, Rumi's remedy requires that we do so *as part of a collective,* acting as metaphorical mirrors for one another, casting and beholding our reflections as reminders of the gold, *the love, the sacred,* within each of us. Sworn testimonies of the human heart, these reflections require a depth of presence, trust, and attention that simply cannot exist online. In other words, your Facebook app may tell you what your acquaintances across the globe are eating for dinner, but it will never feed your soul like the warm embrace of a true friend.

That said, it's often our closest friends whom we're most likely to take for granted. Otherwise, why would we reserve our tightest hugs for those we haven't seen in years and then go a full day without deeply embracing the person we claim to love the most? Proximity—be it physical, emotional, spiritual, or all of the above—breeds presumption, and presumption breeds negligence. For instance, there is no one on earth whom I love more than Matthew, yet sometimes I let days go by without really looking into his eyes or holding him close, because I assume he will be here tomorrow. But of course, none of us is guaranteed tomorrow, and even if we were, we can never actually *live* anywhere other than today.

After more than a year of studying Rumi, I begin to see how easily distracted I can be from everything that is most important to me. So I resolve to focus on what matters, and being human, I start outside of myself: with Matthew. Together, we decide to take a vacation through the opposite corner of the North American continent. It's a part of the country we've both always wanted to explore, so we happily dive into planning a two-week road trip across the Pacific Northwest to celebrate our thirteenth wedding anniversary in August.

It's the first big vacation we've taken in years that doesn't include work for me. Usually we just turn my international speaking engagements into vacation destinations to take advantage of the free flights and accommodations. I'm grateful to be able to take these trips, yet because they always involve work for me, they never *fully* feel like vacations.

All this to say, I can't remember the last time we took a trip somewhere we've always wanted to go *because* we've always wanted to go there. So this is a big deal for us, and we treat it as such. We scour travel sites and order guidebooks and brochures to help us carefully plan out the journey, and we do so in a ridiculously detailed Google doc that includes all the things we want to see and do while we're there.

But like all great adventures, this one laughs in the face of our itinerary. True to form, I drastically underestimated the time it would take to drive from point A to point B. The roads are far higher and windier than either of us expected, and because guardrails appear to have gone the way of the floppy disk here, every hour or so, there is at least one moment when I fear I might accidentally drive over a ledge and send us plummeting to our deaths. So we drive like senior citizens. RVs pass us, truck drivers stick their heads out of windows to shower us with saliva and expletives, and one woman even tosses what I assume is the last remaining cigarette in the entire state of California at us. The first night, we barely drive two hundred miles north of the San Francisco airport.

"So where do you want to stay?" Matthew asks after he cancels the Airbnb we had reserved way farther north. "I found a place in Fort Bragg that looks cute."

"Fort Bragg? What? Did we hit a vortex that sent us back to North Carolina?"

"Right? Who knew California had a Fort Bragg? But the place looks nice, and they have a room available. Should I book it?"

"What's it called?"

"The Living Light Inn."

"Great. Sounds like a New Age cult headquarters. Let's do it! Let's get abducted by zealots on our first night here."

By the grace of God, the Living Light Inn turns out *not* to be a cult compound, and we spend the rest of the evening in the "Serenity Room," canceling every other reservation we've booked for this trip. We have no idea how long it will take to drive these roads, and we don't want to rush just to make it to some cabin or hotel. So we agree to stop when we feel like it and drive as much or as little as we want each day.

"Now you can *really* go beyond the five and six," Matthew says as we essentially toss out the itinerary we spent months perfecting.

"Do you even know what that *means*?" I reply. I've explained the concept of the five and six to Matthew before, but never in detail and never outside the context of poetry.

"Of course I do. It means, you know, um, well, basically . . . ignore the bullshit and do what Rumi would do. Right?" Unlike me, Matthew doesn't need to know exactly what the five and six are to go beyond them.

"It *means*," I reply snootily, "you don't give in to all the distractions that come through your five senses from the six earthly directions. It means you pay attention to what matters and ignore what doesn't. It means you live in the present without obsessing over the past or fretting over the future."

"AKA, *ignore the bullshit and do what Rumi would do*. I was right," Matthew proclaims as he gets into bed beside me.

"Sure. Why not. I bet you could even start your *own* New Age cult around that."

"I'll call it 'White Dudes Misappropriating Stuff'—or maybe just

'America.' Same thing," Matthew replies as he pulls me close, snuggling his face into the back of my neck and squeezing my rib cage as it shakes with laughter.

The night before we flew from Raleigh to San Francisco, I noticed a bug bite that bore a striking resemblance to the state of Florida on the back of my calf. North Carolina is effectively a festival of bugs that love to bite in the summers, and they have always been faithful fans of my blood, so I thought little of it.

The morning I wake up in Fort Bragg, however, I am thinking about it and nothing else. My leg itches mercilessly, and that same "bug bite" has now not only doubled in size, but it has set up a full-fledged colony on the back of my thigh, a mirror image of itself that lines up perfectly when I tuck my leg beneath me. It no longer looks like Florida. Now, Matthew insists, it looks like poison ivy.

"But it *can't* be poison ivy. I'm not *allergic* to poison ivy," I argue.

As a child, I once played soccer in a field littered with poison ivy. All the other kids who played that day spent the next few weeks covered in ugly red splotches they couldn't stop scratching. Incredibly, however, I did not, for as my mom confirmed then—without providing any timeline or expiration date—I was magically not allergic to the stuff.

Until then, I didn't know it was possible to *not* be allergic to poison ivy, so I felt like I'd been blessed with some sort of lifelong superpower, and it's possible that, being somewhat of a brat, I took pains to rub it in when I found out.

Until now, I didn't know it was possible to *develop* an allergy to something you've never before been allergic to, so I feel like I've been cursed by a ruthless vengeful karma, decades delayed.

Mercifully, Matthew is spared the contagion, but I spend the entire trip itching, scratching, trying not to scratch with varied degrees of success, and dousing myself with calamine lotion.

Few things are more immediately and consistently distracting than an incessant itch that no amount of scratching can put to rest. As a result, I have endless opportunities to practice rising above the five and six on this trip, and while I'm not as successful as Matthew—who, for the record, is just naturally far more tranquil and focused than pretty much anyone I know—I still manage to thoroughly enjoy the journey in spite of the constant itching. For this, I credit Matthew's patient company and willingness to scratch, as well as many of the lessons I've learned on my pilgrimage thus far.

Every day here, I find myself drawing more on and from Rumi's verse: connecting with my Source through every living thing, finding the tonic nectar in the bitter sting, making my own way without keeping score, and slowing down to welcome every guest at the door.

Here, in this far-flung corner of the continent I call home, the spotty Wi-Fi and the crappy cell reception appear to facilitate spiritual connection. Here, the ocean breeze and the enormous trees keep drawing me to my knees. Here, in case you've yet to notice it, I'm rhyming without trying the slightest bit. Maybe that's what happened to Rumi—his rhyming being the result, not the cause, of his ecstasy.

Whatever the case, this scares the hell out of me, because the last time I found myself rhyming inadvertently, the day ended with me in a psychiatric facility.

Which, of course, brings me back to Rumi, as I wonder if he was at all like me. Did he constantly see patterns where others saw lunacy? Did he fear losing touch with reality? Did he risk his reputation to be free?

Though this book is the farthest thing from a Rumi biography, I've read enough to suspect the answer would be yes to all three.

Perhaps his rhyming was as much a response to insanity as to rhapsody. And based on Rumi's poetry, I doubt that he would disagree.

But here's the part where things get tricky: If Rumi had taken lithium or lamotrigine, would he have been able to find the Beloved in between? Would the side effects have disturbed his singing and whirling routine? Would his diction, rhyme, and meter have lost their sheen? Would he have been just another scholar, regressing toward the mean?

Of course, I want to disagree, because I write and take my meds religiously. But maybe these words would read and sing more brilliantly if I *hadn't* treated my bipolarity. Maybe I would've written more and better books without the aid of modern psychiatry. Maybe I should've taken fewer trips to the pharmacy.

While I'm learning to dismiss the five and six, these thoughts in my head are harder to fix. The racing and rhyming don't need a plug or a signal to function; they run on a steady supply of inner disruption. Useless at best and destructive at worst, they're the kinds of reflections that make me feel cursed. They zip through my head like delinquents on a crime spree. No registration, no insurance, no plates, no ID. But Rumi made his counsel for this clear in the *Masnavi*, and through the echo of my father's voice, it now returns to me:

> *Abstain from thoughts, my dear friend,*
> *For such abstinence is always the best medicine.*
> *Quit your scratching, as it only makes the itch worse.*
> *Stop it already; free your soul from this curse.*

Standing beside a tree a thousand years older than me, my thoughts finally quit racing and the rhyming relents. It's not gone, but now it feels like more of a choice than a punishment.

Yet that's how this trip begins for me: with lots of rhyming and punning involuntarily. The trouble with introspection, at least if you haven't done it for a while, is that there's always this nasty layer of thought buildup. And no regular household cleaner can put a dent in that kind of psychic mildew. So I follow Rumi's advice and try to quiet my mind. But this route to my heart is littered with barriers built in my head.

Perhaps you're thinking I ought to try meditation at this point, and to that, I say, you're not alone. I've thought exactly the same thing, and after much deliberation and several attempts, I've concluded that I *do* meditate. I just call it prayer, and I happen to stand, bend, kneel, and whisper in Arabic when I "meditate." I've read my Thich Nhat Hanh and my B. K. S. Iyengar, and I know they're full of lovely ideas. But like them, *and like you*, I have my own culture and history full of *its own* lovely ideas too. And there's something to be said about returning to your roots—not because they are inherently better than anyone else's, but because they are inherently *yours*.

> *As usual, we're drunk with Love today.*
> *Evict your thoughts and find a song to play.*
> *Prayers and devotions come in countless shapes and sizes.*
> *Pick the ones the beauty in your soul recognizes.*

So I do my own "meditation" here: I pray atop mountains and beside lakes, in the shower and in the car, on water and on land. And it helps some. But ultimately, what helps most isn't any formal prayer. It's this ancient *tree*. And for the record—though I love trees and have even taken a few photos hugging them—I'm no "tree hugger."

I'm a fan of the environment and I recycle and all that, but you won't find me chaining myself to a redwood or an oil rig or anything—which is why I am surprised to be so taken with this tree. It isn't even

an arboreal celebrity, of which there are many in this part of the coun-
try. My tree has no plaque or ring of tourists taking photos. It's just
swaying by itself in the middle of some Northern California forest.
I don't know its species or precise location. Only that it is massive
and that standing beneath it, I feel at once infinitesimal and infinite.
Something in me knows this tree, and something in this tree knows
me. Through some unidentifiable substance deep within its sap and
my blood, we are connected: family. I know it sounds super woo-woo-
flower-child-pass-the-LSD—which, if you haven't gathered yet, is *so*
not me—but there it is. I'm connecting with a tree, and somehow, it
clears my head.

Now I'm able to join Matthew and fully submit to the sacred
wonder of our surroundings, grateful for the fact that after spending
nearly half our lives together, we're still each other's favorite humans.
Dodging a series of wildfires tearing through the region, we manage
to roam the majestic redwoods, swim under glistening waterfalls, and
marvel at a massive rain forest we never knew existed. We wander
through fields of lavender and bogs of carnivorous cobra lilies. We
climb a giant glacier-laden volcano along the Cascades after staring
into the deepest lake in America, clearer and bluer than any I've ever
seen. Awestruck by this land so new to us both, I find it impossible
not to witness the Beloved everywhere.

That said, it's also impossible not to recognize that all of this
beauty is part of a massive occupation. For one, this land feels so
sacred and the names our maps assign to it feel so *not*: Crater Lake,
Mount Hood, Rogue River, Mount Rainier. Bleh. Staring at these
pristine landscapes and knowing they're all stolen, it almost seems
fitting that they're on fire. You need only inhale to know that this hal-
lowed land is in the wrong hands.

The smoke gets worse at the end of our journey, evoking tears
unlike the many I've shed along the way. This glorious terrain is so

touched by God that it has left me tearing up—if not weeping—spontaneously on several occasions before the smoke ever becomes a factor. These new tears are just as spontaneous and involuntary, but they find their source in horror, not wonder, as we drive on a narrow road sandwiched between two strips of smoldering earth.

In the middle of all of it, I see a sign that reads "Fried Dough." Years ago, I spent a summer working at a resort in Glacier National Park, hiking the sublime mountains of northwestern Montana, consecrated territory of the Blackfeet Nation. While there, I not only enjoyed my first mystical experience on the Canadian side of the park, but I also enjoyed my first fry bread experience on the American side.

"Stop!" I proclaim from the passenger seat on this smoking deserted stretch. "Reverse!"

"Are you kidding? We need to get out of here. It looks like they evacuated. It could be dangerous."

"I saw a sign for fried dough and there's a trailer next to it. There were people there. I *saw* them. I promise. Have you ever had fry bread?"

"Fry bread? You mean like the funnel cakes at carnivals?" Matthew asks.

"No, like *real* fry bread," I respond, as though I'm some fry bread connoisseur despite the fact that I haven't eaten any in more than a decade.

"I guess not."

"It's *amazing*. If we do end up suffocating in the car, then it's even more important. You can't die without ever having tried fry bread."

"I know you think this is a joke, but it's seriously dangerous. We shouldn't stop. We should try to get out of all this smoke."

"*Come on,*" I insist, like an overgrown toddler who isn't getting her way. "We checked this morning. It should be *fine*. And if we stop now, we can ask the people there for information, to see if anything has changed. They're locals. They'll know what's safe and what isn't."

"You're *positive* you saw people there? This place looks totally deserted."

"I'm *positive*. Turn around."

The fry bread trailer is run by a mother-and-son team. The kid takes our orders and Mom cooks.

"Did they evacuate this town?" Matthew asks the son after we order, pointing to the side of a house where someone has spray-painted "THANK YOU, FIREFIGHTERS!"

"Not officially, but a lot of folks left. The firefighters are doing a great job though. We should be okay."

"Do you know if it's safe to drive this road to Douglas City? We're trying to get to a lodge there, and when we called this morning, they said they were open and that the roads were too. But now we have no signal, so we don't know if anything has changed."

"Oh, I think you should be fine. I haven't heard anything about the road closing, but I would try to get there before dark," he says as he hands us our fry bread. "There's powdered sugar and honey on the picnic table."

I head to the table and sit down.

"You can sprinkle it with powdered sugar, but I like it plain," I tell Matthew, who is still standing up.

"We should go," he insists. "We can eat in the car."

"It'll take *five minutes*. You really need to experience this without any distractions. Also, it's *good*. Mom knows what's *up!*" I say, tearing off another piece and shoveling it into my mouth like a starving animal.

"This really *is* good," Matthew concedes, taking a bite and a seat.

"I *told* you!"

. . .

We make it to Douglas City before dark in one piece, and a few days later, we fly home to Raleigh. At the time, I saw the wildfires as an inconvenient reminder of the lasting and suffocating toll of colonialism. I soon realize, however, that the charred earth and soot-filled sky were more than living relics of genocide and occupation. They were burning omens of panic and desecration.

Shortly after we return home, I read the news of the deadly 2015 Mina stampede and crush, where thousands of pilgrims were killed during *Hajj*, and I find myself weeping for entirely new reasons.

Soon after, my parents arrive in Raleigh for a visit, and we all go out to dinner at Flame Kabob, our favorite local Persian restaurant.

"You know most of the people who died were Iranian and African," I say when Ahmad brings up the stampede during dinner. "All those Saudi princes can go to hell. They treat us like garbage, and we still keep going there and spending our money. As long as they control and profit from *Hajj*, we should *all* boycott it. Not a single Saudi died in the stampede. *Not one!* They take care of their own, and they let us die in the street."

"We are happy to never go," Ahmad replies as he douses his kabob with sumac.

"You can't *pay* me to go," my mom chimes in.

"I know. Melody told me about Las Vegas," Matthew says, laughing. Several years ago, presented with the choice of completing the pilgrimage to Mecca or vacationing in Las Vegas, both Ahmad and Jazbi opted unabashedly for the latter.

"We had a great time. We have no regrets," my mom announces as Ahmad nods in agreement.

"You shouldn't!" I say. "I'd rather go to Las Vegas than Mecca any day, and I *hate* Vegas. At least no one is *pretending* to be pious there. You can add up all the sins in the entire city of Las Vegas, and they wouldn't come *close* to matching those of a handful of Saudi monarchs."

"Oh no, we've got Melody started on Saudi monarchs. This could go all night," Matthew says before heading to the self-service tea station in the corner of the restaurant.

"We should call it Haramestan,"[1] I go on. "They're an *insult* to Islam. I don't know how anyone with a conscience can still do *Hajj*. I mean, how can you find any spiritual meaning in a pilgrimage that supports the most unjust and *un-Islamic* regime on earth?"

"You should not judge anyone for doing *Hajj*," Ahmad cautions. "You can decide that *you* will not go, but you cannot say that others are bad because *they* decide to go. You remember the story of Moses? Molana says—"

"Oh no, now we've got Ahmad started on Rumi. *This* could go all night," Matthew jokes as he places two cups of tea in front of my parents and sits back down beside me.

"I was telling Melody a poem Rumi has about the prophet Moses, how one day he walks by a shepherd who is talking to God and saying how he wants to comb God's hair and kiss God's hands and feet. Moses yells at the shepherd for talking to God this way. But later, God yells at Moses, because he was sent to unite people with God, but his words *separated* the shepherd from God. Then God says that it does not matter what words people use to show their love—only that they are *full of love*."

---

1 This is my own made-up word, meaning a land ("stan") that is *haram*. "*Haram*" means "forbidden" in Arabic and is often used in reference to sinful acts, objects, substances, or spaces (as I am using it here in reference to the abominable insult to Islam and great bastion of gender apartheid known as the Kingdom of Saudi Arabia). For reference, *haram* is the opposite of *halal* (permitted). That said, *haram* is also used to refer to the realm of the sacred, set aside, or forbidden to those in a state of impurity.

Forget religious rules and regulations.
Let your heart conduct communications.

"And this has to do with Saudi Arabia how?" Matthew asks.

"It has to do with Melody judging people for going there to do *Hajj*, thinking everyone should think the way *she* thinks and act the way *she* acts," Ahmad replies. "She says no one should go for *Hajj*, because it gives money to the Saudi government. She says it is *haram*."

"I know what you're getting at," I reply. "I don't mean to be judgmental. I just think it's *haram* to pay all that money for *Hajj* when you know it supports this *haram* regime."

"But you *are* being judgmental," Ahmad says. "How do you feel when other people say that what *you* do is *haram*?"

"I hate it," I reply.

"So," Ahmad concludes, "don't do it to *other people*. Worry about yourself. When you criticize someone else for how and where or when she does her prayer or pilgrimage, then it distracts from doing your *own* prayer and pilgrimage."

Indeed, none of us is in a position to judge the validity of another's chosen form of worship, no matter how odd or seemingly blasphemous. We're all pilgrims on different paths leading to the same Source, and judgment is a prominent distraction on every path.

To go beyond the five and six is to admit that love supersedes judgment: that our senses deceive us, prompting the complaints and criticisms that distance us from our Source instead of the grace and gratitude that bring us closer to It.

The Mina tragedy is a reminder of so many lessons I'm learning on my pilgrimage: how ego and intellect—and the judgment they breed—can get in our way; how even though we need not travel far (or at all) to find the Beloved, it helps to follow our hearts (without judging others for following theirs); how it doesn't matter *how* we love (through whatever religions or rituals), but only *that* we love; and how vital (albeit tricky) it is to rise above the five and six, evict those thoughts that aren't serving our souls, and connect with the divine inside.

Dodging the distractions of everyday life—whether they come from the outside world or from our own inner critics—isn't something you can master on a two-week vacation. It's a lifelong effort.

Still, my time in the Pacific Northwest was like a spiritual self-defense boot camp in distraction warfare, and I remember it as such. Yet each new day presents its own unique set of distractions, and if we don't actively practice fending them off—by prioritizing what matters most and dismissing what doesn't—we are bound to lose our way.

As I write this, I've now spent more than four years consciously reciting and applying Rumi's prescriptions, and doing so has helped me curb myriad distractions in my life—television, shopping, and web surfing, to name just a few of the worst culprits. Of course, I still fall victim to these and other distractions—just not as often or as intensely as I used to. This frees me up to focus more on my true priorities: faith, family, friends, art, justice, community, health, and above all, love, reflecting it for others and honoring it within myself.

I now LOL, WTF, and OMG less, while actually laughing, crying, praying, and getting out into the world more. I still use Facebook and Twitter and Instagram; I still text and email and WhatsApp and Skype and FaceTime; and I still even LOL, WTF, and OMG on occasion. I'm just much more thoughtful about all of it now, and as a result, I do it less.

Today, when all these high-tech shortcuts and modes of connection zap my focus, inciting me to disconnect from the greater purpose within myself and those around me, I recite Rumi's counsel to myself and sometimes aloud. It's a constant struggle with no end in sight, but it's worth the effort.

Take this very moment. As I type these words, I have ten tabs open on my web browser: five are relevant to what I'm writing (a few news articles about the 2015 Mina stampede and a couple of translation sites) and five are absolutely not (a *New York Times* article on Vladimir Putin's attempts to control the internet, three travel sites, and Pottery Barn's "Outdoor Event"). I'm not proud of these latter five tabs, but I am grateful to be *aware* of them and mindful of what they represent, because now I can close them. And I do, remembering that—like all of us—I am gold on the inside, teeming with a greater purpose.

In my case, I am here to write. And with the weight of five surprisingly heavy browser tabs now lifted, my fingertips brim with vim and vigor as they chassé and pas de bourrée across the keyboard like Misty Copeland in *The Firebird*. I am free to do the thing I came here to do, and I do it, confident that I have the tools I need.

> *You already own all the sustenance you seek.*
> *If only you'd wake up and take a peek.*

By repeatedly returning to my Source—through learning, reading, writing, teaching, walking, praying, breathing, and browser-tab closing—I've quit wanting so much. It's taken a while and I still need constant reminders, but I now recognize that the sustenance I seek already rests within me: that refilling my creative well relies far more on fresh perspective than on fresh discovery.

The result, among others: I can write again. I am no longer stuck or sinking; I am thinking, feeling, and typing. And though not immune to distraction by any stretch, I'm more conscious and cautious of it now. As a consequence, most every day for more than a year now,

I do what used to seem unthinkable: I come to my desk and write. Instead of seeking or waiting for inspiration, I commit to minimizing distraction. I start a timer; I set my phone to airplane mode; I banish Facebook and Twitter; I do my best.

Still, I sometimes get distracted by the Putins and Pottery Barns of the world. And you may be thinking: Does it even matter? Are Putin and Pottery Barn really the ones preventing you from doing what you're supposed to be doing? Are *they* the ones standing in the way of the important internal work that will bring you closer to where you are meant to be? Are *they* responsible for keeping you from creating and connecting to that sacred space within?

Though neither personally nor exclusively: yes, yes, yes, and *YES!* Those five tabs may seem like minor intrusions, but they represent all of the small impositions on our attention that combine to create a cavernous rift between us and our unique yet universal purpose on this planet.

We all seek spiritual connection, even if we don't label it as such. Some of us do it through words, while others do it through family or food, music or dance, scalpels or paintbrushes, microscopes or telescopes. The means and obstacles along the way vary from person to person, but the end remains the same. We are all here to get past petty distractions and go for the gold: the real gold, the inner gold, the gold that doesn't cost a cent, the gold we already own, the gold that facilitates connection. And while our paths may differ dramatically en route to this most precious spiritual metal, its source remains identical, eternal, and unmistakable: Love.

Dx: Distraction ♣ Rx: Go Beyond the Five and Six

You went out in search of gold far and wide,
But all along you were gold on the inside.

—

Love has no business with the five and six.
Only upon the Beloved are the true lover's eyes fixed.

—

The Beloved has expanded your heart with divine light,
Yet you still seek answers from outside to feel right.
You are a fathomless lake, yet you complain of drought incessantly.
Why settle for a puddle when you have a channel to the sea?

—

Why seek pilgrimage at some distant shore,
When the Beloved is right next door?

—

Abstain from thoughts, my dear friend,
For such abstinence is always the best medicine.
Quit your scratching, as it only makes the itch worse.
Stop it already; free your soul from this curse.

—

As usual, we're drunk with Love today.
Evict your thoughts and find a song to play.
Prayers and devotions come in countless shapes and sizes.
Pick the ones the beauty in your soul recognizes.

—

Forget religious rules and regulations.
Let your heart conduct communications.

—

You already own all the sustenance you seek.
If only you'd wake up and take a peek.

CHAPTER 6

Dx: Anxiety
Rx: Follow the Light of Your Wounds

Your wounds may summon the light hereto,
But this sacred light does not come from you.

"Fruit of the poisonous tree!" I yell, waking myself up.

"What happened? Are you okay?" Matthew asks, stunned yet half-asleep. "Fruit of the poisonous *what?*"

"I'm so sorry. I was in court again. Go back to sleep."

It's been happening for weeks now. Last night: "I move for a directed verdict." The night before: "Objection. Relevance." The night before that, I forget, but it's always the same: I'm defending someone I love against a laundry list of felonies in a state where I'm not licensed to practice, and it feels like I'm losing. This time it's my mom, though my defendants have included a panoply of different friends and family members, as well as Lady Gaga for entirely unapparent reasons.

The nightmares started around New Year's, but it's nearly March now, so they're officially getting old. Matthew is already calling 2016 the year of my "courtroom cold sweats." He can go back to sleep after my outbursts, so it's easier for him to make jokes. I can't, so I'm less amused. And it doesn't help that the nightmares are so pathetically transparent. I get the message. In fact, I got it the *first* time. Yet they won't stop.

Apart from the extraneous psychic bric-a-brac (AKA Gaga), the memo is crystal clear, and not just because I keep waking up soaked in sweat and panic. It doesn't take an MD or a PhD to figure out that these dreams are all about, and on account of, anxiety. And I'm not talking about the butterflies-in-your-stomach variety. Unless those butterflies have ice picks for antennae and razor blades for wings—in which case, I very much *am* talking about those butterflies. Sickening specimens, straight out of some creepy sci-fi series come to life, they enter my pleura as a swarm of fluttering dread, a tangled mess of lepidopteran barbed wire closing in on my heart and lungs until I finally scream myself awake, always between the hours of two and five a.m.

Breathless, I hear my heart pounding furiously inside my ears, and I am as terrified as all those horror film fools who walk through creaking doors when they ought to be running like hell in the opposite direction. But my monster isn't some homicidal clown around the corner. It's failure.

So yes, I know *exactly* why I'm losing sleep, why I'm dreaming of botched cross-examinations, why I'm waking up drenched in sweat, and why it feels like a brutal ballet of barbed butterflies is squatting in my chest cavity every night. I'm worried that I'll fail on every possible front in all the worst possible ways: disappointing my people, disgracing my profession, and defying my purpose.

Right now specifically, I'm worried that this book will never find its way into the world, which will inevitably spell the end of my literary career, and because no one will invite me to speak anywhere ever again, I will ultimately be forced to return to legal practice. Of course, at this point no civil rights firm will take me seriously because every page of my CV will become haunted by the same indelible water-mark: *CRAZY*.

As a result, I will naturally end up in the basement of some cold corporate law firm, redlining contracts until all the tiny particles of my soul—which will have been disintegrating steadily with each new billable hour—finally run out. A pitiful shell of my former self, I will proceed to meet my end by dissolving into a faint but cavernous crack in a mahogany conference table right in the middle of taking a deposition from a dirty day trader who calls himself a "futurist."

All this to say, not only do I know *that* I am anxious, but I also know *what* I am anxious about—in agonizingly specific detail. My insight regarding the source of my sleep-screaming anxiety, however, has done little to alleviate it. Hence, I've moved on to other tactics: therapy, warm baths, Netflix, Ambien, Kit Kats, sex, online shopping, reading, redecorating, journaling, cleaning, sewing, painting, and pacing. But each of these strategies has shown limited success, and none has fully cured my anxiety or banished my nightmares as of yet. Every method, moreover, harbors its own tradeoffs.

Ambien, for instance, seems to make the nightmares less likely, but it also makes other anxiety-provoking behaviors *more* likely—as demonstrated by the four boxes of gourmet fruit leather Amazon delivered to my doorstep yesterday as a surprise gift from myself on Ambien a few nights prior.

In short, my tactics for treating this anxiety, like my sleep, are lacking. So I set them aside and pray that a change of scenery will put an end to the nightmares.

In late February, I return to San Diego to speak at another Iranian American Women Foundation conference—and this time, Matthew tags along. It's been more than a year since I sat on the IAWF "Breaking Taboos" panel that left me feeling so frustrated and isolated in LA. And as if the memories from that conference alone aren't enough to aggravate my anxiety, I'm calculating the time between then and now—nearly sixteen months—and berating myself for not having done more with it. All of this combines to make me feel like an extra-special failure when we get to San Diego, so it's no surprise that the courtroom cold sweats have followed me here.

"I move to strike," I yell at two in the morning as my elbow literally strikes Matthew in the chin.

"Are you *kidding*?" he whisper-shouts, cradling his chin in his palm.

"I am so sorry! I was in court again. Are you *okay*?" I ask, inspecting his chin.

"I'm fine. State or federal?"

"It's always state court and always the wrong state."

"Who was it this time?"

"You actually."

"What were my crimes?"

"Oddly enough, assault and battery," I reply. Matthew bursts out laughing. "Shhh! You'll wake my parents."

"Yeah, pretty sure it's too late for that," he says before falling right back asleep.

I go to the kitchen to get some water, and Ahmad is already there. Silhouetted by the light of the fridge, he is holding open the door and leaning in.

"I'm so sorry. Did I wake you?" I say as he turns around holding an avocado and a tub of feta.

"No, I was getting a snack," he says, pulling two slices of *barbari*[1] out of the toaster. Ahmad's midnight snacks are as routine as his afternoon naps. He can't sleep through the night without waking up to eat *something*, and half the time he isn't fully awake when he does it. I expect a sleep specialist might consider this a problem, but given Ahmad has always been thin and well rested, no one in the family has ever worried about it, least of all Ahmad. As far as he's concerned, we're the weird ones for sleeping straight through the night without stopping midway to refuel. "So what happened? Why did you scream?"

"It's nothing. I just keep waking up with these same nightmares. I'm always in court, defending you or Mom or Matthew or Romana, sometimes friends. It's always a criminal case, and it's always in a state where I'm not even licensed to practice."

"You know what it means?"

"Yeah, it's obvious. I'm just anxious is all. If I can't keep publishing books, eventually I'll have to start practicing law again, and apparently, it's not enough that I'm consciously worried about it. Now my subconscious wants to keep reminding me."

"Worry is like a sharp knife," Ahmad replies, holding up the one he's using to slice up his avocado, and proceeds to recite this verse in Persian:

> *Anxiety is like an ax, so let your worries remit.*
> *They'll cut off your own foot and think nothing of it.*

"You see," he continues. "Your anxiety only hurts you. So why you worry?"

"I can't help it. I work in one of the most unpredictable profes-

---

1   A thick Persian flatbread.

sions on earth. At least when I was practicing law, I always knew what I was getting paid and when. I hated it, but it was secure. There's nothing secure about the book business."

"Security is a fantasy. There is nothing secure about *any* business," Ahmad insists as he takes a bite of his feta, mint, radish, walnut, and avocado sandwich. "This is delicious. You want me to make you one?"

"No thanks, I'm not hungry. I can't get over how *California* you and Mom have become, adding avocados to your *noon-o-paneer*, taking Spanish classes, driving hybrid cars."

"This is the *best* state," Ahmad proclaims. "If you move here, I promise you will not worry so much. Just go to the beach and you can see it: no one is worried."

"Because they're all high or on vacation. Anyway, it doesn't matter *where* I am. I'm always going to be anxious about this stuff, as long as I'm a writer. There's just too much uncertainty in this career."

"That's life, Melody *jan*. It does not matter if you are a writer or a lawyer or a doctor. *Life* is uncertain," Ahmad says, reciting Rumi:

> *Forget your plans and embrace uncertainty.*
> *Only then will you find stability.*

"You see," he continues, "trying to fight uncertainty with a plan that has no room for accident or surprise: this is a big source of anxiety and unhappiness for human being."

"You're right. But admit it, *even you* were worried when I decided to write full-time. Remember how you told me I should go back to practicing law, because writing was a 'hobby,' not a 'profession'?"

"Of course I remember. Also I remember I was wrong. And don't *you* remember what you said to me? You said that in America this was possible, that maybe in Iran writing was just a hobby, but in America, writing can be a *profession*. I thought you were crazy, but you were right. You proved it. Don't you know that?"

"I do. It's just demoralizing to think that no matter how successful I become as a writer, chances are I'll never make nearly as much as I'd have made as a lawyer."

"So *what*? Ever you have run out of money, become homeless, or even hungry? You worry about something that never has happened and never will happen. You sound just like the cow."

"I'm sorry. Like the *what*?"

"Like Rumi's cow. You know, the one who always worries he will run out of grass. That is who you sound like," Ahmad says, reciting a poem I've heard countless times before:

> *A fat cow grazes on a lush green island pasture.*
> *For years she feeds daily; still every night she fears disaster.*
> *You've eaten well since birth; in no nutrient are you deficient.*
> *Quit fretting for tomorrow; your lot has always been sufficient.*

"Just like this cow, always you have had more than you need. But still you worry that one day you might not have enough. So stop," Ahmad concludes, leaning in to kiss my forehead. "Now you go back to sleep. And don't worry. There is still lots of *noon-o-paneer* left for tomorrow. And avocado too."

Miraculously, I manage to fall back asleep for a few more hours, and when I awake, my mom has already proven Ahmad right. The table is teeming with more strawberries, honeydew, cherries, kiwis, and *noon-o-paneer* than any of us could ever eat.

After filling ourselves with fruit and feta, we walk a half mile to the Gaslamp Quarter Westin, the site of this year's conference. Ahmad carries the giant sign from last year and Matthew carries my suitcase full of books. When we get there, they set up my booth in record time while my mom and I mingle.

Within a few minutes, it's clear that the SoCal aunties are out in full force, and the more cheeks I kiss and "*salaam*"s and "*haleh shomah*"s[2] I dispense, the more anxious I become and the less I want to be here. What makes this exceptionally disturbing is the fact that I happen to be one of those bizarre hominids who actually *enjoy* public speaking. But the prospect of discussing my mental health condition in front of a pack of impeccably dressed hypereducated Iranian women makes me deeply uncomfortable. It did last year, and evidently it still does.

As if to remove all doubt, Exhibits A, B, and C all present simultaneously: racing heart, dry mouth, and sweaty palms. I know it's a trite trifecta, but it's new to me. I've never entertained all three at once like this. Even when I had panic attacks in college, my palms never sweat and my mouth never went dry. This synchronized assault within my hands, head, and heart does more than reflect my anxiety; it magnifies it. Now I'm actually *anxious about being anxious,* and apparently it shows. Recognizing my unease from across the room, Ahmad walks over and pretends to have a question about paperback pricing.

"You look like you are going to vomit," he says, holding out his hands in prime prayer/vomit-catching position. I swat them away, laughing.

"I'm fine," I lie.

"*Dooroogh-goo* [liar]*!* What's wrong?" he whispers as he guides me toward an empty couch in the corner of the lobby.

"I just feel weird talking to Iranians about this stuff, like I should

---

be whispering or ashamed or something. I know I *shouldn't* be, but that's still how I feel. They can be so *critical*, you know."

"*They* can be so critical? You mean *you*? They are proud of you, Melody *jan*—just like me and Jazbi. You talk about something no one else talks about, so of course it is hard."

"I know, but when I'm talking about this stuff, it's like I can *feel* them judging me."

"That's *you*, Melody *jan*. It's not them. You think they judge you, but really even if they want to judge you, they are too busy judging themselves. They don't have time to judge you. Remember Molana and the meat," Ahmad says, alluding to a story he loves to tell me before I go on any stage.

It's about Shams instructing Rumi to walk around this busy bazaar carrying a colander of raw ground meat on his head one day, and then telling him to return to the same bazaar the next and ask if anyone remembers seeing him. No one does. Point being: while you're so busy being embarrassed, so sure that the world is pointing and staring at *you*, chances are everyone else is too busy being embarrassed and worried about themselves to even notice you, no matter how ridiculous you look.

"You know that you find that story way more comforting than I do, right?"

"*Chera?*"[3]

"Because I'm not like you. I *like* public speaking. I want people to notice me and remember what I say. It's this *crowd* that makes me nervous. Everywhere else, I feel confident and composed. But here I just feel like a mess."

"Are you crazy?"

"Yes, actually. That's sort of the problem."

---

3   "Why?"

"*Pedar sag!* Anyone would be *lucky* to have your crazy. This is a gift, Melody *jan*."

"I doubt these women would consider it a 'gift.' I mean, think about it. Last year my panel was called 'Breaking Taboos.' This year, it's called 'Overcoming Obstacles.' It's like to them I'm just some big taboo who keeps running into obstacles. Why else would they keep asking me to talk about all the worst things that ever happened to me?"

"They ask you because most people would give up after that, but *you did not.* Remember, Melody *jan*, all the things you talk about, the things that when they happened we thought they were so bad—your tumor, your bipolar, all of it—they made you *better.* What we thought was the worst thing to happen to you became the best," Ahmad says before reciting this couplet in Farsi.

> *Break a leg and the Beloved grants wings to soar.*
> *Fall in a ditch and the Beloved opens a door.*

"It sounds a lot like the prescription you put on my plate the night I got here, when we started. I translated it the other day actually," I say, reciting my translation:

> *Your wounds may summon the light hereto,*
> *But this sacred light does not come from you.*

"Do you remember?" I ask.

"Of course I remember. This is the *perfect* translation, Melody *jan*, and it is the same message: the part of you that you think is the biggest mess, the most broken, it is the part that brings you closer to God. So you are not a mess. You are a miracle."

"Thanks for that," I say, and I mean it, because Ahmad's words have once again combined with Rumi's to put me at ease.

Looking back from here, it's clear that my greatest successes never came about in spite of my wounds—but rather, *because of them.* And since it is indeed our wounds that summon the Beloved's light, the wounded self is ultimately the most sacred one. Thus, to follow the light of our wounds is to surrender our most sacred selves to the Beloved.

By embracing the scars that have made us who we are—and shunning the delusion of perfection en route—we liberate ourselves from deep anxieties around not being "good enough." To accept the radical notion that our scars actually *make us better* is to open a world of possibilities. It's a world where we can finally start inventing instead of imitating, creating instead of craving, being the clouds that make the rain instead of the gutter that carries it to the drain.

With all of this in mind, I now calmly claim my seat among the other panelists as Ahmad claims his in the back beside Matthew. My mom smiles and waves at me from her seat up front, surrounded by a gaggle of aunties whom I now recognize as neither judgmental nor critical, but encouraging and nurturing. In the midst of an animated conversation with Ahmad, Matthew winks at me, and I wink back, happy he is here.

Initially, he was hesitant to come, because he didn't have a ticket, but Ahmad cited his experience crashing last year's conference and successfully recruited Matthew to follow in his footsteps. This is fitting, since Ahmad insists that he was also the first to recruit Matthew to our family. Soon after meeting him during my first year at Wesleyan, my father—who spent my entire adolescence hanging up on every boy who ever called our house asking to speak with me—casually suggested that "it would be okay" if I wanted to date this white American boy from upstate New York. I ignored the suggestion for years, but when Matthew and I finally began dating, Ahmad took credit for being the first in our family to "discover" him.

As I watch them laughing and talking at the back of the room before my panel begins, I overhear Ahmad tell Matthew the story about Shams and the ground meat, and I am struck by how far Ahmad has come. More than a year since I first came here with my suitcase full of Sufi poets, Ahmad has taken what I thought was a temporary license to be fully himself and made it permanent. He now recites even more poetry, even more often, even more loudly, to even more people, for even longer than ever before.

I embarked on this pilgrimage chock-full of intensely selfish motivations: seeking to liberate *my* creative spirit by reclaiming a cultural, spiritual, and literary inheritance I had long ignored. I never considered that my journey might liberate *Ahmad* in any way. But just as the chance to connect with my father—on *his* turf, in *his* language, and through *his* eyes—has changed me, it has also changed him.

As I look out at my own people and share a microphone with three remarkable Persian women who have overcome obstacles as wide-ranging as cancer, religious fundamentalism, patriarchy, xenophobia, and government censorship, I am suddenly overwhelmed by a profound sense of belonging.

Last year when I entered this pride of *sheerzan*s I felt like a misfit: isolated and ashamed. Leaving Los Angeles back then, I resolved to evolve. But evolution takes time, and as usual, the Beloved's timeline didn't match mine.

It isn't until this moment, returning to the same conference nearly a year and a half later, that I recognize the *beginning* of an evolution, a transformation from traumatized misfit to imperfect mystic. While today I still feel like a misfit, I also feel connected and humbled, like one of the pride, a *sheerzan* through and through. Unsurprisingly, my winding path from misfit to mystic retains a crucial asterisk—for a mystic is also a kind of misfit, one who may not belong in any single spot on the globe, but one who has found a perpetual place to belong that defies geography, out beyond the five and the six, at home inside her heart, bound to the Beloved.

Finding a home inside your heart, however, isn't something you can do once and then check off your list. It's something we do every day, again and again, for it takes but an instant to forget where we belong. As humans, we require constant reminders, and the more people we have along the way who can remind us that we belong exactly where we are, the less likely we are to forget it.

"*Khak to saret!*" Ahmad yells at the computer screen. Literal translation: "Dirt in your head." Liberal translation: "I hate technology that I can't grasp immediately."

"Can I help?" I ask.

"It is too late. The world has gone on without me. It is time for me to die," Ahmad says with barely a hint of sarcasm. "I have to register with this new 'CURES' system for my medical license. I don't even know what the hell does that *mean*: CURES. I can't do this."

"Oh my *God*, you're such a *drama queen*, Ahmad. Relax," I say, evicting him from the computer to the adjacent sofa and taking his seat. "I'll ask you the questions and fill them out for you. It says here that CURES stands for the Controlled Substance Utilization Review and Evaluation System. Does that sound right?"

"Yes, it is to track controlled substance prescriptions, so less patients become addicted, overdose, and die."

"Sounds good. Here's to the end of the opioid epidemic," I say as I fill in all the boxes I already know the answers to.

"I wish I could type like you," Ahmad says, wistfully watching my fingers dance across the keyboard.

"Ahmad, you *can*," I say, annoyed. "I signed you up for those online typing lessons. Why don't you do them?"

"I forget. I am old, Melody *jan*. It is too late for me. I told you, it is time for me to die." Partly this is pouting and partly it's just what happens to Ahmad when he is confronted by anything he can't do that didn't exist twenty years ago.

"Ahmad, you've got to stop this. I know you don't mean it, but it's not funny."

"I am not trying to be funny. I *do* mean it. Everything moves so fast now. One day I learn how to use my phone, and the next day there is an update that changes everything, and I have to learn all over again. I am tired. Just watching how fast you type, I am tired."

"So what? I can type. You can do surgery. You can recite half the *Masnavi* by heart. You can deliver babies so they don't suffocate."

"But if I don't do *this* right," Ahmad says, pointing to the screen, "then I cannot even write a lousy prescription."

"Why are you so worried about something that has never happened and will never happen? You still have three months to submit this—and you're pretty much retired anyway. You barely work once a week, and not because you have to, but just to stay busy. *Now* who sounds like the cow? Do you need me to recite the poem for you?"

Before I can finish asking, Ahmad is already reciting the poem from this morning.

> *A fat cow grazes on a lush green island pasture.*
> *For years she feeds daily; still every night she fears disaster.*
> *You've eaten well since birth; in no nutrient are you deficient.*
> *Quit fretting for tomorrow; your lot has always been sufficient.*

"Good," I say after he finishes his recitation. "Now all you have to do is apply it to your life. Not as easy as it sounds, right?"

"True. Not so easy. But thank you for telling me. I try to do better. Really, you make me so happy, Melody *jan*," Ahmad says.

"It's no big deal. I'm glad to help," I say as I continue filling in boxes on the screen.

"No, I am not talking about the computer. I am talking about Molana. It makes me so happy to know that you are learning this. It is something that for the rest of your life it will bring you happiness. You know, I always wished that I could study literature," Ahmad says.

"I know. You told me. And you *did* study literature."

"I mean in *school*: that I could become a professor of literature instead of a doctor," he goes on.

"I promise, school would have ruined it. And remember what Rumi says about regret," I reply, reciting this couplet:

> *Your regrets do you no good, persisting at your own expense.*
> *The past can't be undone, so best live in present tense.*

"*Afareen,*" Ahmad says, smiling.

"It's not me. It's Rumi. Now let's finish this: enter your DEA number," I say, leaning back so he can type it in.

"You see how slow I type," he says as he hunts and pecks at the right keys.

"Ahmad, just do those typing classes already. You could learn in a *day.*"

"*Boro baba!* I can do surgery and deliver baby and recite *Masnavi*. So what if I cannot type?"

"Exactly!" I reply as Ahmad repeatedly enters his DEA number to no avail.

"It won't take my number," he says, shoving the keyboard toward the screen and sitting back down on the sofa.

"Don't worry. We'll figure it out. Is this the right number?" I ask, pointing to what he has already typed on the screen.

"Yes," he replies, folding his arms.

"Okay then, I'll just take a screenshot and send a message reporting the problem."

"What is *screenshot*?"

"It's a picture you take of your screen."

"How you do it? I want to know *how*," he says, leaning toward the desktop, still visibly frustrated. I teach him and write the steps down on a Post-it at his request.

"Ahmad, don't let this bother you," I say, handing it to him. "There's something wrong with their system. It's not *you*."

"I know. But I need to learn. I just feel so far behind," he says, staring at the rug.

"Do you remember what I said before I came here to study with you?" I reply, leaning down toward the floor to catch his gaze. "I said the exact same thing you just said. When I started, I felt a *lifetime* behind. So if *I* can study medieval poetry in a language where I still have to sound out the words when I read, then you can learn how to use a computer. And I'll help you. Any time you have questions, you can call and ask me—just like every time I have a question about a poem, I call and ask you."

"That would be nice. Only I don't want to bother you."

"It's not a bother! I know I can get frustrated sometimes," I say, vividly recalling the time I tried to walk Ahmad through sending an attachment and ended up throwing my cell phone across the room. "But I promise, I'll be more patient. I'm thinking a lot about Rumi's guesthouse lately. I know I should start treating frustration and anxiety as guests with something to teach me, and I'm trying."

> *Welcome every guest,*
> *No matter how grotesque.*
> *Be as hospitable to calamity as to ecstasy,*
> *To anxiety as to tranquility.*
> *Today's misery sweeps your home clean,*
> *Making way for tomorrow's felicity.*

"Bah bah," Ahmad replies, invoking an untranslatable utterance that doubles as the name brand for the most popular air freshener in Iran; it's not as much a word as an expression of approval in response to a pleasant scent, taste, experience, or anything else.

"The guesthouse works for pretty much all the worst emotions," I say. "If you treat them like guests and try to learn something from them, then they don't seem so hostile or permanent. Like all this anxiety I have around my writing—if I see it as a lesson that's worth listening to, then it's not so scary."

"So why don't you do that with your dreams?"

"What do you mean?"

"Why don't you see that *they* have a lesson?"

"I *do*. I just don't know why they keep happening, because I already *know* what the lesson is."

"What is the lesson?"

"To quit worrying so much."

"That is all? It must be more specific. Why you are always in court?"

"Because I'm worried I'll fail as a writer and have to go back to practicing law."

"Chera?"

"Because I hated being a lawyer."

"Chera?"

"Because it was boring and soul crushing."

"Chera?"

"Because I couldn't be creative the way I needed to be."

"Chera?"

"Because practicing law is serious."

"Chera?"

"Because people's lives depend on you getting it right."

"Chera?"

"Because that's the way it is. Stop asking me *why!*"

"I ask why only because I don't think you are getting the message right."

"*Chera?*" I ask back.

"Because I think your writing is serious too. And maybe you are not *taking* it serious."

"What do you mean? I'm taking it *so serious* that I'm having nightmares because I'm worried I might not be able to keep doing it."

"That is what I am saying, Melody *jan*. You don't need *permission* to write. It does not matter if you sell your books for ten dollar or ten million dollar. Already you are a writer, and always you will be a writer. You don't need to worry that you won't be who you already are. Only you need to *be* it. As long as you write, then you are a writer. *Tamoom* [finished]!"

And with that *tamoom* (and all the curt and persistent *chera*s that preceded it), my courtroom nightmares adjourn.

We all need reminders of who we are from time to time, and there is no finer mirror than a true friend. Rumi's take on friendship draws from a saying of the Prophet Muhammad:

The faithful are mirrors for one another.

At the start of this journey, Ahmad and I were father and daughter. Today, we are also friends, translating distinct eras and idioms for one another. While this pilgrimage has freed me to lead less with my head and more with my heart, it has freed Ahmad to quit worrying quite so much, about me and everything else. Now he is no longer the only one dispensing poetic prescriptions. Now I catch myself reciting couplets under my breath. And now when Ahmad gets anxious, I can calm *him* down by reciting one of his poems back at him.

"*Bah bah*," I reply to Ahmad's *tamoom*, smiling. "I wish this Ahmad was around when I *first* started writing."

"I told you, I was wrong to ever push you to go back to law," Ahmad replies, looking into my eyes, his gaze solemn and steady. "I want you to know this, *dokhtaram* [my daughter]. Your writing, it is *important*. I know my English is not perfect, but I know enough to tell that you are exceptional. When I read your writing, Melody *jan*, you cannot *imagine* how proud I am."

His voice cracks on the word "imagine" and I catch a glimpse of myself inside the reflective pools of light coating his dark brown eyes, exactly the same shade as mine.

Dx: Anxiety ♣ Rx: Follow the Light of Your Wounds

Anxiety is like an ax, so let your worries remit.
They'll cut off your own foot and think nothing of it.

—

Forget your plans and embrace uncertainty.
Only then will you find stability.

—

A fat cow grazes on a lush green island pasture.
For years she feeds daily; still every night she fears disaster.
You've eaten well since birth; in no nutrient are you deficient.
Quit fretting for tomorrow; your lot has always been sufficient.

—

Your wounds may summon the light hereto,
But this sacred light does not come from you.

—

Break a leg and the Beloved grants wings to soar.
Fall in a ditch and the Beloved opens a door.

—

Your regrets do you no good, persisting at your own expense.
The past can't be undone, so best live in present tense.

—

Welcome every guest,
No matter how grotesque.
Be as hospitable to calamity as to ecstasy,
To anxiety as to tranquility.
Today's misery sweeps your home clean,
Making way for tomorrow's felicity.

—

The faithful are mirrors for one another.

CHAPTER 7

Dx: Anger
Rx: Fall in Love with Love

If you're in love with Love, don't be bashful.
Be brave and plant your flag!

Upon leaving California this time, I'm as clueless as ever about the future, but I take comfort in the fact that my father, Rumi, and the Beloved are steadily preparing me for it. Grateful to be free of winter's sleep-screaming anxiety and all the nightmares that came with it, I accept my wounds as sacred and surrender to the light they summon.

In other words, I keep teaching my writing workshops inside the locked psychiatric unit in Raleigh, I keep doing weekly therapy with Spiro and weekly Rumi with Ahmad, I keep writing and speaking out against the stigma surrounding mental illness, and I do all of it with considerably less anxiety. For I now have faith that if I fall into a ditch, the Beloved will grant wings—if not to soar above the clouds, then at least to get the hell out of the ditch—not just because Rumi tells me so, but because the Beloved has shown me so.

While following the light of my wounds has done wonders for my anxiety, however, it has done little to tame my temper, especially in the face of injustice. No matter the scale or the reasoning, inequity incenses me. It always has. My first big opportunity to exercise this passion for justice came early, in the form of an unsuspecting ice-cream man who failed to include our small hilltop neighborhood on his regular route.

For weeks, he tortured us with his peppy melodies, announcing his presence, luring us through the woods in our backyards on count-less futile hunts, reminding us that paradise was near—yet always out of reach. I was seven or eight years old, and I was *livid*. To me, this was nothing short of a grave human rights violation. Unable to let it slide, I gathered local stakeholders (AKA a few neighborhood kids) and unleashed my first organized political protest on the world.

Armed with markers, poster boards, and vocal cords, we ventured to the corner of the busy street at the bottom of our hill, held our signs high, and made our voices heard. Within a week, the ice-cream man responded to our appeals by braving the steep incline that led to our homes, and the rest was history. Wooden Shoe Lane would never be the same.

So it was that my first sweet taste of success as an activist ar-rived in the form of a red-white-and-blue Bomb Pop devoured while dancing midstreet to the triumphant tune of "The Entertainer." All sticky hands and faces, we basked in the glory of our victory, and I proudly retired my inaugural handmade protest sign ("Ice Cream Man, Wooden Shoe Wants YOU!").

Ever since, I've been hooked on activism—not because I'm some lofty humanitarian, but because I'm chronically irate with the state of the world. It's why I spent weeks traumatizing my middle school classmates with gruesome photos documenting the Bosnian geno-cide and collecting money at the end of the lunch line when the student council voted to spend our savings on a dance instead of donating it to help build a hospital in Croatia. It's why I founded my high school's Amnesty International chapter and spent my Friday nights standing outside of Shell gas stations holding signs bearing photos of the Ogoni Nine instead of cheering on our Centerville Elks at football games. It's why I have another handmade protest sign in my office right now that reads "DISCRIMINATION IS NOT A 'RELIGIOUS FREEDOM'! IT'S AN INSULT TO GOD AND THE CONSTITUTION." It's also why I became a lawyer, and it's why I write pretty much anything at all, including this.

Yes, seven chapters in, I am finally ready to reveal my radical Islamic agenda: to brainwash you into accepting that . . . I am human!

Seriously though, I have now spent more than a decade of my life trying to persuade strangers to accept my humanity, and frankly, I'm exhausted. Still, I'd rather debate a rabid Islamophobe than preach to some doting choir any day. I'm not ashamed to admit that I revel in a heated argument any more than I'm ashamed to admit that injustice infuriates me. But fury alone can carry you only so far before it begins to burn.

> The seed of hellfire is in your wrath.
> Extinguish this hell inside to follow Love's path.

For Rumi, anger is a trap that can distance us from the Beloved, yet it is also an undeniable part of the human experience. Rumi recognizes that there is a place for justified outrage at personal and global injustice, but he *also* recognizes that anger, however warranted, takes a toll on our souls. Thus, the most healthy and effective way to fight oppression is not to obsess over our *fury for the oppressors*, but rather to unite over our *fidelity to the oppressed*, thereby transforming our anger into love and our love into action.

Ultimately, the most powerful weapon in the human arsenal against injustice isn't anger; it's love. Faith and experience have repeatedly taught me this, so I need no convincing. But there's a big difference between knowing something and putting it into practice. And the violence and bigotry that consume the spring and summer of 2016 fill me with rage.

It begins with the passage of HB2 (AKA House Bill 2, AKA "the bathroom bill"), which singles out transgender and gender-nonconforming North Carolinians for special discrimination. The law is clearly one more step in a long line of concerted attempts by the General Assembly and Governor Pat McCrory to turn the clock back decades in North Carolina: drastically cutting unemployment benefits in a state with one of the highest unemployment rates in the country, refusing billions of dollars in federal Medicaid expansion, passing one of the harshest voter-suppression laws in the nation, trying to subject every woman seeking an abortion to an invasive trans-vaginal ultrasound, embracing racist and illegal redistricting efforts, slashing mental health funding, and generally disregarding the US Constitution whenever it seems to suit them.

Falling squarely into this final category, HB2 passes in a single day in March. After convening a special legislative session costing tax-payers $42,000, the General Assembly rams the bill through the legislature with all but zero debate, and hours later, Governor McCrory signs it into law. The next day, I protest outside the governor's mansion holding up the corner of a banner that reads "MUSLIMS for SOCIAL JUSTICE." I join hundreds of others in the middle of North Blount Street as we chant in unison: "I believe that we will win."

And I *do* believe it, or at least I want to. While I have no idea that our state is now a preview of things to come for the country as a whole, I sense that something big is at stake here. When the *New York Times* editorial board labels North Carolina a "Pioneer in Bigotry" in response to the passage of HB2, I'm compelled to agree: this state I've grown to love is ruled by people who love to hate.

Never in my life have I seen government move so quickly and callously on *anything*, and the fact that it's an unconstitutional attempt to mandate bias and bigotry incenses me all the more.

A couple months and five protests later, I'm somewhere in the Pennsylvania wilderness disabling my phone's GPS when it rings.

"Where are you?" Ahmad asks.

"In a forest outside of Philadelphia. I forget the name, and I can't tell you now because I just turned off my GPS."

"Why?"

"So no one bombs us."

"*What?*"

"I'm at the queer Muslim retreat where I was invited to speak. I told you about it."

"Oh yes, I forgot that is *this* weekend. So who will bomb you if your GPS is on?"

"You know, bigots, *haram* police, evangelicals. The usual suspects. But don't worry, it's safe. We're in the middle of nowhere and they don't advertise this. The organizers are just being extra cautious by asking everyone to turn off their GPS."

"Good. They *should* be. There are so many crazy people out there."

"I know, I'm one of them."

"*Pedar sag!* You know what I mean. You have mental illness; they have mental dumbness. Matthew is with you?"

"Yeah, they invited him as my guest, which was really sweet. But apparently we're the only straight cisgender couple here."

"Cisgender *yani chi* [means what]?"

"*Yani* people whose gender *identity* matches their sex assigned at birth, as opposed to transgender. So cisgender *yani* people like you and me."

"Oh, I see. I never hear this word before. Cis-gen-der. Thank you for telling me. So you see friends there, no?"

"Yeah, we're excited to see them all. But things are a little weird right now. Turns out, some people have issues with my being here as the only straight cisgender speaker. And I get it. Thankfully, it's just a few people, and everyone else has been super welcoming. I just feel bad, and honestly," I say in a whisper, "*yek kam asabaneem kard* [it made me a little mad]. I mean, all of my death threats are for defending LGBT Muslims. How much more committed do I need to be to this cause for them to accept me?"

"They *do* accept you, Melody *jan*. That's why they invite you in the first place. But they have so few spaces for themselves. They are the minority of the minority of the *minority*. However bad it is for us, it is one hundred times worse for them. You cannot be mad for this. It is not *about* you. You have to be compassionate. Rumi says that you cannot be angry without being arrogant. These two, they always come together."

> *Anger never arises in the absence of pride.*
> *Crush both beneath your feet and be sanctified.*

"I don't buy it," I respond. "Not *all* anger stems from arrogance."

"No, it does. You will see. And even if you do not agree, then you have to at least admit that *this* anger you have now is from arrogance. You are mad because it hurts your ego that someone might not want you there. This is the *definition* of arrogance, no?"

"I guess. But what about *other* kinds of anger, like anger against injustice? That's not arrogance. That's *compassion*," I say.

"Only if your *focus is on compassion,* not ego. Rumi tells a story of a man who asks the prophet Jesus what is the hardest thing a human can tolerate. Jesus says it is the anger of God, and that the only way to be free from God's anger is to release yours."

To avoid God's wrath, abandon your own.

"Wow. That's a lot of fire and brimstone for *Rumi,*" I say.

"Brimstone *yani chi*?"

"Actually, I don't really know, but 'fire and brimstone' is a saying for when people preach a lot about damnation and God's wrath. It's just weird to hear Rumi talk about God as anything but love."

"Don't get confused, Melody *jan*. For Molana, God is *always* love. This is why he says to get *rid* of your anger. It is not because he wants you to think *God* is angry, but because he wants you to learn that anger comes from pride and both of these get in the way of God, in the way of *love*. That is all. Now tell me, when do you give your talk?"

"Tomorrow morning."

"Good. It will be *great*. Just remember Rumi and the meat."

"Sure, but for the gazillionth time, I don't find that story nearly as comforting as you do," I reply, rolling my eyes so far inside my head that it's a miracle they find their way back.

"I know. But one day you will," he says.

Less than twenty-four hours later, Ahmad's prophecy is fulfilled.

When I was invited to speak here at the recommendation of my friend Scott—a professor of South Asian and Islamic studies at Emory who literally wrote the book on homosexuality in Islam (it's called, wait for it . . . *Homosexuality in Islam*)—I immediately said yes. This is a community I love, full of old friends and comrades, siblings in Islam *and* activism. So naturally, I jumped at the chance to join and support the queer Muslim community—partly because it's the right thing to do, and partly because it's the only American Muslim community that has ever consistently supported *me*.

It's also a community that I expect Rumi would have adored, regardless of whether he was gay—a topic of intense scholarly debate. What Rumi would have loved most about this vibrant community, irrespective of sexual orientation or gender identity, is that it strives to practice what Rumi preaches: to favor invention over imitation, to welcome every guest, to follow the light of one's wounds, and to fall in love with Love. What's more, they accept and celebrate conduct that would easily earn me a lifetime supply of evil eye in most gender-segregated mosques—like my disdain for dress codes and my refusal to pray in the back of the room or behind a screen or in some decaying basement or balcony full of snotty toddlers and diaper wipes. Not so coincidentally, the queer Muslim community is also the only religious circle in which I've ever felt fully at home.

My friend Faisal helped establish it years before some of the people here were even born, and from the moment we met, he welcomed me into it with open arms. I wrote about Faisal in my first book, *War on Error: Real Stories of American Muslims,* and after interviewing him at a coffee shop, I knew I had found not only the last chapter for my book but a lifelong friend and hero.

So I am especially touched when Faisal introduces me before my two-hour morning session entitled "From Mental Illness to Wellness: A Personal, Spiritual and Political Tale." Full of his classic warmth, charm, and grace, Faisal's introduction immediately puts me at ease by reminding me that I have family here.

I feel *so* at ease, in fact, that I lose track of time. After a couple hours of speaking, answering questions, and moderating discussion, I am both exhilarated and exhausted. I can also barely remember what I've said. The audience applauds and several people come up to me afterward to offer thanks and share their own experiences with various mental health conditions.

Then my doppelganger approaches. Okay, well not exactly a doppelganger per se, but another vaguely brown, ethnically ambiguous girl with big hair and a mouth to match. As she walks closer, I smile at her, reach out my hand, and introduce myself.

"I *know* who you are," she blurts through a scowl so severe it makes Stalin look warm and cuddly by comparison.

She recoils from my hand as though it were radioactive, and I know right away this conversation is doomed. The woman begins by scolding me for my liberal use of the word "crazy"—which, as I'm sure you've figured out by now, I embrace proudly on a personal level, and use freely and deliberately to mean exactly what every dictionary says it does. Recognizing that I'm not going to quit calling myself crazy or identifying irrational events or actions as such, she moves on to berating me for "taking up space."

At this point, I literally step back to create more space between us. The more she speaks, the more my stomach growls and the more the same two words repeat inside my head: *Shut up. Shut up. Shut up. Shut up.* Finally, she shuts up.

"What was she *saying*?" Matthew asks as I take his hand and walk into the hall afterward.

"Was it horrible? Was I a total disaster?"

"What are you *talking* about? You did great," Matthew replies, hugging me and kissing the top of my head. "What did that woman *say* to you?"

"I don't know. She doesn't want me here. I'm sure it's all about her own trauma and has nothing to do with me, but I'm not a fucking punching bag. It's like she thinks I just crashed this retreat as opposed to being invited after a lifetime of activism. Whatever. It's got me thinking, though, about what Ahmad was saying yesterday. I mean, I still don't buy Rumi's argument that anger always stems from pride, but I don't know. Maybe I'm wrong. Like now at least, I'm not angry about the massive societal injustices that might have led her to lash out at me like that. I'm just mad she wouldn't shake my hand. Maybe it *is* all arrogance. Tell me though," I inquire again, my freshly bruised ego still clinging to this grudge and desperate for validation, "I did *okay*, right?"

"Yes! Like I said, you were great, but if you don't trust me, go ask Scott and Faisal. They were there."

I immediately track them down, as well as a few other friends along the way, all of whom reassure me that my session went well, and more than a dozen strangers confirm the same without prompting over lunch. Still, I can't shake the seed of insecurity and indignation planted by my pseudo-doppelganger.

"So what if it *was* a disaster," Matthew finally says in the face of my relentless quest for affirmation. "Remember Rumi and the meat."

"Oh my *God*! No matter how many times I tell Ahmad that I don't find that story comforting, he still keeps repeating it to me. He brought it up again yesterday. And now *you're* bringing it up?"

"Well, maybe it's a sign that you ought to listen to it. Because the story *is* comforting. Think about it: At least ninety percent of the time, people are way too caught up in all their own dramas to notice yours. So even if your talk was a disaster, even if you thoroughly blew it—which again, you did *not*—it still wouldn't matter. People either wouldn't notice at all in the first place or they'd forget an hour or a day or a week later. You seriously don't find that *at all* comforting right now?"

"Fine. Maybe in this one discrete, isolated case it's comforting to think that we're all deeply forgettable. But big picture: it's fucking *depressing*."

"Then forget the big picture for a second and focus on this one. Here, today, right now, Rumi wins," Matthew proclaims, throwing his hands up in the air victoriously.

"I don't know what you're cheering about. Rumi isn't into winning or losing," I say, reciting the following verse, a prescription for haste that applies just as readily for anger, pride, and more:

> *Quit keeping score if you want to be free.*
> *Love has ejected the referee.*

"So why do you get so upset when you can't win over every single person in every single audience?" Matthew asks. "Why not just forget about winning and just enjoy the game?"

I try to follow Matthew's, Rumi's, my father's, and my own advice: forgetting about winning, taking comfort in being at least occasionally forgettable, and enjoying whatever game I'm playing *while I'm playing it*. As a result, I spend the rest of the retreat savoring the experience. I take in the beauty of our surroundings and reconnect with old friends who keep introducing me to new ones. This place feels as far away from Philadelphia as the sun does from the moon. Deer, foxes, squirrels, and bunnies frolic about the grounds, and combined with all the rainbow paraphernalia and the impromptu dance parties, the whole retreat almost feels like it's taking place inside of a progressive Disney movie.

I say *almost* because everyone knows that this is just one weekend out of the year, that a wide spectrum of perilous realities awaits us when we return to our respective homes across the world, that the Muslim Alliance for Sexual and Gender Diversity (MASGD), which is sponsoring this magical weekend, doesn't have nearly as much power or pull as the politicians and preachers who wish us dead if they bother to acknowledge us at all. The outside world may *feel* far away for the time being, but we all know it's not. Turning off your GPS doesn't change your global positioning. It just makes it harder to track.

Still, for now, I feel safe and accepted here, my laughter and tears flowing with more ease and proximity than usual. It's partly because of the strong sense of belonging and fellowship that the MASGD organizers have managed to create through workshops, *zikr*s,[1] group prayers where anyone can stand wherever they want, and kinship and support groups. It's also partly because I keep encountering the power and resilience of the human spirit here, repeatedly bearing witness to others' private mental health histories in their own words. These histories include suicidality and all sorts of unimaginable traumas endured largely as a result of sexual orientation, race, religion, and/or gender identity. The stories make me furious at the individuals and systems that have dehumanized, criminalized, and tortured the bodies, minds, and souls of my friends and fellow humans. But the courage and vulnerability it takes for them to share their stories easily makes me love, respect, and connect with them all the more.

Combined, it is this love, respect, and connection that best serve the pursuit of justice. Indeed, the safest and most effective way to

---

1   *Zikr* literally means "remembrance" or "remembering"; specifically, it refers to a remembrance of the Beloved (AKA God in this context). A Sufi devotional practice that involves repeatedly reciting short prayers, or one or more of the many names/attributes of God (of which Islam recognizes at least ninety-nine), or even poetry—all as a means of remembering the Beloved. *Zikr* is often a communal ritual that involves singing and dancing as well.

overcome oppression is not out of revulsion for our enemies, but out of devotion for our friends. When we focus on our love and empathy for the oppressed—instead of our anger and enmity for the oppressor—we liberate ourselves from the pitfalls of ego and outrage. And in doing so, we pave the way for an enduring, inclusive, and accessible path toward justice.

This isn't me being noble or gracious, as I'm inherently quicker to anger than to love. This is me being *practical*. The greater and more deeply entrenched any injustice happens to be, the higher the likelihood that we'll have to convert some enemies into friends to uproot it. That's just math.

I'm not suggesting we love all our enemies to the point of failing to protect ourselves. Far from it. I'm all for defending ourselves and others in the face of oppression. I just think we ought to be *smart* about it.

To that end, it's worth recognizing that everyone needs love—friends and enemies alike—and that most people who perpetrate injustice don't do it because they want to be cruel, but rather because they want to be loved. It's just that somewhere along the line they forgot that they were *born* loved, and then proceeded to conflate love with power, money, fame, privilege, or all of the above.

Once we recognize the pitiful confusion, longing, and insecurity that drive so many oppressors, we can start being more strategic about how we oppose them and quit pretending that fury alone can produce meaningful change.

Outrage, after all, is not a viable public policy. Love, on the other hand, is. Love commands us to see ourselves in others and others in ourselves, while outrage commands us to see ourselves as *superior to others* and others as *inferior to us*. And the more purportedly righteous our indignation, the more it relies on a relentless dichotomy between "us" and "them." Unlike anger and arrogance, however, love doesn't revel in rank or righteousness; love is free from ego. Magnify love and you get justice. Magnify anger and you get injustice.

Rumi says,

> *Justice waters trees that bear fruit.*
> *Injustice waters thorns at the root.*
> *Bestow bounty where it belongs, no matter where it arose.*
> *Don't just go watering everything that grows.*

But it's not always easy to favor the trees of devotion over the thorns of indignation. The night before we leave Pennsylvania, I stay up well into the next morning talking with a transgender man who is actively suicidal. He has been hospitalized on a psychiatric unit before—where he was raped, held for weeks against his will, and repeatedly violated at the hands of people who were supposed to be treating him.

Nothing I say can convince him to seek help from a system that has already so colossally failed him, and I know that coercing him into another psychiatric facility will be counterproductive at best and lethal at worst. So I do the only thing I can: I listen.

Thankfully, he is ultimately able to get help through friends and family outside of the traditional mental health system, but I am enraged by the torments he has been forced to endure. Not just because they represent serious human rights violations, but also because trans and nonbinary individuals are far more likely to be victims of such abuses. Some people wonder how God lets these horrors happen. I don't. The way I see it, humans are the ones who let it happen, and humans are the ones who need to stop it.

I leave Pennsylvania feeling deeply grateful for the abundant beauty, joy, fellowship, laughter, prayer, and dancing I've enjoyed at this retreat. I feel enlightened and empowered by the souls with whom I've connected, but I also feel exhausted and enraged by the oppression so many have suffered and continue to suffer simply for being who they are.

In short, I *want* to water the trees, but I keep running into thorns.

I'm back in Raleigh when, two weeks later, the then-deadliest mass shooting in modern American history occurs on "Latin night" at a gay nightclub in Orlando. Fifty people die, including the killer; fifty-three others are wounded. The murderer claims to be Muslim. His ex-wife claims he had bipolar disorder. Several people claim he was gay. Reading all of this and anticipating the pain it will cause count-less people in my community and beyond who had nothing to do with it, I have trouble catching my breath.

Everyone agrees that the killer was born in America. Everyone agrees he was raised in America. And everyone agrees that the assault rifle and the nine-millimeter handgun he used to massacre forty-nine innocent people were legally bought and sold in America.

Lots of folks blame Muslims. Some blame mental illness. Others blame guns. No one blames the miasma of homophobia, transpho-bia, Islamophobia, anti-Semitism, racism, sexism, and colonialism that have combined to create modern-day America. No one blames the people who want to restore America's "greatness" via rabid xeno-phobia. No one blames war or testosterone. No one blames America.

I say this, for the record, as a proud Iranian-American-Muslim woman who refuses to lose the hyphens or to believe that keeping them makes me any less American. I say this as the daughter of im-migrants who still think America is magic. And I say it as the sister of countless other Americans with countless other hyphens who believe in the promise of this infant nation, and who want it to grow up and *make something of itself*—not to stagnate like some tantrum-prone toddler, perpetually stuck in the terrible two(hundred)s.

A few weeks later, an increasingly divided United States of America turns 240.

The next day, Alton Sterling is shot dead at close range by two Baton Rouge police officers. He was thirty-seven. He was Black. He was trying to sell CDs.

The day after that, Philando Castile is shot dead in front of his girlfriend and her four-year-old daughter by a Minnesota police officer during a routine traffic stop. He was thirty-two. He was Black. He was trying to drive home from the grocery store.

Watching the camera phone footage of these murders, I realize that I've lost track of how many similar reality horror shows I've now seen, how many Black bodies I've observed go limp on camera, how many extrajudicial executions I've witnessed without ever hearing a single person call them that.

At a fledgling two hundred forty years old, America is still throwing its fair share of homicidal tantrums, and it seems to be picking up speed at an alarming pace. At thirty-seven years old, I'm not sure how much longer I can watch.

Less than two weeks later, Donald Trump's overtly anti-Black, anti-Muslim, anti-immigrant, anti-woman, anti-planet campaign officially wins him the Republican nomination for president. I am so angry I can barely see straight. I can hear the crowd cheering as he accepts the nomination on the television in our living room, but I can't see him or his adoring fans. Foggy splotches of red, white, black, and blue flood my visual field. My tears feel like they're boiling, burning through every inch of skin, muscle, and fat, straight to the bone.

Not long after, a prescription slip arrives in my mailbox, and I need it.

Only Grace opens our eyes.
Only Love calms fury's cries.

Though, as always, the couplet is in Persian, Ahmad has signed his name and written the following in English: "I love you. Twice a day."

I call him right away. When he picks up, I thank him, and he happily recites the poem for me. It requires no translation.

"It's beautiful," I tell him. "How did you know I was so angry?"

"You told me, dummy. Also, I watch the news."

"I know. Can you believe it?"

"Yes. Of course I can believe it. This is why you and Matthew need to move to California. People are not so angry here. Not like where *you* are. Really, I worry about all the guns there. Here it does not matter how much people hate the immigrant, the Black, the gay, the Jew, the Muslim. Because in California, *we* become the majority, and *still* we respect the minority."

"So basically, your solution for everything is just to move to California and start adding avocado to every meal?"

"Yes. It is good for you. You get more freedom *and* more omega-3. Why not?"

"Because California isn't paradise. Besides, Rumi doesn't say the cure for anger is to run away to California. He says it's to *love*. Isn't that what your prescription says anyway? Follow *love* to get to Paradise, not I-40."

"*Bah bah! Afareen! Barikalah!*" Ahmad says, oddly showering me with praise for challenging him. "It is always love, Melody *jan*. Always love."

As anti-Muslim sentiment and hate crimes rise alongside Trump's incendiary campaign rhetoric, every fresh news alert that pops up on my phone feels like it's saying the same thing: AMERICA HATES YOU.

Still, I try my best to water trees instead of thorns, love instead of rage, in the midst of what feels like a hailstorm of hate. Soon enough, it's clear to me that *this* is what my pilgrimage has been preparing me for all along: an era of pure psychological warfare, when the faith and ancestry I share with my father and Rumi have made me more of a target—more hated and unwelcome in my own home—than ever before. While I'm not about to retreat, I know that fury alone cannot safely fuel my fight.

Thankfully, I have now spent nearly two years studying the work of a medieval Islamic scholar and mystic poet who went to great lengths to glorify love above all else in an era of deep political turmoil from within a rich Islamic history, tradition, and perspective. Thus, without realizing it, I've been steadily filling my spiritual savings account with more love than I ever imagined might be necessary. In the face of such intense bigotry, however, I need to cash in, and I thank God for my reserves.

No matter our background or circumstance, we can all use similar stockpiles, as none of us is free from the threat of irrational hatred and hostility. We all have to find a way to live, *and to love,* in a world that allows and at times even seems to reward heartless prejudice and enmity.

For me, this means consciously trying to favor love and compassion over anger and condescension. Admittedly, the latter have always come more naturally to me, particularly when faced with ignorance. Love and compassion take more work, but they also reap more rewards.

A neighbor reminds me of this at the end of the summer. I had

met her once before, at a candlelight vigil in the parking lot behind
Legends Nightclub in Raleigh the day after the Orlando shooting. I
didn't know that she was my neighbor at first, but we got to talking
and I learned that she lived just a few streets over. We were having
a perfectly cordial conversation, discussing how horrified we were
by what had just happened in Florida, when the discussion veered
toward the shooter, and she said, "I heard he was a Muslim, like a
jihadi or something."

   I could feel my face getting hot, but having encountered similar
situations plenty of times before, I kept calm as I delivered my stan-
dard three-minute Islam 101 lecture to a total stranger for what felt
like the millionth time. I informed her that *"jihad"* means "struggle,"
not "holy war," as it is often mistranslated, and that it denotes a deeply
spiritual struggle for peace and justice, not a mandate to kill innocent
people while yelling random fundamentalist clichés in Arabic.

   "Of course," she replied, "but I'm just saying they think he was a
terrorist. You know what I mean."

   "Not really. I'm a Muslim; I'm not a terrorist, and the vast major-
ity of terrorists aren't Muslim. So no, I really don't know what you
mean," I said, trying to control my ire and disappointment.

   "I'm so sorry," she replied. "I didn't know you were Muslim. You
don't *look* Muslim."

I've easily heard those last four words with that exact same intona-
tion at least a hundred times. My instinctive response, one I have
spent years dishing out, one that feels great in the moment, and one
that takes absolutely zero work on my part, has been snark. More
specifically: *You don't look stupid.*

   Every cell in my body wanted to say it and say it loud, especially
given her assertion that she didn't *know* I was Muslim, as if that addi-

tion did anything but make her sound *more* Islamophobic. But then I surprise myself by asking her what a Muslim is *supposed* to look like. It's a weak attempt to engage with love instead of anger, but it's an attempt nonetheless: a sign that, however slowly and inelegantly, I am evolving.

Rumi advises,

> *If you're in love with Love, don't be bashful.*
> *Be brave and plant your flag!*

This tiny concession to worldly and spiritual devotion—asking a question instead of hurling an insult—was indeed my clumsy attempt at planting a flag of love. For despite being a natural born brat, I am also a natural born human, and like every other human, I too long to love and be loved.

Nevertheless, I found myself judging this stranger inside my own head as just another run-of-the-mill bigot while knowing next to nothing about her. Projecting and entertaining my own set of stereotypes, I fully expected her to walk away when I asked what a Muslim was *supposed* to look like. But she didn't.

Instead, she surprised me by genuinely entertaining my question. She actually began to list a whole host of stereotypes about Muslims, and for the most part, she disputed them all before I even had the chance. She even *thanked* me for the "exercise." I was stunned.

For all my efforts to apply love before anger, I know I still must have sounded upset, mainly because I was. The only reason I can imagine for her *not* walking away was the fact that she could tell that I was *trying*, however imperfectly, to employ my higher emotional faculties. So, to her credit, *she tried too*. Nevertheless, I left the vigil with more than a dozen mosquito bites and a growing sense that the world was falling apart.

I didn't think of that woman again for months. But today, she surprises me again: living proof that planting a flag of love can indeed free us from the tyranny of anger and ignorance alike.

I'm taking my daily walk around the neighborhood when a random minivan screeches to a halt beside me. The driver rolls down her window and says, "It's *you!*" I have no idea who this woman is, but she graciously reminds me that we met at the vigil. Her face rings no bells (which is typical, because I have abysmal facial recognition), but her story immediately jogs my memory. I forgot that she was my neighbor. I also apparently forgot that I discussed my work with her at the vigil, that I even suggested she read my first book about American Muslims (which she blessedly didn't find nearly as gauche then as I do now).

She tells me that she has read it, and convinced her partner, her teenage son, and some friends to do the same. She insists the book has changed her mind "on so many things," and thanks me for it.

"Can I give you a hug?" she asks from inside the car. I apparently say yes, because she proceeds to hop out of her minivan and embrace me as though I were a long-lost relative. I am literally speechless. I hug her back, not because it feels like the polite thing to do, but because I want to. I know from experience that anger is contagious, yet her sincere embrace reminds me that so is love.

Dx: Anger ♣ Rx: Fall in Love with Love

The seed of hellfire is in your wrath.
Extinguish this hell inside to follow Love's path.

—

Anger never arises in the absence of pride.
Crush both beneath your feet and be sanctified.

—

To avoid God's wrath, abandon your own.

—

Quit keeping score if you want to be free.
Love has ejected the referee.

—

Justice waters trees that bear fruit.
Injustice waters thorns at the root.
Bestow bounty where it belongs, no matter where it arose.
Don't just go watering everything that grows.

—

Only Grace opens our eyes.
Only Love calms fury's cries.

—

If you're in love with Love, don't be bashful.
Be brave and plant your flag!

CHAPTER 8

Dx: Fear
Rx: Quit Making Yourself So Small

Quit being a drop. Make yourself an ocean.
Abandon your ego and reap the Beloved's devotion.

Partly out of an attempt to channel anger into love, but mostly out of sheer dread, I spend the fall running my mouth nonstop. I sit on three separate panels at UNC, Duke, and NC State challenging Islamophobia. I keynote a three-city tour for the Depression and Bipolar Support Alliance in Baltimore, Seattle, and Akron, challenging the stigma surrounding mental illness. I speak to the BBC World Service from a studio in Chapel Hill challenging the royally regressive Saudi regime. The result?

Islamophobia: still here, just worse.

Stigma surrounding mental illness: still here, just as bad at best.

The Saudi regime: still here, just with way more American weapons.

Unsurprisingly, I feel defeated. It's been a decade since I wrote my first book, aimed at shattering stereotypes around what it means to be Muslim in America in a post-9/11 world. I never imagined things would be *worse* today than they were then, but they are.

For one, I wasn't nearly as afraid back then as I am now. Ironically, the trouble with publicly disputing the irrational fears of others is that it makes you a prime target for those same irrational fears. And bonus, phobics tend to be far scarier than the objects of their phobias. I'd like to say that the Islamophobes who track me down online to berate and threaten me don't scare me, but they do. The only explanation I have for not shutting up is the fact that I'm crazy, prone to suicidal ideations and delusional expectations. Nonetheless, irrational hope is no match for rational fear.

In October, I discover a disturbing consequence of being a registered voter in North Carolina: my home address is publicly available on the internet. I contact the State Board of Elections to seek a formal exemption, citing death and rape threats as my reason for asking them to remove my address from their website. Two days later, I receive a reply: "Dear Voter," it begins. "Unfortunately, voters are unable to choose whether or not to share this information."

With that, Merry Street suddenly seems anything but. The window in my home office overlooks this quiet residential street listed online next to my name. Now, whenever I see a car slow down in front of the house, my heart jumps into my throat, and I have to fight the impulse to duck.

I've never before felt even remotely afraid in my own home. Still, something about this new sense of insecurity feels oddly familiar. Perhaps because I soaked in it as a zygote. Perhaps because I was swaddled in it as a newborn. Perhaps because it isn't new at all.

I was an embryo at the height of the so-called Islamic Revolution, flying from Tehran to London to Chicago in my mother's womb. I was an infant when we traveled through North America, Europe, and

the Middle East searching for a place to call home. And I was a tod-
dler when we finally settled in the US for good. While I've been told
it was a terrifying time, I remember none of it.

Chief among the things I don't remember: I was born in Chicago
in the spring of 1979. Eight months later a group of students stormed
the US embassy in Tehran, taking dozens of Americans hostage and
destroying countless documents inside, including my parents' immi-
gration papers. Shortly thereafter, paperless and in the midst of a
massive shitstorm of anti-Iranian hostility, we returned to Tehran. As
luck would have it, the Iran-Iraq War had started by that point, so in
the hopes of not being killed by an Iraqi bomb, we moved to Athens.
It took two years for my parents to regain entry to the United States,
and the way they describe it is akin to the way athletes describe finally
qualifying for the Olympics. But we did more than flee bombs and
fill out paperwork before returning to America. In that time, I also
learned to speak (first Farsi, then Greek), I evolved from flailing lump
to quadruped to biped, I developed a peculiar penchant for eating
live snails off the walls of our patio in Athens, and I spent a month
building sandcastles on the island of Paros. Again, I remember none
of it. Not the Greek, not the snails, not the sandcastles. Not the revo-
lution, not the hostages, not the war.

Still, as I watch a white Honda Civic slow down to a standstill
directly in front of my office window on a balmy October afternoon
in 2016, there is some part of me that recalls the revolution I fled as
a fetus and the war I fled as an infant—not consciously, but cellularly.
It's the same part of me that has always hidden a waterproof bag full
of important documents in a random location in every home I've ever
inhabited as an adult, *just in case*. No one ever told me to do this, and
I don't remember my parents ever doing it, but I can't imagine a day
when I stop hiding passports and birth certificates any more than I
can imagine a day when I stop sneezing or yawning.

Revolution, war, and exile leave an imprint, even if you're just ges-
tating or learning to walk and talk when you experience them. I don't
expect to have to flee America, but then again, my parents never ex-
pected to have to flee Iran. In any case, you can only be told you're
unwanted in your own home so many times before it becomes irre-
sponsible *not* to prepare for potential expulsion. That's not paranoia.
That's practicality.

I'm still watching the white Civic when my parents call. By the
time I look up and realize it's gone, my fears have morphed and so-
lidified. They no longer revolve around a deranged stranger and a
series of hypothetical political scenarios. They now land on a kindred
sage and a cluster of recklessly proliferating cells.

"You are on the speaker," my mom says. "Ahmad is here too."

"*Salaam*, Melody *jan*," he says, sounding somehow smaller and
farther away than usual.

"There is no reason to be afraid," my mom continues.

"What are you talking about?" I ask, confused. How could she
know I was afraid?

"It's nothing," Ahmad replies. "I have a small cancer in my thy-
roid. They will cut it out, and I will be fine."

"What are you *talking* about?" I repeat, though I heard exactly
what he said. Tears fill every corner of my eyes, heavy drops of salty
panic plummeting onto my desk.

"In a few weeks, he has a surgery in Denver," my mom says matter-
of-factly. "Romana found us the best doctor. October twenty-sixth
they do it. Already it is scheduled."

"It is better to do sooner than later. You do not need to come. We
just want to tell you so you know," Ahmad says.

"What do you mean '*you do not need to come*'? Of course we're com-
ing. I'm just trying to digest this. It's *treatable* then, right?"

"*Highly* treatable. Ninety-nine point nine nine *nine* percent *curable*," Ahmad says, invoking his favorite percentage on earth and rendering me 100 percent doubtful. "Almost it is a benign cancer. They should not even *call* it a cancer."

"A *benign cancer*? Did he just make that up? What's he talking about, Mom?"

"Don't confuse her, Ahmad. Of course it's a cancer, Melody *jan*, but it's a cancer that is very easy to treat with surgery. No radiation. No chemotherapy. Just surgery and then he takes a medication every day for the rest of his life. That is all."

"Are you sure the diagnosis is *accurate*?" I ask, having grown eternally and incurably suspicious of pretty much all medical diagnoses since my pancreatic tumor was initially misdiagnosed as pancreatic cancer and my bipolar disorder was initially misdiagnosed as unipolar depression.

"Yes, yes. I check it. Romana check it. Robert check it. We sent to our friends; they all check it. Everyone agrees it is cancer. It's not like *your* tumor. This is *not* a misdiagnosis," my mom confirms.

Romana is an endocrinologist, and her husband, Robert, is a pathologist like my mom. I'm grateful to have so many doctors in the family, but it also puts me at a constant disadvantage when it comes to all things medical.

"I just want to be sure we're doing the right thing," I reply. "It scares me to think that there might be something I don't know, because I'm not a doctor."

"Always there is something we do not know, Melody *jan*. It does not matter if you are doctor or not. But I promise you: there is no reason to be afraid," Ahmad says, repeating my mom verbatim, almost as if they've rehearsed this, though I know they haven't.

"Honestly, the more you tell me there's no reason to be afraid, the more I feel like there is a really good reason to be afraid: like something you're not telling me or forgot to tell me or assume I already know. You don't need to protect me. I want to know everything. Promise me you're telling me *everything*," I plead.

Among Iranians and plenty of other non-Westerners, it's not uncommon to withhold a diagnosis from family members or even patients themselves in an effort to preserve hope and optimism. The idea is that labels and diagnoses carry weight and can make us feel sicker or more depressed. Thus, withholding a patient's diagnosis ideally extends their life, because (the argument goes) people are less likely to feel sick or treat people like they're sick *if they don't know they're sick*. Even if there were stellar data to support this theory (which there aren't), I don't care. I want to be fully informed, and not having been so in the past about other friends and family members makes it harder for me to trust that my parents are being entirely honest now.

"I promise we tell you everything. It is normal to be afraid, Melody *jan*, but it is not *necessary*. Remember," Ahmad says, and proceeds to recite Rumi:

> *When you walk atop a towering wall,*
> *You wobble, because it's so terribly tall.*
> *Even if its crest is strong, stable, and two yards wide,*
> *Your heart trembles as you imagine falling off the divide.*
> *But know that this fear is your own creation:*
> *The mischievous child of imagination.*

"You see," Ahmad continues, "don't imagine what can happen tomorrow. Enjoy what happens today. This is why I am so glad that you read Rumi. No matter what happens to me, always for the rest of your life, you have Molana."

"Except I still can't understand half of what I'm reading. I hope this isn't your way of saying 'It's okay if I die,' because *it's not*. Aside from the fact that I love you and you're my father, you *can't* die, because we have *work* to do!"

"Work to do? I am *retired!* I have *no* work to do. I read Rumi because I enjoy it. This is not *work* for me. It is more fun than playing poker or riding my bike. Anyway, it does not matter. I am not dying because of a *choss*[1] of a thyroid tumor."

"Good. You *can't* die. That's all I wanted to say. Matthew and I will get our tickets; we'll do whatever we need to do, and we'll be there."

"*Merci,* Melody *jan.* It will be nice. We will all be together."

But before we can all be together—before I can buy our tickets, before I can process my terror at the possibility of losing my father, and before I can consider how devastating it would be to live in a world without him in it—Hurricane Matthew hits North Carolina.

As a result, we lose power for nearly a week and are forced out of our home. We book the last room at a nearby Holiday Inn and spend the next week arranging our flight to Denver and researching thyroid cancer. As a former investment banker turned teacher turned education researcher, Matthew finds the statistics highly comforting. As a former patient turned lawyer turned author, I don't.

For years, I listened to doctors repeatedly use the phrase "one in a million" to refer to the likelihood that I would get the type of pancreatic tumor I got, that I would get it at the age that I got it, and that I would need the surgery that I needed to get rid of it.

"The data are great," Matthew tells me from the bed of our hotel room. I'm hanging up dresses, and he is in the midst of a seemingly endless Google Scholar search.

"Oh yeah? What are the data on seventy-one-year-old men under-

---

1   A *choss* is a silent fart. A *gooz*, for reference, is a fart that makes noise.

going general anesthesia? On thyroid hormone replacement meds? On infection? On pain? On blood clots? On shock? On hurricanes kicking us out of our own home that happen to be named after *you*?"

"Ouch! Hashtag too soon," he replies, laughing. "But I forgive you, because I know you're not a huge fan of stats. But this is what I *do*, and I'm telling you, the stats are *way* in our favor. We really have no reason to be afraid."

"Why does everyone keep *telling* me that? For future reference, you should know that the easiest way to scare the hell out of me is to tell me that there is no reason to be afraid, because there's *always* a reason to be afraid. When you tell me there's not, then all I know for sure is that you're lying to me. I'm a thirty-seven-year-old Iranian-American Muslim woman living in North fucking Carolina; I have half a pancreas, no gallbladder, high cholesterol, bipolar disorder, migraines, dyslexia, a vagina, and brown skin. I've lost track of all the shit I ought to be afraid of!"

"I know," Matthew says, grabbing a handful of my hair and examining it. "You totally left out split ends."

"Divorce!" I proclaim, trying (and failing) not to laugh as he pulls me onto the bed.

Over the next few weeks, I try to remember what Rumi and Ahmad have taught me. Most notably:

> *Every storm the Beloved unfurls*
> *Permits the sea to scatter pearls.*

Our home is unscathed. The power comes back. The odds are indeed in our favor. I try to see and appreciate all of these pearls, but more often than not, they're dwarfed by my growing suspicion that a bigger storm is brewing just beyond the horizon.

I spend the four-hour flight to Denver praying and reviewing old audio files from my poetry lessons with Ahmad in San Diego. An hour and a half into one, Ahmad stops me and says, "*Hala*[2] I give you fifteen minutes break."

But before I can shift or get up to take advantage of this alleged break, he converts from Fanglish to Farsi and offers to tell me something funny. I accept and he recites Rumi's poem about a housefly.

Floating on a strand of hay in a revolting pool of donkey piss,
The fly lifts his head like a proud captain cluelessly steering amiss.
He mistakes the strand of hay for a yacht, the puddle of piss for a sea.
He thinks he's a big shot, but he's just floundering in pee.

Deluded by ego and his own limited interpretation of the world around him, the fly mistakes the puddle of urine for an ocean, the hay for a yacht, and himself for the captain. Like countless humans, the fly is so caught up in his own tiny territory, so busy making himself and his world so pathetically small, that he doesn't even notice that he is effectively swimming in sewage, let alone that there is a bigger and more beautiful world beyond the puddle of waste he calls home. The poem goes on to note that if the fly could quit imposing his narrow interpretations onto the world, then fortune would turn him into a phoenix. But the fly is oblivious to this glorious potential for transformation within himself. He is simply afraid of trading what he

---

2 "Now."

knows for what he doesn't, so he protects his miserable abode with all the bluster and bravado he can muster.

Such is the curse and the irony of ego. As our heads grow bigger, our worlds grow smaller. Afraid of losing our own pitiful piss pads, we settle for being small.

Rumi's counsel:

> *Quit being a drop. Make yourself an ocean.*
> *Abandon your ego and reap the Beloved's devotion.*

Inspecting the mercifully receding puddle of piss that helped inspire my pilgrimage—writer's block—I detect the product of an egocentric, overachieving mentality that has plagued me since birth. Like so many children of immigrants and other so-called minorities, I was trained to believe that to succeed, I would have to work at least twice as hard, to *be* at least twice as *good*, as my white male counterparts.

After decades of following this mantra, I emerged with a psychiatric diagnosis, exhausted, and stuck. The more success I gained as a writer, the harder it became to write. Afraid of not writing the *best* sentence, knowing mine would have to be better to be "equal," I wrote no sentences. Like some obnoxious diva, I panicked at the pressure, dropped the mic, and ran offstage. Consumed by ego, I made myself and my world so pathetically small, and thus made my spiritual and creative burnout all but inevitable, simply because I feared failure.

But it's fear that makes us small, not failure. Combine failure with love and you get resilience, not weakness. Hence, just as fear makes us small, love makes us big.

I have now spent two years learning to connect with the Beloved within—not through some spontaneous mystical experience, but through actively working to learn from and share in Ahmad's love for

Rumi's verse, allowing my father to serve as my guide and mirror en route.

While each of us will have different spiritual guides and routes to follow, we all share the same longing for love and union with something greater than ourselves. I generally call it the Beloved, oftentimes God, sometimes Khoda, occasionally Allah. You may call it the Universe or Science or Christ or Nature or Truth or something else entirely. But these distinctions are etymological, not essential.

Rumi notes,

> *It's names and labels that make us disagree.*
> *Look beneath the words and make peace with me.*

We may call the Beloved by millions of different names or by one. But whatever we call It, Its pull is always there, drawing on our need to connect with something greater. When we follow this longing toward connection instead of the temptation toward fear, we allow our hearts, our lives, and our worlds to grow bigger instead of smaller. It's how a fly becomes a phoenix, how a break for laughter becomes a lesson in love, and how a terrified daughter becomes a little less terrified.

But I've only begun to quit making myself so small. I'm still a sucker for wanting, isolation, haste, depression, distraction, anxiety, anger, and fear. I'm still so full of ego that I genuinely believe my birthday ought to be a national holiday. I'm still a floundering pupa—evolutionarily way closer to the fly than the phoenix. In short, *I still need my father, my guide, my friend.*

This is what I'm thinking about when Matthew nudges my arm right in the middle of an "*Allahu akbar.*"[3] Without noticing it, I had

---

3 "God is greater."

started praying out loud. For the record, I pray on every flight I take, but usually, I'm aware of it and keep it to a whisper tops.

"Shit! I didn't even realize," I say.

"No worries. I'm sure they're sending an air marshal now," Matthew replies, laughing. "It's only a matter of time."

Thankfully, it isn't, and we make it to Denver intact and without incident.

Ahmad's birthday was last week, so I bundled his present in bubble wrap, stuffed it in my carry-on, and brought it with me. It too has mercifully arrived intact and without incident, so the next morning, before we leave for the hospital, I give Ahmad his birthday gift: a cookie jar filled with individually wrapped salted caramels. An ardent caramel fan, Ahmad only recently learned that it can be purchased in isolation—outside of ice cream, candy bars, and cakes. Still, the caramels aren't the gift; the jar is. It's a ceramic yellow house with a red door and matching shutters.

After carefully unwrapping it, Ahmad lifts up the house and says, "My *yellow* house!"

"I know I promised it would be a *real* house, but this is all we can afford for now. I hope you like it."

"I *love* it," Ahmad says, and stands up to hug and kiss Matthew and me.

"Look inside," Matthew says. Ahmad lifts the roof off the house and sees all the caramels.

"These are my favorite—thank you. But *the house is the best,*" he says, putting the roof back on and lifting up the jar to examine it more closely.

"*You* did this?" he asks me, pointing to a sign next to the front door that reads "THE MOEZZI HOUSE."

"Yup. It said Nestlé Toll House, but I painted over it."

"It is *perfect*," Ahmad replies. "You know, Matthew *jan*, ever since Melody she was a child, she always promise me and Jazbi that she will buy us a *yellow* house. She said it will be close to her house, so we will never be far apart. Right, Melody *jan*?"

"Right," I say, smiling. "So we will never be far apart."

Ahmad sits up in his hospital gurney as my mom tightens the strings at the top of his gown. I can tell he feels uneasy, if not afraid. When I ask him about it, he showers me with Rumi, which I suspect is as much for his own benefit as for mine.

As usual, it's all in Farsi. But in a rare move, he drops the standard translations and extended explanations, and instead punctuates each poem with a sentence or two of his own. I can't tell if it's the sedatives talking or the knowledge that he is headed for surgery soon, but whatever the reason, Ahmad is on a lyrical bender, and I can't keep up.

He begins with this couplet, after which he concludes, "I am in love. I am not afraid."

> *In the face of Love, fear is slighter than a single hair.*
> *In the faith of Love, sacrifice is everywhere.*

Then he proceeds to dozens of other verses, including ones by Hafez, Saadi, Khayyam, and Attar—I think. Among them is the following from Rumi, after which Ahmad concludes, "*Har chi khoda bekhad khoobeh.*" Translation: "Whatever God wants is good."

> *From doubt, the Beloved grants certainty.*
> *From hatred, kindness; from fear, security.*

Before they wheel him off, it's clear that the sedatives are working, as he is both unusually blissful and slurring his words. He kisses my mom, whispers something in her ear, then holds her hand and tells her, "You are everything." After that, he kisses all three grandchildren, then Robert, then Romana, then Matthew, then me. I lean down to hug him, and he kisses my forehead before leaving me with one last couplet.

> *When I die you will kiss my grave without hesitation.*
> *Why not kiss my face now that we share a location?*

I kiss his cheek once more, and he is gone.

The surgery is only a few hours, yet it feels like an eternity. I try to play rummy with everyone, but I can't. Instead, I head to the empty hospital chapel alone, where I spend my time praying and reliving random memories: our family trip to Epcot, including our parents' refusal to visit Disney World, because it was apparently overly provincial and insufficiently educational; a hot-air balloon landing behind our old house in north Dayton; my cousin Mersedeh's wedding in our newer old house in Centerville; playing hide-and-go-seek-in-the-dark in the basement of that same house. And on and on and on—until I stumble upon a memory that isn't a memory, at least not in the traditional sense. Technically, it's my mother's, but I've been told the story so many times now that it feels like mine.

Ahmad was working in a hospital in Tehran when I was born in Chicago. While he was planning to join us in America soon, that plan fell apart after the hostage crisis, and we eventually ended up leaving the US to join him in Iran instead—which is where this legend begins, en route and between two worlds.

On the way to Tehran, during a layover in London's Heathrow Airport, my mother became frustrated, apparently visibly so, at an airline counter while holding me in her arms. A tall, well-built man approached her, asking if he could help and offering to babysit while she dealt with whatever new hassle the airline representative had presented. Just to be clear, under most circumstances, my mother never would have handed me off to a stranger in an airport, but this wasn't most circumstances and he wasn't just any stranger. This was the early 1980s, and he was Muhammad Ali.

However famous and revered Muhammad Ali is and was in the United States, multiply that by ten, and you'll begin to understand how famous and revered he is and was in Iran and among Muslims worldwide, regardless of their chosen sect or level of practice. From converting to Islam to changing his name to speaking in poetry to becoming the heavyweight champion of the world to refusing to fight in Vietnam, he became an international symbol of indomitable strength and poise in the face of brutality and imperialism. For Iranians, Muhammad Ali was a faithful poet first, a fighter second, and an artist always.

Where some saw him as arrogant or egotistical, we didn't. We just saw him as a man who wasn't afraid to sacrifice his own liberty and livelihood to oppose injustice, who was proud of where he had come from, and who wasn't about to let anyone steal that away from him. In other words, we saw him as a brother who refused to make himself small—and in doing so, inspired us to do the same. So of course my mother happily handed me over to Muhammad Ali, if only so a bit of his greatness might rub off on me.

In 1972, when David Frost asked the poet, boxer, and activist what

he'd like people to think of him after he was gone, Ali responded
in verse:

> *He took a few cups of love,*
> *He took one tablespoon of patience,*
> *One teaspoon of generosity,*
> *One pint of kindness.*
> *He took one quart of laughter,*
> *One pinch of concern,*
> *And then, he mixed willingness with happiness.*
> *He added lots of faith,*
> *And he stirred it up well.*
> *Then he spread it over a span of a lifetime,*
> *And he served it to each and every deserving person he met.*

After Muhammad Ali's death a few months ago, I couldn't stop
"remembering" this story—and ever since, it has taken on more
meaning for me.

Now, when I feel afraid, I increasingly find myself recalling this
encounter I cannot remember—like my subconscious recalls my
years in Tehran, like my heart recalls my parents' years in Iran, like
my soul recalls *their* parents' years in Persia. I call them all back, every
phantom memory, like a sacred shield of armor.

This way, wherever I am, it's not just me: it's Jazbi, it's Ahmad, it's
every Mostashfi and Moezzi, it's Muhammad Ali, it's Rumi. This way,
wherever I turn, I always find a home. This way, wherever I go, I never
travel alone.

I am wrapped in this invisible armor when the doctor tells us that
Ahmad's surgery was a success.

He wakes up a few hours later still groggy from the anesthesia, and he is in tears. First thing, he asks for his mom. All of us are here: my mother, my sister, me, our spouses, the grandkids. But we are no substitute. At seventy-one years old, my father is crying for his mother, like the reed flute crying for the reed bed, like the soul crying for the Beloved.

I will never be prepared to lose Ahmad, but today, I remember how blessed I am to have him here now, as a father and as a friend, teaching me about love in a time so full of hate, hope in a world so full of fear. Sitting at his bedside, I admit that I am still afraid. But fear is a prerequisite for courage, and amid all the love in this room, I feel brave enough to quit making myself so small, to plant my flag of love, and to follow the light of my wounds. Grateful, I wipe away my father's tears and kiss his cheek.

Dx: Fear ♣ Rx: Quit Making Yourself So Small

When you walk atop a towering wall,
You wobble, because it's so terribly tall.
Even if its crest is strong, stable, and two yards wide,
Your heart trembles as you imagine falling off the divide.
But know that this fear is your own creation:
The mischievous child of imagination.

—

Floating on a strand of hay in a revolting pool of donkey piss,
The fly lifts his head like a proud captain cluelessly steering amiss.
He mistakes the strand of hay for a yacht, the puddle of piss for a sea.
He thinks he's a big shot, but he's just floundering in pee.

—

Quit being a drop. Make yourself an ocean.
Abandon your ego and reap the Beloved's devotion.

—

It's names and labels that make us disagree.
Look beneath the words and make peace with me.

—

In the face of Love, fear is slighter than a single hair.
In the faith of Love, sacrifice is everywhere.

—

From doubt, the Beloved grants certainty.
From hatred, kindness; from fear, security.

—

When I die you will kiss my grave without hesitation.
Why not kiss my face now that we share a location?

CHAPTER 9

Dx: Disappointment
Rx: Wake Up

You already own all the sustenance you seek.
If only you'd wake up and take a peek.

"Are you OKAY?"

"I know this must be really hard on you."

"Whatever we can do to help, we're on it."

"Call me if you want to talk."

"We'll get through this together."

"You're in my prayers."

"I'm here for you."

"I have no words."

"Are your parents okay?"

"I'm thinking about you."

"I'm so sorry!"

"I love you."

I have never received so many condolences over text, email, or social media in my life. It feels weird—and not just because no one died, but because underlying this cascade of sympathy rests a shared premise: now that Trump has won the presidency, we're worried for your safety.

I know, because other messages are less subtle:

"Run!"

"CalExit w/ us."

"They have guns."

"Muslimahs Unite!"

"I won't let them ban you."

"This Jew will stand with you!"

"They did it to the Japanese. They'll do it to us."

"I'll say I'm Muslim too if they come for you."

"Come over. My basement [in Canada] is empty."

"Perhaps we should all just pretend
to convert to Christianity."

"If you return [to Iran] as a refugee,
maybe they won't put you in jail."

"If anyone invites you camping, don't go.
Could be a whole different kind of camp."

"The kids [Romana's] were asking: Can he truly
ban Muslims from entering the country?"

Amid this flurry of messages, Ahmad sends a simple and predictable one:

"Come to California."

So the day after Trump's election, Matthew and I distract ourselves by planning a weeklong trip to San Diego in February. This is the most "running" I do in response to the election—though I admit, I did consider it.

But I'm an American. As much as I hate the colonialism, genocide, slavery, and rape upon which this nation was built, I love the promise and possibility that it represents—not in its power structures or its stone monuments, but in its people and its natural wonders. I have lived in Ohio, Illinois, Connecticut, New York, Massachusetts, Montana, Georgia, and North Carolina, and I have visited every state save Alaska. So I know better than to underestimate the beauty of this land or the spirit of its people, myself included. I refuse to run away, because this is still my home, and I have yet to set foot on the Last Frontier, our wildest state, roughly the same acreage as the entire nation of Iran. I still stand in awe of America's unbridled promise and possibility. I still love this country. I still have hope that we can be better, and I'm still acting on that hope.

Like the majority of Americans, I find Trump's xenophobic rhetoric inane, bigoted, and indefensible. Being a member of more than one of the groups he loves to hate, I experience his election as a threat to my body, mind, and soul. After all, his dream policies would undoubtedly restrict my freedom to control my own body, to speak my own mind, and to practice my own religion.

Fortunately, Rumi and Ahmad have given me an opportunity to cope with this threat and the disappointment it has evoked: a chance to implement one of the many lessons I've learned on this perpetual pilgrimage into the past that could be neither more relevant nor more reassuring in the present. So after I finish crying, pacing, praying, and booking our tickets to San Diego, I do my best to apply Rumi's counsel, which Ahmad mercifully repeats to me on this day:

Welcome every guest,
No matter how grotesque.
Be as hospitable to calamity as to ecstasy,
To anxiety as to tranquility.

> *Today's misery sweeps your home clean,*
> *Making way for tomorrow's felicity.*

I try to welcome the calamity that is Donald Trump and all the anxiety and disappointment it evokes, in the hopes that he will inadvertently sweep our country clean of bigotry—presumably and paradoxically by bringing its horrifying consequences to life.

Considering the fact that so many Americans had no problem voting for this man so enamored of apartheid walls and travel bans, it's clear that his vicious vitriol represents a much bigger problem in American society than most of us ever wanted to admit.

Thankfully, however, this epidemic—and its copious consequences that spread far beyond politics—happens to be one that Rumi specializes in treating: *disaffection*. Broken down, "dis" is a Latin prefix meaning "apart" or "away," while "affection" denotes love. Indeed, faced with rancor and hostility, many of us have actively *distanced ourselves from love* without realizing that this disaffection hurts *us* most of all.

Our only hope for recovery—culturally, politically, personally, and spiritually—is to reverse course. That is, to draw ourselves nearer to love and to draw our love nearer to those who lack it. If we don't, we may well incinerate in the flames of our own outrage. For however righteous or justified our indignation, it still burns—not just the people we're aiming it at, but *ourselves*—which brings us right back to Rumi's prescription for anger:

> *If you're in love with Love, don't be bashful.*
> *Be brave and plant your flag!*

So I *try* to plant my flag in the middle of this disaster zone and to invite others to do the same. I write an article that calls for exactly that, I commit to attending ever more protests, and I try to apply Rumi's prescriptions for depression and anger liberally across my life. In other words, I welcome this disappointment as best I can. Sure, I'm not exactly rolling out the red carpet, but I'm not slamming the door in its face either. I recognize it as a formidable blend of every other diagnosis herein and resolve to apply all of Rumi's prescriptions accordingly: to go to the Source, to favor invention over imitation, to slow down and quit keeping score, to welcome every guest, to go beyond the five and six, to follow the light of my wounds, to fall in love with Love, and to quit making myself so small.

But that's a lot to cover all at once, and in my effort to do everything, I achieve next to nothing. More specifically, I forget to connect all of these prescriptions through the highest prescription, which is love. As a result, my disappointment quickly realizes that it's not that welcome after all, so it does what most houseguests do upon realizing they're unwelcome: it holds a grudge. And in return, I hold a bigger one. So now, as I set out on the protest circuit, I'm not just disappointed. I'm *bitter*.

The day after Trump's inauguration, I take part in the biggest one-day protest in American history. I hang a sign around my neck that reads: "TINY HANDS OFF MY CAROLINA VAGINA!" and head to Moore Square with Matthew and my friends Krista and Aliya. It's easily the twentieth mass demonstration I've attended in Raleigh, and I can safely say that I've never seen a crowd like this.

Shortly after we moved here, the Moral Monday protest movement took hold: religious leaders and the North Carolina NAACP, led by the Reverend Dr. William J. Barber II, joined forces to call for an end to racist, classist, sexist, homophobic, and transphobic policies in North Carolina, insisting that the purportedly "Christian" lawmakers promoting these policies were not only violating the US Constitution left and right, but also the basic tenets of their own faith. Spiritually and strategically speaking, it was a brilliant move, and I'm proud to have taken part—and to continue taking part—in this momentous movement.

What I'm not proud of amid this sea of pink pussyhats, however, is how recognizably absent so many of these predominantly white women have been in the Moral Monday movement. I speak with women who say this is the first time they've ever protested anything, and while I congratulate and thank them, I also want to shake them.

I want to ask them where they've been all these years. I want to ask them why it has taken the dawning of the apocalypse just to get them off their asses. I want to ask them how they justified staying at home when our state government passed HB2, when it slashed unemployment benefits, when it endorsed voter suppression, when it refused to accept much-needed Medicaid expansion, and when it let corporations dump everything from coal ash to pig shit into our waterways.

I want to ask all of this, but for once, I hold my tongue, because I am *trying* to take Rumi's advice and apply love and mercy instead of anger and anxiety. Nevertheless, I know that the fact that I still have these instincts is a sign of my unchecked bitterness and disappointment. In no way do I feel the same sense of hope and solidarity that seems to be swelling inside of so many of the women here.

Instead, I am seething—and not just with disappointment and bitterness, but also with wanting, isolation, haste, depression, distraction, anxiety, anger, fear, and pride. In short, I am brimming with all the diagnoses I'm trying to treat here, and having overlooked love as the overriding prescription for every one of them, I am colossally failing to treat all of them.

. . .

It only gets worse after Trump issues his first travel ban. Matthew and I respond by attending a protest outside Raleigh-Durham International Airport. As usual, Matthew uses it as an opportunity to take photographs for his ever-expanding online protest portfolio, while I join the other protesters, sporting yet another handmade sign around my neck: "THIS PROUD IRANIAN-AMERICAN MUSLIM WILL NOT HIDE OR SHUT UP! I WILL RESIST!"

But I spend much of the protest in tears, too choked up to speak. Between begging my parents to cancel their upcoming trip to Iran and worrying about friends and family stuck in this mess at airports around the world, I am too busy calculating the personal consequences of this ban to sing and chant.

My sign speaks for me, but inside, I feel like I'm breaking. Then I spot my friend Maryse running to join me, arms outstretched, holding a sign that makes me smile: "QUEER JEW against RACISM, FASCISM & ISLAMOPHOBIA."

Several things, in addition to friends like Maryse, have kept me from going mad in this maddening time: Rumi, my family, medication, prayer, therapy, writing, music, books, chocolate, activism, laughter, tears, daily walks, weekly poetry lessons with Ahmad, and weekly writing workshops inside the locked psychiatric unit in Raleigh.

While I still have a lot of work to do in terms of more effectively applying Rumi's prescriptions to my daily life, I am trying, and while I still fail frequently, I am failing better on average. This is partially the result of a concerted effort on my part, but mostly, it's the result of grace: the right people showing up with the right reminders at the right time, day after day after day. When I forget love's indispensable role in every viable treatment and prescription, they show up to remind me.

. . .

A week later, grace arrives in the form of six incredible psychiatric patients. When I walk onto the ward, two new patients are watching television in the room where we normally hold workshop.

"You *see* this," one says, motioning toward the screen, which happens to be tuned to a news station covering yet another "unpresidented" tweet. "He's crazier than all of us in here combined, and he's the *leader of the free world*. If that's what sanity looks like, then count me out!"

"No argument here," I reply, laughing as I pull tables together and organize my papers.

"I'm Mo," he says. "And that's Leo in the corner."

"I'm Melody," I reply, shaking their hands.

"Why you here?" Leo asks, still looking up at the television.

"I'm teaching a writing workshop. I come every Thursday."

"Do you know Johnnie Cochran?" Leo asks me.

"Not personally. Why?"

"He's my lawyer, *that's why*. He's coming to get me outta here," Leo says, putting his feet up on a chair, blissfully unaware that Cochran has been dead for more than a decade.

"That's nice," I say, knowing from personal experience that delusions don't respond to argument. When I was delusional, no one could have convinced me that I couldn't fly or that I wasn't a prophet or a high-level advisor to Barack Obama or *sane* for that matter. Only antipsychotics could banish my delusions, so I know better than to waste time arguing with anyone else's.

"Wasn't Johnnie supposed to visit yesterday?" Mo asks Leo, grinning.

"He visits me *every* day. You just don't *see* him."

"I'm sure he does, Leo," I say. "But listen, in the meantime, we'll need to turn off the TV in a few minutes when the other patients show up for workshop."

"*What?* Fuck that. I'm *watching* this," Leo says.

"I know, but it's just for a couple hours, and besides, I'd love for you to join us. You don't have to write or read. You can draw or talk or just listen even," I say. About a quarter of the patient population here is either illiterate or too disabled by illness or medication to read or write, so there isn't always that much "writing" going on during workshop. Having been struck illiterate by mania myself, I try to keep my lessons as broad, flexible, and cooperative as possible.

"Fine, I'll stay," Leo says, "but only because you're *pretty*. There's nothing but ugly chicks in here." Leo is short, pale, and skeletal. He is thirty, but thanks to the malice of meth, he looks at least sixty.

"Don't be creepy, Leo," Mo says. "She wants to help us. You can at least be polite." Mo is tall, dark, and strapping. He is forty, but thanks to the magic of melanin, he could easily pass for half that.

"Creepiness aside," I respond, "it's not okay to reduce people to their appearance. My workshops are safe spaces. Plus, none of us is looking or feeling our best when we're locked in a place like this."

"What do you mean '*us*'?" Leo says. "*You're* not a patient."

"Not now and not here, but I've been a patient on other locked wards before. I have bipolar disorder."

"Me too!" says Mo. "I'm type one, though. I bet you're type two, right?" Type I is often considered the most severe form of bipolar disorder, because it includes at least one acute manic episode, while type II includes only hypomanic (or mildly manic) episodes. The truth is, however, the overall severity of bipolar disorder (or more precisely, bipolar disorder*s*) can vary dramatically across individuals, regardless of the type they happen to have.

"Nope. I have type one. Just like you."

"No kidding? And you *work* here now?"

"Nah, I'm a writer. I just volunteer here."

"So you're filling a community service requirement, then?" Leo asks skeptically.

"Nope. Never been arrested. I'm a lawyer actually," I say, laughing.

"Like a *real* lawyer or just a paralegal or something?" Leo asks.

"Yes, a *real* lawyer, like Johnnie."

"So you lost your license then?" Mo asks.

"No, licensed and in good standing. And the two of you would make great lawyers, by the way, because this is beginning to feel like a cross-examination."

"I just can't believe they let people like us become *lawyers* is all," Mo says.

"*Let us?* Some of the best lawyers I know have mental health conditions," I say. "I write and teach because I find purpose in it. No one is preventing me from practicing law or forcing me to volunteer. I'm here because I want to be."

"*Why?*" Leo asks, incredulous.

"Because I felt invisible and hopeless when I was a patient, and I don't want y'all to feel that way," I reply.

"That's *exactly* how I feel," Mo says, staring at his shoes.

"Me too," Leo concurs.

"I feel like some of the staff think we're contagious or something. They barely talk to us, and when they do, you can tell they look down on us, like we're not even human or something," Mo says.

"I've been there, and I hate that it's still like that, but I promise, you're not alone," I say, launching into what has become a well-rehearsed speech for me by now. "The way I see it, there's something extra-ordinary, *by definition*, about having a brain that works differently. We have problems other people don't, but we can see solutions other people can't. I wish someone had told me that and heard me out when I was a patient. So yeah, I guess that's why I'm here: to remind you that you're extraordinary and to listen."

"Thanks, Melody," Mo replies sincerely as the room begins to fill with patients. "I'm happy you're here."

"You're telling me! *Helloooo, Melody.* I'm Alex," says another new patient, a short young white kid with a mustache, a spare tire, and a Confederate flag tattoo on his right forearm. He grabs a chair next to mine, spins it around, straddles it, and sits down, resting his chin on the back of the chair and staring at me.

"Leave her alone," Mo says.

"So, what *are* you? Mexican? Indian? Mixed?" Alex asks.

"I'm *American*," I reply. "I grew up in Ohio. Where are *you* from, Alex?"

"Come on. You're not *really* American. Where's your people from? Like your *tribe* or whatever?" Alex asks, scooting his chair closer, still staring at me with his beady blue eyes.

"Don't be an ass, Alex," says Kiara, a grad student at NC State who was admitted a few weeks ago after a suicide attempt.

"It's okay. Let's just relax," I say, holding up my hand. "Alex, I'm also from Iran."

"Eye-ran? You ISIS!" he proclaims, jumping out of his seat and pointing at me.

"Are you *kidding* me?" I whisper, dropping my head in my hands and taking a moment to breathe and collect my thoughts before saying something I'll regret. Then I look up and speak slowly and deliberately: "Alex, my workshop is a safe space. We don't call each other names or point at people. We don't draw conclusions based on zero evidence. And we don't judge one another. If you can't respect these rules, I'm going to have to ask you to leave."

"You hear that? ISIS bitch thinks she can tell me where to go in my own country! What do you think of *that*?" Alex says, scanning the room for support.

"I think if you don't shut up, I'll beat the shit out of you," Mo says as he stands up, leans forward, cocks his right arm, and punches into the air, catching it with his left hand. At this point, a health tech outside the room notices and walks in, threatening to remove Mo. I explain the situation, and Mo apologizes and sits down while Alex makes no apologies whatsoever. Without sharing details, I tell the health tech that Alex is the one creating trouble, being rude and disruptive, and that he is no longer welcome at workshop today. The tech agrees to escort Alex back to his room, but before they leave, Leo stands up.

"He can't go until he apologizes to Melody."

"That's okay, Leo. Alex isn't feeling well," I say.

"*None* of us is feeling well," says Mo. "Leo is right. Alex needs to apologize."

Then Kiara stands up and chimes in: "Yeah, apologize to her, Alex." Before I know it, all of my students are standing up and staring at Alex, demanding that he apologize to me. And he does. First quietly, and then louder, because Mo insists his apology wasn't sufficiently audible.

If you've never had six psychiatric patients demand that a bigot apologize to you, I *highly* recommend it. I can't remember ever having my hope in humanity revived so swiftly. I couldn't have cared less about the apology. But watching my students—all in the midst of their own serious mental health crises—take the time and energy to stand up for *me*, even after I assured them it wasn't necessary, floods my heart with hope and gratitude.

After class, as I'm packing my bag to leave, Norah comes up to me. She has been a patient for a couple months now, and while she attends workshop religiously, she barely ever speaks. But now she surprises me by asking for a hug, and I gladly oblige. She probably weighs no more than a hundred pounds, yet from her hug alone, you'd easily guess she weighed twice that.

"I see God in you," Norah whispers into my ear as she squeezes my rib cage. "I see God in *everyone*. They think I'm crazy, because I can see what they can't. I know you see it too though."

Before I can even begin to respond, Norah is gone. But her words hang in the air like holy particles of dust, sparkling in the ray of light that is the aftermath of her embrace. I close my eyes for a moment and absorb the warmth around me. In the midst of this cold, locked, windowless ward, I feel like a cat blissfully rolling about in a sublime stretch of sunshine, and as happens more and more these days, Rumi comes to mind:

> *Open your arms if you want to be embraced.*
> *Break your idols, drop your ego, and behold the Beloved's face.*

I walked into this ward and began today's workshop feeling drained and disappointed with the state of the world, but I walk out humbled and hopeful. While I try my best to prepare helpful lessons, prompts, and exercises, I am under no delusions: I know full well that the patients here are teaching me far more than I am teaching them.

Rumi notes,

> *For all the degrees you scholars may attain,*
> *You'll never learn to love 'til you're insane.*

I have met many mystics on the ward since I started teaching here, and it's clear today that Norah is one of them. She no doubt needs psychiatric medication, but she also needs spiritual consideration. Her wounds have indeed summoned a light, and unlike so many of us, she not only recognizes that light as sacred but *submits* to it.

For years, I ignored that light within myself, including the mystical side of my own manic experiences, because it scared me. But to find love in madness as Rumi advises, we must face the fear and arrogance that underlie two widespread delusions. First up is the delusion that this light is not present within *all of us*, because it is. And second is the delusion that any of us could produce such a light in the absence of the Beloved, because we can't.

While Rumi considers lunacy a mark of divine favor, he distinguishes between different types. The madness he promotes is rooted in ecstatic love; the one he condemns is rooted in petty fear. The former creates a mystic, the latter a lunatic. In short, love makes all the difference. As disappointing as it is to know that my fellow Americans have elected a lunatic to lead our nation, it's heartening to know that all of us—even lunatics—are capable of evolution through love. I'm grateful to Ahmad, Rumi, and my students for reminding me of this—and to the Beloved for continuing to drop mystics into my life for inspiration.

Among writers, rejection is a rite of passage, a perpetual nuisance, and an inescapable reality. We'd all like to say that our responses to it are always healthy and rational, but often, they're not.

Still, there are writers who will tell you that they are so used to rejection that it doesn't bother them, that they've grown a "thick skin," that they're actually *good at it*. They'll insist that rejection doesn't crawl into every crevice of every cell in their "thick-skinned" bodies—that it doesn't grate at every Golgi apparatus, maraud every mitochondrion, and rankle every ribosome. Bless their hearts, but they're lying through their teeth. Rejection hurts, and pretending it doesn't is asinine. I know, because I've tried the whole "thick-skinned" approach, and it's crap.

The only way to overcome rejection is to acknowledge all the emotions it evokes—from disappointment to anxiety to fear to isolation to whatever else. For Rumi, these are all guests we should welcome, because when they get recognition and appreciation, they sweep our souls clean, making way for joy and celebration.

And if you don't believe Rumi and me, then you should know that science backs us up here. Research shows that upon sensing distressing emotions, people who *accept, feel, and label* them are far less likely to employ maladaptive coping strategies such as self-harm, aggression, or binge drinking. Not only do these people experience a reduced severity in depression and anxiety, but they actually demonstrate less neural reactivity in response to rejection.[1]

Furthermore, if you can survive failure and rejection without letting them define or derail you—*by accepting, feeling, and labeling the emotions they evoke* instead of pretending you're immune to them—then success and acceptance become that much sweeter when you finally *do* attain them. In Rumi's words:

Opposites invigorate one another.
Honey is only sweet because you've tasted vinegar.

Even still, it's hard to believe you'll ever taste honey again when it feels like you're pickling in vinegar. And despite all the mystics the Beloved keeps dropping into my life, that's how I'm beginning to feel. My agent has finally sent out my proposal for this book, and every day, it seems like a new publisher passes. I try to accept, feel, and label the disappointment I sense amid this festival of rejection, but it's not easy.

Nonetheless, I've learned a lot throughout my career as an au-

1   T. B. Kashdan, L. F. Barrett, and P. E. McKnight, "Unpacking Emotion Differentiation: Transforming Unpleasant Experience by Perceiving Distinctions in Negativity," *Current Directions in Psychological Science* 24, no. 1 (February 2015): 10–16.

thor that should help here. I've been told ad nauseam that my stories are either "inaccessible" or "unrelatable," which I now know is code for not white enough (NWE). I've been told that I'm "too political," which I now know is *also* code for NWE. And I've been told that I'm "too foreign," which is delightfully devoid of code at all, as it clearly and unapologetically shouts NWE from the rooftops. One would hope that knowing all of this would make my rejections sting a little less, but it doesn't. Nor does it help to compare myself to others, which is worth noting, because unchecked, disappointment quickly begets jealousy. After all, when we find ourselves disappointed, it's often because we didn't get what we wanted, and when we tire of lamenting the fact that *we* didn't get it, we routinely move on to envying those who did.

Rumi advises,

> *Envy is the toughest companion to ditch on your journey.*
> *But ditch it now, for it's the devil's defense attorney.*

Of course, like everyone else, I'd love to be 100 percent free of jealousy. But I'm human—and worse yet, a *writer*. Athletes have nothing on us when it comes to envy. Basketball games end at the buzzer, while literary feuds can fester for eternity. Though I've never engaged in any heavy literary rivalries, I know that I'm just a couple Ambien and a rash tweet away from starting a war with any number of writers with whom I disagree on any number of issues. Then there's that more banal and embarrassing breed of envy: the one that pops up when someone you *should* be cheering on gets something you don't have and want. For writers, it's usually an award or a contract, but it could be anything.

I remember being in my publicist's office at Penguin years ago, around when my last book was published. While there, I saw a bunch of marketing materials all over her office for a brilliant graphic memoir by Ellen Forney that I had read, loved, and even blurbed. Like me, Ellen is also a bipolar writer, a woman, and a Wesleyan alum—so I should have been thrilled. But her book had recently hit the *New York Times* bestseller list, and mine hadn't.

So, naturally, I hated her. Until we met a few years later in Ann Arbor, at a screening for a PBS documentary on bipolar disorder that had featured both of us. There, I quickly realized that I loved Ellen just as much as I loved her writing. She was kind, smart, witty, and just a blast to be around. I had a choice: ditch my envy and gain a friend, or keep my envy and gain an ulcer. I chose the former, and I'm better for it.

Looking back, I now realize that to reach this decision, I applied Rumi's prescriptions for disappointment and wanting: waking up to the blessings I already had, including the opportunity to make a new friend, and going to my Source by consulting my intuition, which confirmed that this potential friendship was worth far more than any petty rivalry.

I was right. Ellen and I became dear friends after that—so much so that she will eventually become my "accountability buddy" for this very book. I will send her chapters to review before anyone else, and she will help hold me accountable to the deadlines I set for myself. In the process, she will also send me adorable emails and texts full of her own original artwork, cheering me on with refrains like "Thassright, writer warrior!" These messages will serve as steady reminders of how mutual encouragement, admiration, and friendship beat envy, disappointment, and bitterness any day.

But I don't know this yet. What I do know is that in the midst of all the disappointment this year has brought—between Trump's election and my seemingly endless stream of rejections—it helps to have friends.

It also helps to know that whatever becomes of this book, I will be fine, because the process of writing it has taught me to serve the Beloved within instead of seeking approval from without, to accept that the Almighty's plan—however inscrutable—has always proven better than mine in the end, and to trust that it always will.

I no longer need anyone else to validate me or my work: I am valid because the Beloved lives within me. Just as you are valid because the Beloved lives within you. We can choose to surrender to that divine light within, or we can choose to dismiss it. Either way, it's still there, summoned by our deepest and most sacred wounds, waiting for us to accept Love's invitation. No terms or conditions apply. No expiration date exists. No entry fee required.

"*Beeya, beeya,*"[2] Ahmad whispers through a crack in the door. We arrived in San Diego late last night. It's barely six in the morning, and Matthew is still sleeping, but I'm awake, sitting up in bed, checking email on my laptop as Ahmad whispers at me from the hallway.

"Come where?" I whisper back.

"Molana!" he says as he lifts his arms up in the air like a conductor inviting the orchestra to rise and take a bow. Then he heads to the kitchen. I'm not exactly inspired to study Rumi right now, but I throw on my sweats and follow him anyway.

"So is this how it's going to be from now on? Every time I visit, we'll have to spend our mornings with Rumi?" I ask Ahmad as I sit down at the same round glass dining room table where we first started studying this poetry together.

"Of course not. Sometimes, we do Hafez."

---

2   "Come, come."

"Wow, way to expand your horizons, Ahmad," I reply, laughing though I know he isn't kidding.

This morning's lesson revolves around a porcupine:

A pure soul is like a porcupine.
The more it's prodded, the more it shines.

"I don't get it. What kind of fool attacks a *porcupine*?" I ask.

"Life. *We* are the porcupine. *Life* attacks *us*, but if we follow the Beloved within and not our own thoughts and ego, then instead of getting smaller, we puff up and our defense is greater. Your soul is like this animal, because the more it is attacked, the stronger it becomes. Rumi says this is why all the prophets, they suffer more than anyone, because it makes them stronger."

"So he wants us to seek suffering?"

"No. He wants us to know that when we suffer, our defense becomes greater, stronger. We do not suffer for no reason. It brings us closer to God."

"Okay, I get it. I guess I just wasn't feeling the porcupine."

"Good. You have to be a dummy to *feel* porcupine."

"It's a figure of speech, Ahmad. 'Feeling' *yani* 'enjoying' or 'appreciating,' not actually *feeling*."

"Then why you don't say 'enjoying' or 'appreciating'?"

"Because I wasn't feeling 'enjoying' or 'appreciating.' I was feeling 'feeling,'" I reply, laughing.

"*Boro baba!* I am *feeling* hungry. *Beeya*, let's have some *noon-o-paneer*."

Aside from eating and reading and reciting Rumi, we spend our time in San Diego visiting old family friends, playing Rummikub, yelling at cable news anchors, and trying to pull my mom away from *Shahrzad,* her latest favorite Persian television series. Eventually, she recruits Matthew to join her, which he happily does, convinced that watching these shows will improve his minimal Farsi. By the end of our trip, she has him so hooked that when Ahmad and I try to get them to join us for one last walk around Seaport Village, they both refuse.

So the two of us walk together along the San Diego harbor, just as we have countless times before. We talk life and death, mysticism and fundamentalism, love and fear, depression and disappointment—and as always, Ahmad recites poems. But this time, I'm familiar with nearly all of them, so I draw our focus to my favorite:

> *Bread on your head and knee-deep in a river,*
> *How are you so starved and withered?*
> *You already own all the sustenance you seek.*
> *If only you'd wake up and take a peek.*

I interpret this poem as a warning against cluelessness and an invitation to quit sleepwalking through life, to wake up and appreciate what's right in front of me, and to live in the present. Ahmad, on the other hand, interprets it as an invitation to visit a panoply of past regrets—failing to see how he is defying the very lesson he is trying to teach me.

"You know, I never forgive myself for this. If I was truly awake, I would notice that you were sick before everyone else. I could have caught the pancreatic tumor *and* the bipolar so much sooner. You could have been saved so much suffering," Ahmad says.

As a father and a physician, Ahmad has always found his initial inability to perceive or prevent my maladies doubly disappointing. I know it wouldn't have made a difference, and I've told him so, but it's

easier to overcome our disappointment with others than it is to over-
come our disappointment with ourselves. To this day, it's still hard for
Ahmad to see me as "well," because historically, I haven't been—and
however unfounded his reasoning, I know that he blames himself for
that. Though it's been almost a decade since my last hospitalization,
I know he still worries, and I recognize that my pilgrimage is just as
much about Ahmad's healing as my own. Perhaps by passing down
these poems, he will finally accept that I'm okay now—and perhaps,
if I wake up and appreciate what's right in front of me, I can allow
myself to do the same. As I learn to wake up to Ahmad's reality and
to help him wake up to mine, our realities overlap, and we become
mirrors for one another, reflecting a stronger resemblance than either
of us ever imagined. I hold his hand before I reply.

"But you forget, Ahmad, my soul is like a porcupine. The more I
suffer, the more it shines!"

"*Bah bah! Afareen!* This is true, but it is also true that no one
wants to see their child suffer. Many times, we take for granted those
who are closest to us and we don't really *see* them. You know?"

"Sure. Why do you think I spent more than twenty years ignoring
all the poetry you've been reciting to me my entire life? I had to be
on the other side of the country before I figured out that your poems
might be useful."

"But it is okay for you. *You* are the child. *I* am the adult—and I
am a physician. If I really had my eyes open, I would notice your
illnesses sooner, so we could *treat* them sooner. I am so sorry, Melody
jan. I will *never* forgive myself for this."

"There's nothing to be *sorry* about. No one could have predicted
that I'd develop two rare conditions back-to-back like that. Just *please*
forgive yourself already," I say as I walk up to a concession stand and
order two soft pretzels and two large waters. Briefly, I am blessed with
the rare opportunity of applying my lessons while learning them. For

a moment, Ahmad and I reverse roles: he becomes the student and I the teacher.

"*Look,*" I go on, handing Ahmad his food and drink. "We've got everything we need right here: bread *and* water! *Wake up!*" And he does. We both do.

When I started this journey, California was experiencing its worst drought in recorded history. Today, as we walk home through the Headquarters, it begins to rain, and before we know it, San Diego is in the midst of its biggest downpour in more than a decade. We watch from the condo between episodes of *Shahrzad*.

During a lull in the storm, I step out onto the balcony, lean over the railing, and look up. Warm raindrops land on my face like installments of hope, reminders that disappointment and desperation *can* end, caustic California droughts included.

On the way to the airport, Ahmad hands me another prescription. As usual, it's all in Farsi and too long and messy for me to read and understand immediately.

"Keep it. We do this poem next week on the Skype," he says, reminding me that pilgrimage is an unending process, a repetitive ritual of constantly choosing to come back to the Source, back to the Heart, back to the Beloved.

Dx: Disappointment ♣ Rx: Wake Up

Welcome every guest,
No matter how grotesque.
Be as hospitable to calamity as to ecstasy,
To anxiety as to tranquility.
Today's misery sweeps your home clean,
Making way for tomorrow's felicity.

—

Open your arms if you want to be embraced.
Break your idols, drop your ego, and behold the Beloved's face.

—

For all the degrees you scholars may attain,
You'll never learn to love 'til you're insane.

—

Opposites invigorate one another.
Honey is only sweet because you've tasted vinegar.

—

Envy is the toughest companion to ditch on your journey.
But ditch it now, for it's the devil's defense attorney.

—

A pure soul is like a porcupine.
The more it's prodded, the more it shines.

—

Bread on your head and knee-deep in a river,
How are you so starved and withered?
You already own all the sustenance you seek.
If only you'd wake up and take a peek.

CHAPTER 10

Dx: Pride
Rx: Return to the Source

Seek the tonic nectar in the bitter sting.
Go to the source of the source of your spring.

The upside of disappointment, when we welcome it, is that it wakes us up. And upon returning to Raleigh, I'm awake. My sense of gratitude, hope, and adventure resurrected, I resist fear, quit making myself so small, and try something new. Wondering what it would be like to teach outside of psychiatric facilities and welcoming the prospect of becoming, in Matthew's words, "beach people" for a year, I apply for a position as a visiting professor of creative nonfiction at UNC Wilmington. Lacking an MFA or a PhD, I know the odds are against me, so I'm surprised when the hiring committee requests a phone interview. It goes well, so naturally, I get cocky and suggest a day trip to check out Wilmington before anyone offers me the job—which is why Matthew has spent the entire two-hour drive here trying and failing to keep my expectations in check.

"Just don't get your hopes up," he says as we drive by Flaming Amy's Burrito Barn. "Obviously it would be amazing to live by the beach and they'd be lucky to have you, but getting a university job without a PhD is pretty much impossible these days."

"Shows what you know: *lots* of creative writing professors don't have PhDs. Most of them have *MFAs*," I say before considering the obvious implications.

"*And* did you go get one of *those* while I wasn't looking?" Matthew asks, raising an eyebrow.

"For your information, I did," I say, pausing for a few seconds to make something up while attempting to keep a straight face. "When I went to pick up our takeout last night, I stopped by the Fiction Kitchen Diploma Drive-Thru and got my very own Master of Fine Afterthoughts. I was saving it as a surprise, but now you've ruined it."

"Master of Fine *Afterthoughts*? Really? They should give you the gig just for that. Seriously though, you know it's the university administrators I doubt, not you. I just don't want you to be disappointed."

"I know, and you're right. But I don't care if I'm disappointed next week. Just let me have a little hope today. Plus, the posting said MFA, PhD, *or equivalent*," I say as I parallel-park at the end of Market Street. "*That's me.* I'm equivalent. Fuck that, I'm better than equivalent. I'm exceptional. They'd be fools not to hire me."

A few days later, they offer me the job—making it that much easier to dive headfirst into the *least* exceptional variety of madness on earth, the source of the wanting that first prompted my pilgrimage, and my most ruthless and relentless obstacle along the way: ego.

Rumi warns,

> *Ego is the soul's worst affliction.*
> *No one lives outside its jurisdiction.*

The second we consider ourselves superior, we distance ourselves from the Beloved. In order to entertain a sense of superiority, we must first forget the common Source of our humanity. And when we forget our Source, we instantly become vulnerable to all the most routine and disastrous human diagnoses: wanting, isolation, haste, depression, distraction, anxiety, anger, fear, disappointment, envy, bitterness, and of course, ever more pride.

For Rumi, ego is not only the worst of our spiritual afflictions, but it is also *the root of all of them*. His notion of ego, or *nafs*, includes far more than mere ego*ism*. It includes our entire sense of the self as a creation somehow *separate* from the Beloved. Like mystics across so many faith traditions, Rumi promotes the *annihilation of the ego*, or *fana*, because the only way to fully unite with the Beloved is to set aside our delusions of a separate "self" disconnected from every other "self" and from the Source of all "selves."

For most of us, this doesn't happen for good until our hearts stop beating—which is why the anniversary of Rumi's death is also known as his "wedding night," for he envisioned death as his ultimate re-union with the Beloved. Likewise, it's why Rumi encourages us to follow the Prophet Muhammad's advice to *die before you die*.

The hope is to achieve ego death before physical death, because when we die before we die, we learn to make the most of life: we free ourselves from the torture chambers of our own egos, finding refuge and security in the Beloved within.

> *The same glorious feathers that spark the peacock's pride*
> *Attract hunters from every side.*

Like predators stalking a peacock for its vibrant plumage, pride stalks the soul for its inner gold, heightening our susceptibility to all the most distressing human afflictions. Certainly, there are valid and productive expressions of what we often call pride—check out your local gay pride parade for proof. But that's not what Rumi is referring to when he addresses what he calls pride or ego.

Gay pride, for example, aims to replace the internalized shame and self-loathing reinforced by oppressive systems and societies with the mutual respect and self-love reinforced by connected communities. Certainly this is *not* the "pride" that Rumi denounces. On the contrary, it is the love that he endorses.

Remember, Rumi extols justice as an expression of divine love, encouraging us to *bestow bounty where it belongs, no matter where it arose*, and warning us against *watering everything that grows*. The ego commits a grave injustice against our souls by isolating us from love, and as such, we would be wise not to water it.

Of course, we are not always wise, nor are we always aware that we're watering our egos until we notice hemlock sprouting where we were hoping for honeysuckle—which is eventually what happens after I start teaching.

In August, Matthew and I rent a furnished upstairs apartment in a historic two-story Victorian on Front Street and split our time between Raleigh and Wilmington, though we spend most of our weekends at the beach. I teach two days a week, and never before 3:30 in the afternoon. It's the cushiest job I've ever had, and I can barely believe they're paying me to do it.

The only drawbacks to Wilmington are the zero Persian restaurants, the copious Confederate monuments, the intense racial segregation, the overall lack of diversity, and the toxic water laced with a carcinogen called GenX (courtesy of a DuPont spin-off known as the Chemours Company) and a disturbing amount of pig and chicken excrement (courtesy of eastern North Carolina's vile "concentrated animal feeding operations" masquerading as "farms").

Other than that, I love most everything about this place: my students, my colleagues, my neighbors, my home, my office, the Ping-

Pong table at the entrance of the creative writing department, the wraparound porches *everywhere*, the Riverwalk, the Spanish moss, the ocean, the massive oaks at Airlie Gardens, the estuaries, the sunsets over the Cape Fear River, the beaches, and the tiny hole-in-the-wall on Market Street that serves the best pho I've ever tasted.

Most of all, however, I love teaching. One of the benefits of never being taught anything about your own culture, history, or literature in school is that you realize how important it is to make room for others to learn about *theirs* when you're in a position to do so.

As a result, I incorporate Show and Tell into every one of my classes: at least once during the semester, each student shares and presents a reading that speaks to them, and we discuss it as a class. I've learned at least as much from and about my students this way as they've learned from and about themselves, their classmates, and world literature. It has also helped me heal some of the pain I felt upon realizing how lacking my formal education was when it came to learning anything about the place and the people from whom I descend. I never considered how much power rested in the simple act of creating a syllabus, but I now recognize it as an invitation to help myself and my students heal.

All of my syllabi include the following under "Course Goals & Descriptions": "In this class, as in life, I strongly advise you to *invent, not imitate*: in Rumi's words, to *become the sky and the clouds that create the rain, not the gutter that carries it to the drain.* The hope is to learn from and be inspired by other writers, writing, and categories of writing without being so unduly limited and influenced by them that you abandon your own unique creative signature. In other words, learn from others, but *do you*."

There's an extra Show and Tell spot in my fall fiction course, and my students encourage me to use it, so I "do me" by assigning the song of the reed flute from the start of the *Masnavi*. Ahmad is elated by my choice, and for weeks before my Show and Tell, he keeps calling with ideas about how to best present Rumi to students who've never read his work: from "take your time" to "recite the Farsi, so they hear the music" to "take them outside if the weather is nice" to "dress professional" to "let them ask questions."

I listen to my father's advice, but ultimately, I follow my instincts. I take my time, I entertain questions, and I recite some Persian verse to impart Rumi's musicality. But I don't take my students outside, because it's too dark, and I don't "dress professional," because it's not my style. Instead, I share a box of Persian desserts and wear my finest purple pullover, complete with rainbow holographic lettering that reads "ALWAYS BE YOURSELF UNLESS YOU CAN BE A UNICORN."

Teaching this poetry is a trip, and teaching it to graduate fiction students as a first-time professor with no formal writing training just makes it trippier. So I begin my Show and Tell on the song of the reed flute by leaning on my ancestors, telling my students what my father told me: you could spend a lifetime exploring these opening lines of Rumi's *Masnavi*. I concede that I have indeed spent my life exploring these verses, albeit mostly unwittingly, and I invite them to do the same deliberately.

My fiction students are smart and open-minded; they are also largely white and American. So as I lay my inheritance before them, I do so with hesitation. I provide countless disclaimers about the dangers of translation and the importance of cultural, historical, and literary context. But finally, I let the verses speak for themselves:

> *Listen to how the reed flute sings its song,*
> *Lamenting a separation gone on too long:*
>
> *"Ever since I was torn from the reed bed,*
> *My cry has multiplied and spread.*

I want a chest split open and apart,
To convey the pain that burns my heart.
All those severed from their source
Yearn to return as a matter of course.
In every gathering, I played my mournful hymn,
Consorting among the gleeful and the grim.
All befriended me of their own accord,
But they left my secrets unexplored.
My greatest secret lives within this song,
Yet eyes and ears will get it wrong.
Between body and soul there is no separation.
Nonetheless the soul defies observation."

The reed sings of those who've been torn from a friend,
Piercing their hearts so that they can ascend . . .
It warns of a harrowing path rich with blood,
Relating Majnun's[1] tale of passion's flood.
But the message of this melody stands classified,
Reserved only for those who in madness reside.

Teaching these verses to students who have never been instructed to consider Rumi as part of any noteworthy literary canon heals something deep within me that I didn't know needed healing. Not once in my life have I presented Rumi's work as anything other than my father's lifelong hobby, a seemingly endless oral tradition as central to my upbringing and identity as my DNA.

Now I present Rumi's *Masnavi* as the great work of literature I know it to be, and my students accept it as such. Even in translation, they call it tender, lyrical, powerful, arresting. I know all of this is true,

---

1   Majnun (meaning "insane" or "possessed") is the moniker given to a famous character from the ancient love story "Leyli and Majnun," popularized by the twelfth-century Persian poet Nezami Ganjavi.

yet hearing my students say it out loud feels like nothing short of a spiritual coup.

I still sing the song of the reed flute, but now I do so with a new confidence, for connecting with my students by teaching them what Ahmad has taught me allows me to remember the reed bed and all of the history and divinity it represents.

Of course, there's a difference between confidence and arrogance. Simply put, confidence comes from the knowledge that we are all connected, while arrogance comes from the delusion that we are not. Confidence requires a profound appreciation for those who created you—from your ancestors all the way back to your ultimate Source. By contrast, arrogance requires an appreciation for the fiction that you alone created yourself—that all of your successes and failures are solely your own doing, that you travel this earth alone, and that you have only yourself upon whom to rely.

Hence, confidence springs from love (for yourself, for others, and for your Source), while arrogance springs from fear (of yourself, of others, and of the mistaken notion that you have no Source). Reconsider Rumi's prescription for fear in this light:

> Quit being a drop. Make yourself an ocean.
> Abandon your ego and reap the Beloved's devotion.

Where confidence frees us to become an ocean, arrogance detains us in a drop. In the latter case, we are not small, but we *feel* that way, because our ego keeps us wanting, isolated, hurried, depressed, distracted, anxious, angry, afraid, disappointed, jealous, bitter, and prideful.

When we abandon our ego and remember that the Beloved is within us, we *can't* be insecure any more than an ocean can be insecure. When we forget, however, *watch out!* Suddenly, we become like

Rumi's housefly, wading in donkey urine: We mistake our strand of hay for a yacht and our puddle of piss for the sea; we think we're big shots when we're just floundering in pee.

The transition from healthy confidence to prideful pee-floundering, moreover, can be quick, because as humans, we are a highly forgetful lot. Being no exception to this rule, my transition from confident to arrogant occurs almost overnight.

Since I teach only two days a week and my classes don't start until midafternoon, I spend most of my mornings writing. As a result, I've revised the proposal for this book by late October, when my agent begins sending it out to publishers again.

This time around, I'm the belle of the literary ball. Perhaps it's because the revised proposal is just that much better, perhaps it's because Beyoncé has now named her baby Rumi, perhaps it's because the wave of white guilt that has been growing since Trump's election has finally hit the world of publishing, or perhaps it's some combination thereof. There's no way of knowing for sure, but I don't care, because I've never felt so sought-after in all of my professional life, and it feels *amazing*.

Ahmad is so over the moon that he calls at least three times a day until the book is sold, and even *he* starts getting cocky about it. When I correct him on the name of one of the publishers (he keeps calling HarperCollins HarborCollins), he replies, "Tell them to change it to Harbor; it sounds better. What is a 'harper'? Someone who plays harp? It makes no sense. If you let them buy it, then we tell them to change the name to Harbor."

All the while, editors keep calling and writing letters to gush about the way I weave words together. One makes the mistake of suggesting

I "tone down the Persian part" over the phone, and in response, I tell him that asking me to tone down the "Persian part" would be like asking Dostoyevsky to tone down the "Russian part." Not only does this editor *not* hang up or scoff at my conceited comparison, he back-pedals faster than a tobacco executive at a cancer convention, agrees with me, and then proceeds to beg my forgiveness.

In short, the whole experience is such an absurd ego trip that by the time the book finally sells at auction, I'm so full of myself that I nearly forget that I still have to finish *writing* this book—as the proposal includes only a single sample chapter.

The day after the sale, I drive to the mountains to speak at a Creative Writing Studies conference near Asheville. I'm so deliriously pleased with myself that when, on the morning of my panel, I wake up with a few mosquito bites, I think nothing of it despite the fact that it's November.

By the time the panel is over, I realize I have at least twenty more bites to match. Naturally, I freak out and alert the front desk that I think I've been a "victim" of bedbugs and insist that housekeeping inspect my room. The result: *one* bedbug. Allegedly.

"But it's not possible to have just *one*. These things travel in packs, don't they?" I ask the manager.

"I don't know what's *possible*, but they looked everywhere and found only one," she replies, impressively composed and indifferent as I scratch my elbow raw.

"How did it *get* there? Aren't you going to warn the other guests?"

"It was a single bug. And for all we know, *you* brought it in," she says to me. It takes every last shred of restraint I have left not to throw a full-blown tantrum. Somehow, I manage to maintain a modicum of composure as I tell the manager that she should expect a lawsuit. Then I discreetly inform the conference organizers of the situation and immediately get the hell out of there.

I drive straight to Raleigh and call Matthew on the way. He spends the entire day researching all things bedbugs, so by the time I get home, he is waiting for me next to the washer and dryer in the back of the garage. He dumps all my clothes in the washing machine and throws away my suitcase in the trash bin outside. Then we both strip naked, add our clothes to the wash, and run directly to the shower. Matthew carefully washes and combs my hair with Nix as he sings "One Is the Loneliest Bedbug" and "Owner of a Lonely Bedbug." Between my protests of "too soon" and "not funny," I can't stop laughing.

By the time I get out of the shower, I'm perfectly clean. But I won't *feel* clean for a long time. Not until a prednisone pack makes the swelling retreat, and not until I know for sure that no bedbugs have followed me home.

For weeks I'm terrified that the bastards will show up in Raleigh or Wilmington, but mercifully, they don't. They do, however, humble me. My face, neck, chest, back, and arms are all covered in bites. They itch like hell and are downright impervious to concealer. But now that I look and feel hideous, I'm finally able to recognize just how much the sale of this book and this new job combined to overinflate my ego.

Rumi cautions,

> *Worse than all the lies that plague humanity*
> *Is the ego lurking inside of me.*

Ego is indeed the greatest liar of all time, as it dupes us into disconnecting—from ourselves, from one another, from nature, and from the Beloved. Oddly enough, both success and failure have a powerful knack for awakening the ego within. But *true* success or failure—unlike the misleading societally constructed varieties—

cannot be measured by worldly pursuits, because regardless of the results, such pursuits tend to distract us from the blessings before us, leaving us wanting instead of appreciating, consuming instead of creating, taking instead of giving. When we measure success and failure based on how the world reacts to us instead of on how *we* react to the world, we cheat ourselves *and* the world.

By spring, thanks to the bedbugs and the insights they inspire, my ego has floated back down to earth, and I am better for it. I haven't annihilated my ego by any stretch, but I now recognize that tackling pride—like tackling every other diagnosis herein—will require consistent *work* on my part. After all, these emotional diagnoses are chronic conditions inherent to the human experience, and these prescriptions are lifelong therapies, not one-time cures. While my diagnoses respond well to the regular treatments I find in my father's Rumi prescriptions, they cannot be cured or eliminated, because they are central to our existence as human beings. In other words, they are all recurring guests in the guesthouse of the soul.

With this in mind, I apply for the permanent tenure-track position for my current job, and I get it. At the same time, Matthew is accepted into the PhD program at Harvard's Graduate School of Education. For years, he has wanted to go back to school, and for years, he has put it off. Over that time, he worked as an investment banker, a paralegal, a public school teacher, an education researcher, and the cofounder of an education technology startup—all while helping support me through law school, the bar, a master's, a suicide attempt, and a psychotic break.

So when Matthew calls to tell me that he has been accepted to Harvard, there is no doubt in my mind that I will turn down the professorship and we will move to Boston. After more than three years of studying Rumi's poetry, I've learned at least enough to know that when you get a chance to move for love, *you take it.*

But true to form, Matthew has done the math, so he is cautious. He insists that we should stay in North Carolina, because the chances of my getting an offer like this are significantly less than his chances of getting into Harvard. I'm touched by his instinct to run the numbers and the attempt to do what he thinks is best for me, but I'm not buying.

"Um, I'm sorry, but you're *going* to Harvard. You read statistics textbooks for *fun.* You're the biggest nerd I know. You *belong* there," I tell him as I shut my office door and shriek like a maniac. I detest the cold, and I'll take the Bible Belt over New England any day, but there is nothing I love more on this planet than Matthew, and I know that he wants this even though he won't admit it.

"But we can just as easily stick to the plan and stay in North Carolina," Matthew continues. "I can go to school here, and you can take the job at UNCW. Seriously, think about it: Boston is so expensive, and I'll be *forty* by the time I start classes. It just seems kind of . . . *irresponsible.*"

"Smoking *meth* is irresponsible, Matthew. Going to Harvard is *duh.* It's fully funded; they'll pay you to go, and with the money we have saved plus my advance, we can swing it. How many more signs do you need? It's a no-brainer. Besides, when has sticking to the plan ever worked out for me anyway? If I stuck to the plan, I'd still be drafting contracts. I'd never have written any books or spent a *day* as a professor, let alone a year. Rumi says, 'Forget your plans and embrace uncertainty, for only then will you find stability.' So screw our plans. Let's take a leap. Let's move to Boston."

In August, after more than fifteen years of living in the American South, Matthew and I pack a twenty-four-foot Penske with all our belongings, sedate our cats, and drive seven hundred miles north. We move into a second-floor apartment on a quaint tree-lined cul-de-sac in Cambridge. It's lovely, but we miss North Carolina. We had so many friends there, not to mention sunshine and steady incomes. Here, we have far fewer friends, a bit less sunshine, and a lot less cash.

Little about this place feels familiar, but we're adapting. I keep busy writing this book, inevitably going through some version of every diagnosis in the process of writing about it; Keshmesh and Nazanin keep busy exploring and colonizing windowsills and closet corners; and Matthew keeps busy attending classes and completing coursework. He is thrilled to be back in school, and while he is the oldest student in his cohort by nearly a decade, he also appears to be the happiest. What's more, his joy is contagious. Watching Matthew gleefully immerse himself in something he has wanted to do for so long delights and inspires me beyond measure.

As the trees strut dazzling autumn reds and golds that never make their way down South, we find time to make new friends and reconnect with old ones here. Our neighbors across the hall, Sherry and Jim, invite us to celebrate the Jewish harvest festival of Sukkot in an effort to welcome us to the building, and we become fast friends. Bita, my sister's best friend and a longtime staple of the Dayton Iranian crew, lives nearby with her family in Brookline and goes out of her way to make us feel welcome. At the end of September, when my parents visit for a few days, she insists on inviting us all over, and together with her mom—Auntie Fati to me—they cook a bona fide feast.

My parents are here to join me on a trip we've been planning since the summer. In June, Omid Safi—my friend, a fellow *irooni*, and the same professor who kindly welcomed me to crash his Rumi seminar at Duke a few years ago—invited me to join one of his "Illuminated Tours" to Turkey in the fall. He had just published a beautiful book called *Radical Love: Teachings from the Islamic Mystical Tradition*, and the tour description noted a special focus on Rumi this year.

Ahmad and I had just finished reading *Radical Love*, so we were in right away. My mom agreed to come after confirming the "luxury accommodations," and while Matthew, Romana, and Robert were all interested, none of them could join us on account of school and work commitments.

So it was just Ahmad, Jazbi, and me. Unlike my parents, I've never done—nor wanted to do—group travel. But Omid is a friend, a seeker, and an esteemed Rumi expert who has been leading this tour for years. I knew that if we were going to visit Rumi's shrine, *this* was the way to do it. Ahmad agreed, and he hasn't been able to stop talking about the trip since we booked our tickets. Even now, at Bita's house, less than twelve hours before we board our flight to Istanbul, he *still* can't stop talking about it.

"I never in my life experience what it feels like to be going on a pilgrimage," he says to me after taking a bite of Auntie Fati's famous raisin cake, "but *now* I do. I feel like I am going for real *ziyarat*.[2] I cannot tell you how happy this makes me. It is like I am living in a dream."

The night we arrive in Istanbul, we meet our tour group at a restaurant on the banks of the Bosphorus. Twenty-six brave souls make up what Omid calls "our little caravan of lovers," and none of us is here

---

2   "Pilgrimage."

merely to sightsee. We are all seeking something more than our rods and cones can perceive, something out beyond the five senses and the six directions Rumi warns against, something deep within our souls, with countless different names but stemming from the same shared intuition.

Though our labels for the Beloved vary dramatically, we share an underlying connection that extends far beyond our present geography. Among our little caravan of lovers, there is an Australian atheist, a Sufi Unitarian Universalist minister and her precocious teenage daughter, a Methodist educator and peace advocate, an American Sufi CDC epidemiologist, a Pakistani nuclear-nonproliferation organizer, an American retired obstetrics nurse, an Armenian-Iranian-American human rights activist, a Bangladeshi-British scientist turned Royal Society international affairs director, and a "retired" American couple doing community development work in Kenya—and that's just the short list.

We each take a few minutes to introduce ourselves at the restaurant, and when Ahmad's turn arrives, he stands up and says, "My name is Ahmad Moezzi, and unlike all of you, I start studying Rumi to get rich."

The whole caravan laughs, and he proceeds to tell a story I already know: about his father offering to pay him and his five siblings to recite Sufi poems by heart. But this time, Ahmad elaborates: "Almost like one hundred American dollars was what my father he offered us. And I was only seven years old, maybe less. I tell you, it was *a lot of money.* But of course, there was a condition: for every mistake we make, my dad, he takes a ten percent deduction. In the end, I did not make a cent."

"I never knew you didn't make *anything,*" I tell Ahmad on the short walk back to the hotel from the restaurant that night.

"Are you kidding?" he replies. "I made *everything.* Just no money."

Despite our detailed itinerary, I don't realize quite how mosque-heavy this trip is until we're in the middle of it. We visit a slew of imposing historic mosques throughout Turkey, full of elaborate calligraphy and tilework, yet every time we walk into a new one, I immediately want out.

This should be no surprise, as I hate mosques—all houses of worship really, but mosques especially, on account of the rampant gender segregation and the routinely neglected women's sections. The way I see it, if we turned every mosque, church, and temple into free public housing, we'd all be better off for it. The idea that God needs an address anywhere outside of our own hearts has always struck me as inane.

So I spend as little time as possible inside the mosques. Instead, I stroll the streets, making friends with stray dogs, cats, and strangers, confident that they are all lovelier than anything I could encounter inside any formal house of worship.

Still, my parents insist that my disappearing acts are rude, that they make us look bad as a family, and that they are an insult to Omid, who takes thoughtful care to provide impressively thorough and entertaining contextualized histories of every site we visit. I don't want to be rude or disrespectful, so I try to force myself to stick with the group, but inevitably, I fail.

In Bursa, I bail on a mosque tour to commune with a family of feral cats outside. Ahmad shows up minutes later, right after a local shop owner empties a small bag of cat food onto the ground and smiles at me as at least a dozen cats bolt to my feet.

"I thought I find you here," Ahmad says.

"I'm sorry. I just *can't* anymore. It's mosque overdose. I'm tired. I would rather be with cats—not because I don't like spending time with you or Mom or Omid or the rest of the group. I just like cats more than I like buildings. Is that a crime?"

"Of course not, but, Melody *jan*, these buildings, they mean something for a lot of people. This is the only reason I say you need to show respect."

"I know. And I'm trying, but they just keep getting uglier and uglier to me. Like, you see that skinny cat over there?" I say, pointing to a mangy calico with one eye and half a tail. "To me, this cat is ten times more beautiful than anything inside of that mosque."

"That is fine. Good for you. You see *zibaeey* [beauty] where you see *zibaeey*. All I say is that you should try to see beauty *everywhere*, not just where it is *obvious to you*. Like now, I try to see the *zibaeey* in this cat that looks so *zesht* [ugly] to me—because *you* see it. It is hard for me to see this animal's beauty, but I try to look with *your eyes*, because here, looking at this cat, your eyes, they are better for me."

"And inside the mosques, then, *your eyes are better for me*? Is that what you're saying?"

"Yes."

"It's a nice idea, and I'd love to see the mosques through your eyes, but I can't. When I walk inside a mosque, I put on my head scarf to be respectful, but I still hate it. The minute I cover my hair, I feel like a pushover and a hypocrite, and because I feel that way, then whatever is *ziba* [beautiful] becomes *zesht*. That's why no matter how *ziba* these mosques may be, they're all *zesht* to me. Because I remember every fool who has ever told me to cover up or pray in the back, and it's over for me. I can't stand it."

"You are right not to stand it, but you are *not right* to let it ruin all the beauty that is here for you. Every old building made by human being is full of ugliness—maybe slaves were forced to build it, or maybe woman could not enter it, or maybe people were abused inside of it—but still you can look at these buildings and say, 'This is beautiful.' Only God is one hundred percent beautiful. Everything else—like you and me and this mosque and these cats—is part *zesht*, part *ziba*. They mix together. You have to *choose* beauty," he says, and proceeds to recite Rumi:

> *You're like a pearl asking where the ocean lies,*
> *All the while soaking in its tides.*

"The beauty of Love is all around you. Only you have to *see* it—and to not let one ugly part make *everything* look ugly. It is your ego that does this to you. Like the shell that prevents the pearl from seeing the ocean, your ego prevents you from finding beauty and feeling love. To evolve as human being, you must go beyond the shell of your ego," Ahmad says before reciting another poem:

> *When you dedicate each breath to yourself,*
> *You ache with every labored gasp.*
> *When you surrender each breath to the Beloved,*
> *Nothing is beyond your grasp.*

"I get it," I reply, kneeling down to pet the cycloptic calico who is now dining at my feet.

"*Vai, nakon* [Ew, don't]*!*" Ahmad says, cringing as he swats my hand away from the feral feline. "This cat probably has hundred diseases."

"Now *you* get it," I reply, scratching under the calico's chin. "It may have a hundred different diseases, but ego isn't one of them."

"This is true," Ahmad admits. "But also it is true that there are worms all over his butt, so maybe you want to stop touching him and go wash your hand."

On the bus rides from Istanbul to Bursa to Ankara to Cappadocia to Konya, our caravan grows closer. By the end of the journey, Ahmad is holding court at the back of the bus, reciting and interpreting Rumi for anyone who wants to listen. Watching my fellow travelers—strangers less than two short weeks ago—hang on Ahmad's every word, I can't imagine feeling any more grateful to call him my father.

Nor can I imagine feeling any more Persian pride than I do in this moment. With every verse Ahmad recites for this rapt international audience of new friends, I feel the internalized shame and self-loathing reinforced by a society where a Muslim ban is now the law of the land replaced with self-love and respect for where I come from and who I am.

As we approach Konya, fresh off the heels of a magical evening communing with whirling dervishes in Cappadocia, Ahmad is downright giddy. By the time we get to Rumi's shrine, he is like a child who cannot be contained. He practically skips through the front entrance. My mom and I follow him, having already informed Omid that Ahmad is following another tour guide entirely and that we have no way of controlling him.

"Of course," Omid replies, smiling. "You don't have to explain to me. You just have to look at him, and you can see he is in love."

At nearly seventy-three years old, my father has never appeared younger to me than he does today. He takes my hand as we approach the brilliant green dome under which Rumi is buried, and he recites the same poem he recited to me four years ago the day after I landed in San Diego. He sang it to me then, in the dawn after my arrival in California, upon finding me facing the Pacific during my morning prayers, bowing west instead of east. He sings it to me now, in the evening after his arrival in Konya, as we enter Rumi's earthly resting place:

Your homeland flows in every direction.
Why pray facing one minuscule section?

"Sing your *own* song in your *own* direction," Ahmad continues. "Always. You promise me."

"I promise you."

Satisfied with my assurance, Ahmad proceeds to inform my mother and me that he will be spending untold hours in this place, that we should leave whenever we bore of it, that he will meet us at the hotel when he is finished, and that we need not worry about him.

None of us speaks Turkish or has ever even been to Turkey before this. We are foreigners here, but Ahmad feels right at home. For about twenty minutes, my mom and I watch him as he sits on a ledge in front of Rumi's tomb, in what looks like a trance, eyes closed, quietly whispering Molana's verse to Molana.

This whole time, a security guard keeps asking others sitting on the same ledge to get up, making it clear that people aren't supposed to sit there, but he leaves Ahmad alone. Presumably, he can tell that my father is somewhere else.

My mother and I agree that this is the highlight of the trip for us. Not the experience of visiting Rumi's sarcophagus, which incidentally happens to be under construction and is therefore completely obscured and inaccessible, but the experience of watching Ahmad sit before it, blissfully oblivious to the time, the terrain, or the tourists swirling about.

In all, Ahmad spends two hours mesmerized, whispering to Rumi. In that time, my mom and I visit the gift shop, drink tea, eat ice cream, chat with our fellow travelers, and roam the gardens around the mausoleum—where Ahmad ultimately catches up with us.

He is ecstatic.

"A man gave this to me," Ahmad says with tears in his eyes, holding up a set of amber prayer beads as we stand together in the shade of Rumi's iconic emerald dome. "When I opened my eyes, he was there, looking at me, and then he put this *tasbi* in my hand and said *hediyeh. Hed-i-yeh!* Can you believe it?"

"*Hediyeh*" means "gift" or "present" in Farsi—*and*, as it turns out, in Turkish and Arabic too.

"You could not pay me one million dollar for this *tasbi*," Ahmad says, smiling and holding it up to the sun, spellbound by the light as it dances across every shimmering bead.

Packing my things the night before we return to the States, I realize that I've amassed too many books here—so many that they require an extra bag. As I fill it, I express some concern that my books might get lost in transit. At this, Ahmad recounts a tale of Rumi's first meeting with Shams. The story is legend and there are many differing accounts, but tonight, Ahmad's goes like this: One day, Rumi, already a much-revered scholar, is reading by a garden pool, a pile of his treasured books beside him. Shams passes by and inquires about what's in the books. Rumi, the scholar, replies that Shams wouldn't understand. Shams, the mystic, then tosses Rumi's books into the pool. Naturally, Rumi is devastated over the destruction of his beloved books, and in response, Shams proceeds to pull them out of the water, perfectly dry and undamaged. Amazed, Rumi asks Shams his secret, and Shams replies by telling Rumi that *he* wouldn't understand.

It is at this point, setting aside books in favor of experience, that Rumi the scholar becomes Rumi the mystic. After recounting this story, Ahmad remarks, only half kidding, "Maybe you are *ready* to lose your books."

. . .

Upon embarking on this pilgrimage, I thought it was about reclaiming a cultural and literary inheritance in the hopes of overcoming a nasty case of writer's block and sorting mysticism from madness in my own experience. But now I realize that my journey has always been about love, as every prescription here has turned out to be a different incarnation of love and every diagnosis a different incarnation of ego as an obstacle to love.

To connect with the Beloved within ourselves and one another, we must learn to love as freely and selflessly as possible. This means tossing timidity aside and leaving our reputations behind, slowing down and not keeping score, finding the Beloved right next door, welcoming every guest, going beyond the five and six, following the light of our wounds, falling in love with Love, abandoning our ego, waking up to the blessings before us, and returning to our Source. In other words, it means not only *reading* Rumi's prescriptions but *filling them*.

Our instinct to seek healing and wholeness is a direct product of the Beloved within, whether we recognize it or not. We may all want different things in life, yet all of those things inevitably represent the same common uncontrolled substance known as love. Where we falter isn't in our ultimate *aim*, but in our failure to recognize that it's ultimately the same. While many of us may *appear* to be after money or fame or sex or power or success, when we stop to investigate the engine that drives all of these quests, we find that underlying every one of them is a *longing to love and be loved*.

Of course, the path we choose to fulfill this longing varies for each of us—which is why this book is a memoir and not a manual. Still, I'm not writing it because I want you to know *my* story. Rather, I'm writing it because I want you to know *yours*. For by knowing your own story—where you come from, what you're made of, and how you came to be—you learn how to safely steer your soul toward Love.

Sharing in my father's fondness for Rumi and filling his lyrical prescriptions has helped me do exactly that. As has recognizing that the way *I* fill my prescriptions can and will vary from the way he does—or the way *you* do. Sure, there will be some overlap, but in the end, my decision about how and when to fill these sacred prescriptions is up to me—just as yours is up to you.

In my case, I have found a few steady practices that have helped along the way. They include accumulating experiences and relationships instead of things; convening with the Beloved facing any number of different directions at least once a day; creating fine and not-so-fine art; listening to music; learning; teaching; reading; taking deep breaths; keeping a journal in an odd and ever-expanding spreadsheet to track and enhance my mood, sleep, prayers, charity, goals, and gratitude; turning off my phone, closing my inbox, shutting down tabs, and logging off social media more often; giving myself permission to laugh, cry, and pray at will—as well as license to continue seeking psychiatric help and taking medication as needed; sending thank-you notes to friends and family; taking walks in the wilderness; and more.

Together, these habits have helped me treat every diagnosis herein, but they're not one-size-fits-all solutions by any stretch. In sharing how the words of an ancient mystic poet have changed *my* modern manic life, I know better than to promote any single path toward changing *yours*. For one, no such path exists. And just as well, because the goal here isn't to follow some rigid uniform map. Rather, it's to create our *own*: to customize our own rites and rituals as we apply Rumi's counsel to our own lives—guiding us to *our* source, *our* inner gold, *our* purpose, *our* Beloved.

Rumi didn't whirl because he wanted others to whirl like him. He whirled because his heart led him to it—just as he composed poetry and recited Quranic verses while whirling because his heart led him to that.

Thus, to follow the Rumi prescription is *not* to whirl like Rumi or to recite the same words he recited. Rather, it is to liberate yourself from your own ego, to stop asking "What would people think?" and to start following the divine spark uniquely expressed within *you*. Point being, when it comes to filling Rumi's prescriptions, make them your own and apply them from within.

Seek the tonic nectar in the bitter sting.
Go to the source of the source of your spring.

Having sought the tonic nectar in the bitter sting, I keep returning to the source of the source of my spring, confirming that it's not a place but a feeling. Deep at the "root of the root of myself" (an alternate and more literal translation), I have found a Source that is rooted in devotion and grace, not time and space. I know, because I've encountered It just as readily in California as in North Carolina, in Cambridge as in Konya.

Since setting out on my journey, Ahmad and Rumi have guided me toward this Source by helping me evolve from a traumatized misfit who could feel at home nowhere to a budding mystic who is beginning to feel at home everywhere. They have taught me that we are all refugees, fleeing the tyranny of the ego and seeking comfort in a common Home, albeit one with endlessly diverse names.

Their prescriptions have allowed me to move from wanting more to appreciating more, from taking more to giving more, from consuming more to creating more, from worrying about outcomes and income to focusing on process and wellness, from being constantly connected online to being personally connected with the divine, and from relying almost exclusively on my mind and intellect for my sense of self to trusting my heart and intuition to lead. This progression from head to heart has propelled my journey forward—or, more precisely, inward—over the past four years. It has helped me realize just how much ego—that brutal sense of narcissism and self-importance that so often leads to debilitating fear, insecurity, isolation, and all the worst available spiritual diagnoses—can get in our way, and more specifically, just how much it has gotten in *my* way over the years, contributing to everything from indigestion to writer's block to anxiety to depression.

Trading intellect for intuition by accepting my father's guidance while filling Rumi's prescriptions for myself and prioritizing love above all else, I am slowly learning to quit reducing myself to my thoughts and achievements, to quit comparing myself to others' carefully curated Facebook personas, to quit striving for perfection to the point of creative stagnation, and to quit chronically trusting reason over faith.

By returning to my roots (to my parents, to my heart, to the Beloved) I have discovered a newfound sense of love and gratitude for where I come from—personally, culturally, and spiritually. Applying that to myself and the world around me by filling Rumi's prescriptions has helped me reduce the wanting, insecurity, ego, and ambition that first led me on this journey. In the process, it has also mercifully reignited my creative spark, bringing me back from a madness far more common and insidious than manic depression, back from the trappings of my ego, back from fear and insecurity, and back to the joy of creating for its own sacred sake, not my own errant egocentric one.

Even so, the perpetual practice of filling my prescriptions has presented some challenges. Most notably, I can't just walk into a pharmacy, hand over a poem scribbled on one of Ahmad's old prescription slips and say: "I'd like a refill for the 'root of the root of myself' please. What's the wait?"

Instead, I've had to mix and administer my own meds, constantly concocting more effective ways to practically apply Rumi's poetic prescriptions to my everyday life. But the Beloved is indeed all-merciful, for as I approach the end of this phase of my pilgrimage, I now realize that every one of the prescriptions herein works off-label for every other diagnosis. Unlike standard pharmaceuticals, Rumi's prescriptions don't include contraindications. In fact, they are all *complementary*, such that following the prescription for pride also helps treat every other diagnosis and vice versa.

Still, to avoid feeling overwhelmed, I apply one prescription at a time, reassured by the recognition that they all work in tandem while trusting the Beloved's track record. Of course, none of this is easy, and I still fail. *A lot.* But now, when I fail, I have a legacy to fall back on. Now I have a treasure trove of priceless prescriptions with unlimited refills meant to be shared. Now I have a documented reservoir of timeless teachings from my own faith and culture that transcend both. Now I claim my inheritance; I fill my prescriptions, and I pass them along.

I thank God that my father is still here to see me appreciate and share what he has taught me, but I know that this journey is preparing me for the day that he isn't. While I agree with Ahmad and Rumi that it is better to be of the same heart than of the same tongue and that Love has no exclusive language, culture, or religion, I also know that my heart has expanded considerably as I've further embraced the language, culture, and religion of my ancestors through this perpetual pilgrimage.

Wherever our roots lie, however near or far, they summon us. When we answer their call and reconnect, we remember what connects us *all*, a power that transcends every physical sense and global direction, a memory time can't erase, a force too personal not to be universal: Love. Just like memories, some capabilities sink into the bloodstream, passing through generations, showering blessings upon those who return to their source. We do not know them by direct recollection or experience, and we cannot recite them at will. Nonetheless, we know them by heart.

Our flight lands in Boston on a drizzly mid-October night. Thankfully, Turkish Airlines comes through with all our luggage, including my books. Even if I were "ready to lose" them—*which I am not*—I don't want to, so I am relieved when I spot the purple carryall we bought in Istanbul rolling down the conveyor belt at baggage claim.

My parents are staying here for a couple nights before returning to San Diego, so Matthew picks us all up at the airport.

"How was it to finally visit Rumi?" he asks Ahmad on the drive home.

"Matthew *jan,* I cannot tell you. It was a *dream.* We have to go again, all of us together, the whole family. It is such a beautiful country. The people, the history, the nature—everything was wonderful!"

"How was the *food*?" Matthew inquires, ever the epicure. "People always rave about how great the food is there."

"It was not *bad,* but not great," Ahmad replies, and my mom and I agree.

"Yeah, it was the one letdown for me," I admit. "I think it's because the food was so close to Persian, *but not quite.* It always felt like something was missing: the rice needed saffron; the kabob needed *advieh*; the *khoresht* needed lime.[3] Plus, I think we were super spoiled by that dinner at Bita's the night before we left, which was way better than anything we had in Turkey."

---

3 *Advieh* is a Persian spice mixture. *Khoresht,* again, is Persian stew; it comes in many varieties (including my aforementioned favorite, *ghormeh sabzi*) and is traditionally served over rice.

"But to be fair, Bita's was probably better than any meal I've had all year," Matthew adds. "So maybe you *were* spoiled?"

"You are right, Matthew *jan*. We are *all* spoiled," Ahmad says. "Always the best things are at home, but sometimes you have to go to the other side of the earth so you can notice."

"*Ey ghomeh beh Hajj rafteh: Kojaeed? Kojaeed? Mashoogh hameenjast. Biyayid, biyayid,*" I say, reciting Rumi.

> *Why seek pilgrimage at some distant shore,*
> *When the Beloved is right next door?*

"*Bah bah,*" Ahmad proclaims as Matthew parks in front of our house. "I told you this poem in the car after you first came to San Diego to study with me. You remember?"

"Of course," I say. "Do you remember my response?" Ahmad gets out of the car, opens the passenger door, and reaches for both of my hands to help me out.

"You ask why you have to cross the whole country to see me if the Beloved is right next door, and I tell you 'because one day I will be dead,'" Ahmad replies, laughing as he clutches my hands tightly in his, a firm familiar grip to steady me. I step onto the moonlit sidewalk and see myself reflected in my father's eyes.

"I can't believe you remember that."

"Of course I remember that. And when I die, *you remember it too.*"

Dx: Pride ♣ Rx: Return to the Source

Ego is the soul's worst affliction.
No one lives outside its jurisdiction.

—

The same glorious feathers that spark the peacock's pride
Attract hunters from every side.

—

All those severed from their source
Yearn to return as a matter of course.

—

Quit being a drop. Make yourself an ocean.
Abandon your ego and reap the Beloved's devotion.

—

Worse than all the lies that plague humanity
Is the ego lurking inside of me.

—

You're like a pearl asking where the ocean lies,
All the while soaking in its tides.

—

When you dedicate each breath to yourself,
You ache with every labored gasp.
When you surrender each breath to the Beloved,
Nothing is beyond your grasp.

—

Your homeland flows in every direction.
Why pray facing one minuscule section?

—

Seek the tonic nectar in the bitter sting.
Go to the source of the source of your spring.

—

Why seek pilgrimage at some distant shore,
When the Beloved is right next door?

GLOSSARY

Advieh—Persian spice mixture.

Afareen—Well done, good job.

Agha—Mister, sir.

Allah—"God" in Arabic.

Allahu akbar—"God is greater" in Arabic.

Baba—Father.

Bahaneh—Excuse.

Bah bah—An untranslatable utterance that doubles as the name brand for the most popular air freshener in Iran and what the English internet calls an "auditory compliment."

Barbari—A thick Persian flatbread.

Barikalah—Well done, bravo.

Bayt—Couplet.

Beeshoour—One lacking sense.

Beetarbiyat—One lacking upbringing.

Beeya—Come.

Bolbol—Nightingale.

Boro baba—Literally "Go Dad," but the connotation is roughly equivalent to a playful "Get outta here!"

Chera—Why.

Cheshmet ra baaz kon—Open your eyes.

Choss—A silent fart.

Dokhtaram—My daughter.

Dooroogh-goo—Liar.

Eh—More of an exclamation with a meaning akin to "oh" than a word unto itself.

Ein kolah bardarhayeh pedar sookhteh daran telephone meekonan—Literally "The people who take off hats and have burnt fathers are calling." Meaning: These infuriating fraudsters are calling.

Ey ghomeh beh Hajj rafteh: Kojaeed? Kojaeed? Mashoogh hameenjast. Biyayid, biyayid—Literally "Oh, group bound for *Hajj*. Where are you? Where are you? The Beloved is right here. Come. Come."

Fana—The annihilation of the ego.

Ganj—Treasure.

Ganjeh bee-maar—Treasure without snakes (*ganj*—treasure; *maar*—snake; *bee*—prefix meaning "without").

Ghebleh *or* **qiblah**—The direction Muslims face during daily prayers, toward the Kaaba in Mecca.

Ghormeh sabzi—Only the best meal ever. From the text: "a dish full of every green imaginable that takes forever to make and even longer to exit your system."

Gol—Flower.

Goleh bee-khaar—Flower without thorns (*gol*—flower; *khaar*—thorn; *bee*—prefix meaning "without").

Gooz—A fart that makes noise.

Hajj—Pilgrimage to Mecca. Muslims who are capable (physically, emotionally, and financially) are expected to perform *Hajj* at least once in their lives. Along with faith, charity, prayer, and fasting, *Hajj* is one of the five pillars of Islam.

Hala—Now.

Haleh shomah [chetoreh]?—How are you?

Ham-deli az ham-zabani behtar ast—Better to be of the same heart than of the same tongue.

Haram—Forbidden. Opposite of *halal* (permitted). Also can mean "sacred."

Har chi khoda bekhad khoobeh—Whatever God wants is good.

Hediyeh—Gift.

Irooni *or* irani—Iranian. Literally a person or a thing from Iran.

Jan *or* joon—A term of endearment, often added after someone's name. It connotes a combination of "life," "essence," and "spirit" while serving as the rough equivalent of "dear" in everyday conversation.

Johaar—"Essence" or "heart" in a literary context; "ink" in an everyday context.

Kaaba—Often referred to as the most sacred site in Islam, the Kaaba is the cube at the center of Masjid al-Haram (AKA the Sacred Mosque or the Great Mosque) in Mecca. Described in the Quran as the first house of worship, it is central to the performance of pilgrimage (*Hajj*) and establishes the direction for daily prayers (*qiblah* or *ghebleh*).

Khak to saret—Dirt in your head (mild curse).

Khoda—"God" in Persian.

Khoresht—Persian stew; it comes in many varieties and is traditionally served over rice.

Konkour—Iran's notoriously grueling university entrance exam.

Lamazhab—One lacking religion (mild curse).

Maar—Snake.

Mageh—As if. Though its meaning varies with context, *mageh* is a kind of emphatic way to ask a question.

Mageh kholeey?—What are you, a fool? (*Khol* means "fool.")

Maghz—Marrow, center, brain.

Man cheh meedonam—"What do I know?" or "How should I know?"

Molana—Another name for Rumi; an honorific meaning "our master" that is most often used to refer to Rumi when speaking Persian.

Nafs—Ego.

Nakon—Don't.

Namaz—Prayer.

Noon-o-paneer—Bread and cheese, standard Persian breakfast fare.

Nowruz—The Persian New Year; coincides with the vernal equinox, usually around March 21.

Pedar—Father.

Pedar sag—A mild curse. Literally, "Your dad is a dog." Figuratively, "Brat."

Poost—Skin, peel, rind.

Reseedeem—"We have arrived," or "Have we arrived?" as an interrogative within the text.

Rumi—Another name for Molana; means "Roman" in Persian and Arabic.

Salaam—Hello, peace.

Sheerzan—Lioness; also, courageous and spirited woman.

Shehr—Poem, song.

Shirazi—A person or a thing from Shiraz.

Sufi/Sufism—Sufis are Muslim mystics; Sufism is Islamic mysticism.

Tamoom—Finished.

Tasbi—Prayer beads.

Vai—An expression that vaguely translates to "wow." It can indicate awe, grief, pleasure, or disgust, depending on the context.

Velam kon—Leave me alone.

Yani—Means, meaning, as in.

Yani chi?—"Means what?" or "What does it mean?"

Yek kam asabaneem kard—It made me a little angry.

Zar talab gashti. Khod aval zar bodi—Literally "You went out in search of gold. You were gold already from the start."

Zereshk—Barberries.

Zesht—Ugly.

Ziba—Beautiful.

Zibaeey—Beauty.

Zikr—Literally means "remembrance" or "remembering"; specifically, it refers to the remembrance of the Beloved (AKA God). A Sufi devotional practice that involves repeatedly reciting short prayers, or one or more of the many names/attributes of God (of which Islam recognizes at least ninety-nine), or even poetry—all as a means of remembering the Beloved. *Zikr* is often a communal ritual that involves singing and dancing as well.

Ziyarat—Pilgrimage.

ACKNOWLEDGMENTS

I thank the following intrepid souls for helping me and this book come to life:

Rumi for bringing me closer to my father, myself, and the Beloved. Ahmad for being my friend, guide, *baba*, and cotranslator. My mom for giving me life and saving it too. My sister, Romana, for her friendship and encouragement. My husband, Matthew, for being my first and finest editor, as well as my favorite human. My gay husband, Mario, for always showing up for me. My nieces and nephews—Cyrus, Roxana, Noah, Luka, Mila, and Matteo—for allowing me to keep passing these prescriptions down through our family.

Nobar Elmi for being my best friend from the womb—and insisting that I recite Rumi at her wedding, which helped spark the idea for this book. Dena Sanam Behi, Krista Bremer, Ellen Forney, Katelyn Freund, Layton Green, Roxana Jafarian, and Levi McLaughlin for their priceless friendship and editorial feedback. My cats, Keshmesh and Nazanin, for keeping me company while I write.

Danielle Durkin and Lilly Ghahremani for being my literary fairy godmothers—both of whom have gone above and beyond to make my writing career possible. Larry Malley and Mike Bieker for having the guts to publish my first book and to continue standing behind it. Larry Schenk and Barry Peters for teaching and inspiring me to write before I knew I was a writer.

Nina de Gramont, David Gessner, Melissa Crowe, Clyde Edgerton, Philip Gerard, Bekki Lee, Malena Mörling, Anna Lena Phillips Bell, Wendy Brenner, Robert Anthony Siegel, Emily Louise Smith, Beth Staples, Megan Hubbard, and Lisa Bertini for welcoming me into their magical UNCW creative writing community. All of my students at UNCW, on the locked psychiatric unit in Raleigh, at Skyland Trail in Atlanta, and at all the workshops and seminars I've taught over the years.

Scott Siraj al-Haqq Kugle, Ashley Monique Lee, Ayesha Mattu, Nura Maznavi, Maryse Mitchell-Brody, Asra Nomani, Steven Petrow, Andrew Reynolds, Jeff Sebo, Laurel Snyder, Deonna Kelli Sayed, Lee Smith, Samia Serageldin, and Kulsum Tasnif for their creative camaraderie.

Bita Tabesh, Carlos Estrada, Auntie Fati, Tom Levenson, Katha Seidman, Sheila Moeschen, Marjan Kamali, Kandeel Javid, Nadia T. Madden, and Sherry and Jim Leffert for helping me to find warmth and community in the coldest city I've ever inhabited.

Reynold Alleyne Nicholson, Arthur John Arberry, Coleman Barks, Abdul Ghafoor Ravan Farhadi, Ibrahim Gamard, Alan Godlas, Camille Helminski, Kabir Helminski, Zara Houshmand, Jawid Mojaddedi, Majid M. Naini, Omid Safi, and Shahram Shiva for their remarkable translations and interpretations. Alan Godlas and Omid Safi especially for their kindness, patience, and willingness to answer my questions over the years. Farhad Nowroozi for generously sharing his library.

Aja Pollock for her copyediting wizardry and Rachel Ayotte for her priceless assistance throughout the publication process. Lindsay Gordon, Casey Maloney, Katie English-Macloed, and Roshe Anderson for their marketing and publicity prowess. Linet Huamán Velásquez and Jess Morphew for this dazzling cover.

Megan Newman for publishing this book and the one before it—and for combining and applying her extraordinary expertise and empathy all at once. Marian Lizzi for editing this book, bringing her incomparable skill and insight to every page, and for having the courage and foresight to see just how universal the message of *The Rumi Prescription* could be. Everyone else at TarcherPerigee and Penguin Random House who helped nurture this project and get it out into the world. And above all, Ayesha Pande for her intelligence, integrity, and insight; for never asking me to downplay my identity or compromise my dignity; for always finding the perfect homes for my work; and for unwaveringly looking out for me.

CITATIONS

The verses translated herein are from either Rumi's *Masnavi* or his *Divan-eh Shams* (also known as *Kolliyat-eh Shams-eh Tabrizi* or *Divan-eh Shams-eh Tabrizi*)— specifically from one of the three books cited below (all of which are in Persian). The *Masnavi* citations use standard format: the book followed by the line number(s). All the numbered ghazals and quatrains are from the *Divan-eh Shams*, numbered in reference to either the original Furuzanfar critical edition (labeled "F") or Taw-fiq Subhani's collection based on the Furuzanfar edition (labeled "S"). As always with Persian texts, words, and names, please note that spellings vary in English due to the disparate alphabets.

Rumi and Badiozaman Furuzanfar. *Kolliyat-eh Shams-eh Tabrizi* or *Divan-eh Shams-eh Tabrizi*. Tehran: Amir Kabir Press, 1957–66.

Rumi and Tawfiq Subhani. *Kolliyat-eh Shams-eh Tabrizi* (based on Furuzanfar critical edition). Tehran: Qatrah, 2002.

Rumi and Karim Zamani. *Masnavi; or, A Comprehensive Commentary of Mathnavi e Ma'navi.* Tehran: Etelaat, 2004.

Author's Note

Better to be of the same heart than of the same tongue. *Masnavi*, I:1207.

When it comes to love, the pen breaks. *Masnavi*, I:114.

Chapter 1—Dx: Wanting ♦ Rx: Go to the Source

Love's nation of origin is separate from all creeds. For the lovers, the Beloved comprises all religions and nationalities. *Masnavi*, II:1770.

Don't retreat, come near. Don't lose faith, adhere. Seek the tonic nectar in the bitter sting. Go to the source of the source of your spring. Ghazal #120-S.

In love with insanity, I'm fed up with wisdom and rationality. *Masnavi*, VI:573.

Lamenting a separation gone on too long, the reed flute sings its tender song . . . But the message of this melody stands classified, reserved only for those who in madness reside. *Masnavi*, I:1–14.

If a thorn gets stuck under a donkey's tail, the ass knows only how to neigh and flail. But this drives the spike deeper still, the flesh further torn. It takes a sage to dislodge that pesky thorn. *Masnavi*, I:154–57.

Why seek pilgrimage at some distant shore, when the Beloved is right next door? Ghazal #648-S.

Die before you die (Rumi citing the Prophet Muhammad). *Masnavi*, VI:754.

Your wounds may summon the light hereto, but this sacred light does not come from you. *Masnavi*, I:3223–27.

Chapter 2—Dx: Isolation ♣ Rx: Invent, Don't Imitate

Your homeland flows in every direction. Why pray facing one minuscule section? Ghazal #1821-S.

We have taken the fruit of the Quran, the marrow of its verses. We have left the rinds and the bones, the waste for the asses. (Though often ascribed to Rumi and prevalent in the Persian oral tradition, this couplet is likely apocryphal. There are different versions of it in the oral tradition. There is one version, for example, that mentions "asses" where another mentions "others," and one mentions "bones" where another mentions "rinds." My translation takes both versions into account. The following is the Persian transliteration for reference: *Mah zeh Quran maghz ra bardashteem, poost* [or *ostokhoon*] *ra bareh kharan* [or *deegaran*] *bogzashteem*.)

The pen writes and writes in frantic haste, but when it comes to love, the pen breaks. *Masnavi*, I:114.

Though the song of the nightingale you may learn to compose, you still can't know what it sings to the rose. *Masnavi*, I:3358.

Become the sky and the clouds that create the rain, not the gutter that carries it to the drain. *Masnavi*, V:2490.

Since hearing my first love story, I pursued the Beloved with every part of me. But could lover and Beloved ever be separate, subject to division? No, they are one and the same. I just had double vision. Quatrain #1168-S.

Toss timidity aside and leave your reputation behind. Ghazal #213-S. Also see *Masnavi*, II:2331.

Chapter 3—Dx: Haste ♣ Rx: Quit Keeping Score

I have spoken the language of madness, full of whys and hows and wherefores. Obsessed with reasons, I spent a lifetime knocking at this door. When at last it opened, my soul replied. All along, I had been knocking from the inside. Quatrain #1249-F.

Better to be of the same heart than of the same tongue. *Masnavi*, I:1207.

On the road to enlightenment, wise and mad are one. In the way of Love, self and
other are one. For those who drink of the wine that connects souls, in their
religion, the Kaaba and the house of idols are one. Quatrain #306-F.

Be it an hour or a hundred thousand years, they are one and the same, however
the math appears. *Masnavi*, I:3504.

Quit keeping score if you want to be free. Love has ejected the referee. Quatrain
#116-F.

Patience, not haste, gets you where you belong. Slow down and heed the
Beloved's song. *Masnavi*, I:4003.

You went out in search of gold far and wide, but all along you were gold on the
inside. *Masnavi*, I:2305.

Chapter 4—Dx: Depression ♣ Rx: Welcome Every Guest

Where there is treasure, snakes come round. Where there are roses, thorns
abound. In the grand bazaar of life, joy without sorrow cannot be found.
(This couplet is likely apocryphal. Though my father has one version of the
Masnavi, published by Moasesseh Nashr Kotob Akhlagh, wherein it appears
at V:2360, the book is old and missing pages with the exact publication date
for a full citation. As a result, and for reference, I am providing this Persian
transliteration: *Ganjeh bee-maar o goleh bee-khaar neest; Shahdi-eh bee-gham dar
ein bazaar neest.*)

For a viable cure, pain is the key. Your injury invites the remedy. *Masnavi*, II:1939
and III:3210 (this exact same verse appears in both places in the text).

Welcome every guest, no matter how grotesque. Be as hospitable to calamity as
to ecstasy, to anxiety as to tranquility. Today's misery sweeps your home clean,
making way for tomorrow's felicity. *Masnavi*, V:3644–46, 3676–84.

Wherever streams go, life grows. Wherever tears go, mercy flows. *Masnavi*, I:820.

Every storm the Beloved unfurls permits the sea to scatter pearls. *Masnavi*, I:506.

With Love, bitter turns sweet and copper turns gold. With Love, pain becomes
healing manifold. *Masnavi*, II:1529–30.

Chapter 5—Dx: Distraction ♣ Rx: Go Beyond the Five and Six

You went out in search of gold far and wide, but all along you were gold on the
inside. *Masnavi*, I:2305.

Love has no business with the five and six. Only upon the Beloved are the true
lover's eyes fixed. *Masnavi*, VI:5.

The Beloved has expanded your heart with divine light, yet you still seek answers
from outside to feel right. You are a fathomless lake, yet you complain of
drought incessantly. Why settle for a puddle when you have a channel to the

sea? *Masnavi*, V:1066–70. (This poem alludes to the ninety-fourth sura of the Quran, "The Expansion.")

Why seek pilgrimage at some distant shore, when the Beloved is right next door? Ghazal #648-S.

Abstain from thoughts, my dear friend, for such abstinence is always the best medicine. Quit your scratching, as it only makes the itch worse. Stop it already; free your soul from this curse. *Masnavi*, I:2909–11.

As usual, we're drunk with Love today. Evict your thoughts and find a song to play. Prayers and devotions come in countless shapes and sizes. Pick the ones the beauty in your soul recognizes. Quatrain #82-F.

Forget religious rules and regulations. Let your heart conduct communications. *Masnavi*, II:1784.

You already own all the sustenance you seek. If only you'd wake up and take a peek. *Masnavi*, V:1076.

Chapter 6—Dx: Anxiety ♣ Rx: Follow the Light of Your Wounds

Anxiety is like an ax, so let your worries remit. They'll cut off your own foot and think nothing of it. Quatrain #1624-S.

Forget your plans and embrace uncertainty. Only then will you find stability. Ghazal #323-S.

A fat cow grazes on a lush green island pasture. For years she feeds daily; still every night she fears disaster. You've eaten well since birth; in no nutrient are you deficient. Quit fretting for tomorrow; your lot has always been sufficient. *Masnavi*, V:2855–56, 2868.

Break a leg and the Beloved grants wings to soar. Fall in a ditch and the Beloved opens a door. *Masnavi*, III:4808.

Your wounds may summon the light hereto, but this sacred light does not come from you. *Masnavi*, I:3223–27.

Your regrets do you no good, persisting at your own expense. The past can't be undone, so best live in present tense. *Masnavi*, IV:2244. See also: *Masnavi*, V:1409; Quatrain #1787-S.

Welcome every guest, no matter how grotesque. Be as hospitable to calamity as to ecstasy, to anxiety as to tranquility. Today's misery sweeps your home clean, making way for tomorrow's felicity. *Masnavi*, V:3644–46, 3676–84.

The faithful are mirrors for one another (citing the Prophet Muhammad). *Masnavi*, I:1328.

Chapter 7—Dx: Anger ♣ Rx: Fall in Love with Love

The seed of hellfire is in your wrath. Extinguish this hell inside to follow Love's path. *Masnavi*, III:3480.

Anger never arises in the absence of pride. Crush both beneath your feet and be sanctified. Ghazal #2198-S.

To avoid God's wrath, abandon your own. *Masnavi*, IV:113–15.

Quit keeping score if you want to be free. Love has ejected the referee. Quatrain #116-F.

Justice waters trees that bear fruit. Injustice waters thorns at the root. Bestow bounty where it belongs, no matter where it arose. Don't just go watering everything that grows. *Masnavi*, V:1089–90.

Only Grace opens our eyes. Only Love calms fury's cries. *Masnavi*, III:838.

If you're in love with Love, don't be bashful. Be brave and plant your flag! Ghazal #213-S.

Chapter 8—Dx: Fear ♣ Rx: Quit Making Yourself So Small

When you walk atop a towering wall, you wobble, because it's so terribly tall. Even if its crest is strong, stable, and two yards wide, your heart trembles as you imagine falling off the divide. But know that this fear is your own creation: The mischievous child of imagination. *Masnavi*, III:1560–1.

Every storm the Beloved unfurls permits the sea to scatter pearls. *Masnavi*, I:506.

Floating on a strand of hay in a revolting pool of donkey piss, the fly lifts his head like a proud captain cluelessly steering amiss. He mistakes the strand of hay for a yacht, the puddle of piss for a sea. He thinks he's a big shot, but he's just floundering in pee. *Masnavi*, I:1082–90.

Quit being a drop. Make yourself an ocean. Abandon your ego and reap the Beloved's devotion. Quatrain #1465-S.

It's names and labels that make us disagree. Look beneath the words and make peace with me. *Masnavi*, II:3680.

In the face of Love, fear is slighter than a single hair. In the faith of Love, sacrifice is everywhere. *Masnavi*, V:2184.

From doubt, the Beloved grants certainty. From hatred, kindness; from fear, security. *Masnavi*, I:546–47.

When I die you will kiss my grave without hesitation. Why not kiss my face now that we share a location? Ghazal #1535-S.

Chapter 9—Dx: Disappointment ♣ Rx: Wake Up

You already own all the sustenance you seek. If only you'd wake up and take a peek. *Masnavi*, V:1076.

Welcome every guest, no matter how grotesque. Be as hospitable to calamity as to ecstasy, to anxiety as to tranquility. Today's misery sweeps your home clean, making way for tomorrow's felicity. *Masnavi*, V:3644–46, 3676–84.

If you're in love with Love, don't be bashful. Be brave and plant your flag! Ghazal #213-S.

Open your arms if you want to be embraced. Break your idols, drop your ego, and behold the Beloved's face. Ghazal #2577-S.

For all the degrees you scholars may attain, you'll never learn to love 'til you're insane. Quatrain #1729-S.

Opposites invigorate one another. Honey is only sweet because you've tasted vinegar. *Masnavi*, I:3211.

Envy is the toughest companion to ditch on your journey. But ditch it now, for it's the devil's defense attorney. *Masnavi*, I:429–36.

A pure soul is like a porcupine. The more it's prodded, the more it shines. *Masnavi*, IV:98–99.

Bread on your head and knee-deep in a river, how are you so starved and withered? You already own all the sustenance you seek. If only you'd wake up and take a peek. *Masnavi*, V:1076.

Chapter 10—Dx: Pride ♦ Rx: Return to the Source

Ego is the soul's worst affliction. No one lives outside its jurisdiction. *Masnavi*, I:3214, 3216.

The same glorious feathers that spark the peacock's pride attract hunters from every side. *Masnavi*, V:641–47.

Listen to how the reed flute sings its song. . . . Reserved only for those who in madness reside. *Masnavi*, I:1–14.

Quit being a drop. Make yourself an ocean. Abandon your ego and reap the Beloved's devotion. Quatrain #1465-S.

Worse than all the lies that plague humanity is the ego lurking inside of me. *Masnavi*, I:906.

You're like a pearl asking where the ocean lies, all the while soaking in its tides. *Masnavi*, V:1080.

When you dedicate each breath to yourself, you ache with every labored gasp. When you surrender each breath to the Beloved, nothing is beyond your grasp. Ghazal #323-S.

Your homeland flows in every direction. Why pray facing one minuscule section? Ghazal #1821-S.

Seek the tonic nectar in the bitter sting. Go to the source of the source of your spring. Ghazal #120-S.

Why seek pilgrimage at some distant shore, when the Beloved is right next door? Ghazal #648-S.

MELODY MOEZZI is a writer, speaker, activist, commentator, columnist, attorney, and award-winning author. Her books include *War on Error: Real Stories of American Muslims* and, more recently, *Haldol and Hyacinths: A Bipolar Life,* which earned wide critical acclaim and broke new ground as the first mainstream mental health memoir by either a Muslim or a Middle Easterner. Moezzi is a blogger for *Ms.* and a featured regular columnist, blogger, and vlogger for *bp* [Bipolar] magazine. She maintains her own YouTube channel and video blog, *A Saner Spin,* answering readers' questions and addressing a variety of issues, including mental health, wellness, and spirituality. Moezzi's writing has appeared on NPR and CNN and in *The New York Times, The Washington Post, The Christian Science Monitor,* the *Daily Beast, The Guardian, Hürriyet,* and the *South China Morning Post,* among many other outlets.

melodymoezzi.com
🐦 MelodyMoezzi